At the Point of the Bayonet

The Peninsular War Battles of Arroyomolinos and Almaraz 1811-1812

Robert Griffith

Helion & Company

Helion & Company Limited
Unit 8 Amherst Business Centre
Budbrooke Road
Warwick
CV34 5WE
England
Tel. 01926 499619
Email: info@helion.co.uk
Website: www.helion.co.uk
Twitter: @helionbooks
blog.helion.co.uk/

Published by Helion & Company 2021
Designed and typeset by Mach 3 Solutions Ltd (www.mach3solutions.co.uk)
Cover designed by Paul Hewitt, Battlefield Design (www.battlefield-design.co.uk)

Text © Robert Griffith 2021
Illustrations © as individually credited
Maps © Robert Griffith 2021

Cover: The 92nd Foot, the Gordon Highlanders, charge into Arroyomolinos on the morning of 28
October 1811. Original artwork by Christa Hook (www.christahook.co.uk) © Helion & Co. 2020

ISBN 978-1-913336-52-3

British Library Cataloguing-in-Publication Data.
A catalogue record for this book is available from the British Library.

For details of other military history titles published by Helion & Company Limited,
contact the above address, or visit our website: http://www.helion.co.uk

We always welcome receiving book proposals from prospective authors.

Contents

Preface

In the town of Shrewsbury, in the county of Shropshire, stands a forty-metre high Doric column with a five-metre high statue of a general at its top. The statue of Rowland Hill overlooks the town, but the man himself has long been overlooked by history. Those with a keen interest in the Napoleonic Wars will know of Hill, but many of the inhabitants of Shrewsbury who walk in his shadow will not. It was Hill's fate to always be in the shadow of the Duke of Wellington, under whose command he served during the long Peninsular War in Portugal and Spain from 1808 to 1814. Mention of Hill in the history books is often couched in terms of his being a competent subordinate, and will probably also include his concern for those he commanded, which led to his nickname of 'Daddy' Hill.

However, there was much more to Hill than that. The battles of Arroyomolinos (1811) and Almaraz (1812) reveal a skilled commander, willing to drive his men hard, be aggressive, and take risks when needed. They were the making of Hill's reputation and a large part of the fame that led the people of Shrewsbury to want to celebrate him and recognise his service to the country. The two battles were relatively minor affairs in the broad sweep of the two decades of war against France. They have sometimes merited a chapter in one of the larger multi-volume histories but are usually covered in just a few pages. Plenty of books have been written on the war as a whole, on the main battles, the generals and some of the regiments involved. Those seeking to cover the entire war necessarily paint with a broader brush. Even those covering a single one of the large battles may cover the minutiae of the action but they seldom have space to focus too long on any one unit. On the other hand, regimental histories, such as my own *Riflemen*, allow that focus on the men and the unit but have to condense a long war into one book.

Focusing on two smaller actions has enabled me to provide a detailed history of them, the events that led up to them and their consequences, but also to cover in more depth the units and men that fought them. The allied troops involved in both battles were broadly the same units and so I have been able to follow, through memoirs and other sources, an eight-month segment of the war for those regiments. The book is written from the British perspective, but I hope I have also done justice to the Portuguese and Spanish troops who were part of the allied army, and also to their French foes.

I would like to thank my editor, Dr Andrew Bamford, for his invaluable advice and patience once again. My thanks also go to José Manuel Rodríguez Gómez for translating so many of the Spanish sources for me, to Sara Fragoso Delgado for her expert local knowledge of Arroyomolinos, and to Matt Lund from Cumbria's Museum of Military Life at Carlisle Castle, Captain Dicky Bird at The Light Dragoons Regimental Association, Prof. Charles Esdaile, Dr Mark Thompson, Ruí Moura, and Eamonn O'Keeffe for their assistance and support, as well as the staff at The National Archives, the British Library, the National Army Museum, the Hampshire Archives and the Gloucestershire Archives.

Robert Griffith, November 2020

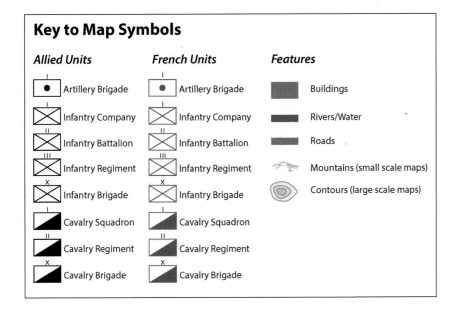

1

Rowland Hill

On 1 June 1811 Lieutenant General Rowland Hill resumed command of the 2nd Division of Wellington's Anglo-Portuguese army. The division was headquartered at the small Spanish town of Almendralejo, 40 miles south-east of the besieged fortress of Badajoz. The once-prosperous town had already changed hands several times between the allies and the French, and as each army arrived they billeted their troops in the houses, requisitioned food, and levied taxes. The town and surrounding countryside became progressively poorer; and the olive groves and vineyards went untended as the population were conscripted, abandoned their farms to join the guerrillas, or just left to find a home free of the ravages of the war. Soon after Hill arrived the townspeople would exchange their British guests for French occupiers once again. A soldier of the 71st Foot was not keen on the town, commenting: 'Almandralajo is a low swampy place, the worst town I ever was in in Spain: our men called it Almandralajo Craco, (cursed.)'[1]

Hill had succumbed to a severe fever in December of the previous year. He had initially gone to Lisbon to recover, staying in Wellington's house there, but after developing jaundice his doctor urged him to return to Britain for a change of air.[2] He had arrived at Falmouth in early February and then spent his leave at his home in Shropshire. As soon as he felt adequately, although not fully, recovered he sought to return to the Peninsula and was waiting impatiently for a ship to Portugal by the middle of May.[3] He landed in Lisbon around the 23rd, which was probably when he first heard news of the Battle of Albuera; an allied victory but one that came at a very high cost. He hurried to re-join the army and by 30 May was at Wellington's headquarters in Elvas. The next day he wrote to one of his sisters:

> I have the pleasure to acquaint you that after a prosperous journey, we arrived here yesterday, and as I have been but one fortnight coming from Spithead to this place, little time has been lost. Indeed, I believe few ever made the voyage and

---

1   Anon., *Journal of a Soldier of the 71st* (Edinburgh: W. & C. Tait, 1819), p.149.
2   Hill to Wellington 13 January 1811, British Library Additional Manuscripts (BL Add.MS), 35059, p.358.
3   Hill to sister 12 May 1811, BL Add.MS, 35061 pp.62-3.

journey in less time. Beresford's Battle, which you will have heard of long before this reaches you, has been a bloody one, and as the French retired, we claim the victory, but alas! it has been a dear bought one.

When I was in England, and heard that the French had possession of Badajos, I said I thought I should be in time to see it retaken. The opportunity exists, and the enemy seems determined to keep it as long as he can, in consequence of which preparations are making to besiege it, and it is the general opinion that it will fall in about ten days. In the mean time, my corps, which I shall resume the command of tomorrow, will prevent the enemy from relieving the Place. I saw Lord Wellington yesterday, and shall dine with him today. He is as usual very civil, and expressed pleasure at my return. I assure you, I never felt better in health than at present, and trust I shall continue well.[4]

Hill was one of Wellington's most trusted subordinates, and the allied commander would have felt that the force covering his siege of Badajoz was in good hands. However, the division that Hill came back to was a shadow of the one that he had left behind. The 2nd Division had suffered over 50 percent casualties at Albuera.[5] Many of the men Hill had worked closely with over the preceding three years were dead, or badly wounded. Lieutenant Moyle Sherer of the 34th wrote of his experiences at Albuera:

To describe my feelings throughout this wild scene with fidelity, would be impossible: at intervals, a shriek or groan told that men were falling around me; but it was not always that the tumult of the contest suffered me to catch these sounds. A constant feeling to the centre of the line, and the gradual diminution of our front, more truly bespoke the havoc of death. As we moved, though slowly, yet ever a little in advance, our own killed and wounded lay behind us; but we arrived among those of the enemy, and those of the Spaniards who had fallen in the first onset: we trod among the dead and dying, all reckless of them.[6]

Officers, many of them senior, wrote letters home severely criticising the allied commander at Albuera, Hill's temporary replacement *Marechal* Beresford, for his handling of the battle and blaming him for the heavy losses.[7] Hill would have to rebuild both the numbers and the morale of his command, whilst keeping an eye on the French and protecting Wellington's flank.

Rowland Hill was born 11 August 1772 at Prees Hall in Shropshire. He was the fourth of 16 children born to John and Mary Hill, 13 of whom survived childhood.[8] Five of his six brothers also served in the army. His uncle, Sir Richard, was a baronet and owner of the nearby Hawkstone estate. Hill appears to have been a gentle, kind and good-natured child, who was said to faint at the sight of blood. However, when he was aged 17 he wrote to his mother:

4   Hill to sister 31 May 1811, BL Add.MS, 35061 pp.64-5.
5   C. Oman, A *History of the Peninsular War* (Oxford: Clarendon Press, 1902), Vol.IV, p.631.
6   M. Sherer, *Recollections of the Peninsula* (London: Longman, 1827) pp.220-1.
7   G. Dempsey, *Albuera 1811* (Barnsley: Frontline Books, 2008) pp.246-7.
8   E. Sidney, *The Life of Lord Hill* (London: Murray, 1845) p.3.

Last Wednesday I received your very kind letter, in which you desired I would let you know what profession I should really like best. I know it is your's and Papa's wish that I should be in the law, but I hope you will forgive me if I say I should not like that line of life; for, indeed, I have a dislike to the law, and am sure I should neither be happy, nor make any figure, as a lawyer. The profession which I should like best, and I hope you and Papa will not object to, is the army.[9]

His father quickly replied:

Immediately on seeing your letter, I consulted those whom I thought most likely to inform me on the best plan for a young man to pursue who went into the army. What is most recommended is to go to a foreign academy for about two years, where strict attention to the several studies necessary to cut any figure in the profession must be attended to. By great favour, a commission may be purchased before you go abroad, with leave of absence, whereby you may stand a chance of creeping a little forward towards rank, the same as if you was with the regiment. This, to be sure, is a more expensive plan than I can well afford; but as I have not a doubt but you will make every proper return, I will exert myself to put it, or something of the sort, into execution (provided you continue in your present resolution); for I much dread the idea of a young man starting in any line of life without his being determined to use his utmost endeavours to advance in it, which I am well assured no one can in the military line, any more than any other, without a proper previous education. It is true a commission may be purchased for a few hundreds: but what a miserable situation for a young man of spirit, with scarce any thing but three and sixpence per day, to saunter about from town to town, unless he has a good prospect of advancing from it.[10]

He also urged his son to 'attend as much as possible to your French.'

Hill was commissioned as an ensign in the 38th (1st Staffordshire) Regiment of Foot on 31 July 1790.[11] Rather than joining his regiment he followed his father's plan and attended a military academy in the French city of Strasbourg until January of the following year. He returned to Britain after obtaining a lieutenancy by raising 12 recruits for an independent company, whom he joined briefly in Kent, before exchanging into the 53rd (Shropshire) Regiment of Foot and then returning to Strasbourg.[12] Raising men for advancement in rank was an alternative to purchasing the promotion, or waiting for promotion by seniority. He had only been in France for a few weeks when his uncle, Sir Richard, and his elder brother John, arrived on their way back from Italy. Given the political turmoil in France Hill decided to return with them to Britain, via a pleasant tour down the Rhine, and then he remained on leave in Shropshire for the rest of the year.

---

9   R. Hill to M. Hill 6 March 1790, in Sidney, *Life of Hill*, p.8.

10   J. Hill to R. Hill, undated, in Sidney, *Life of Hill*, pp.9-10.

11   Army List 1790, The National Archives (TNA), WO 65/40, p.114.

12   Army List 1791, TNA, WO 65/41 p.129.

He finally joined the 53rd on 18 January 1792, at Edinburgh, and for the first time took up his military duties in earnest.[13] The regiment moved to Ayr on the west coast and Hill commanded a detachment of 18 men at Ballantrae. Despite his foreshortened military education, he seems to have rapidly taken to life in the army. Major Mathews, commanding the regiment, wrote to Sir Richard that:

> [A]as an officer, his talents, disposition, and assiduity are of the most promising nature; and that his amiable manners, sweetness of temper, and uncommon propriety of conduct, have not only endeared him to the regiment, but procured him the most flattering attentions from an extensive circle of the first fashion in this country.[14]

France declared war on Britain on 2 February 1793 and Hill, taking advantage of the sudden demand for more men, raised his own independent company and in March secured himself a captaincy in the 86th Regiment of Foot.[15] In April Hill delivered his men to the 38th Foot in Ireland, but then did not join the 86th and instead returned to Shropshire in June.[16] Later in the year he decided to travel to the Mediterranean to take up a diplomatic post at Genoa, but on his arrival there in September he persuaded Brigadier General Lord Mulgrave, sailing from Genoa to join the British force besieging the French port of Toulon, to take him on as an aide-de-camp.

The British support of the Royalist uprising at Toulon in the late summer of 1794 was woefully under-resourced and the British were quickly hemmed in by the Revolutionary army. The four-month long campaign gave Hill his first experience of combat; he had several near misses and was slightly wounded. Mulgrave praised Hill's intelligence, activity and courage. At the end of the siege he was chosen to take the dispatch announcing the British withdrawal to London.[17]

Amongst Hill's fellow aides in Toulon was 46-year-old Scot, Thomas Graham, who was serving as a volunteer after persuading various friends and relations in the Royal Navy and British Army to allow him to accompany them. Following his return from Toulon Graham decided to raise a regiment; the 90th (Perthshire Volunteers) Regiment of Foot. Graham was commissioned as lieutenant colonel commandant and offered Hill a majority, if he could raise a quota of recruits. Hill replied to Graham's offer pledging to do everything he could to merit the faith he had shown in him.[18] He fulfilled his quota and when the 90th was augmented to 1,000 men shortly afterwards Hill was promoted on 13 May 1794 to be the junior lieutenant colonel of the regiment.[19] He was still only 21 years old.

---

13 Sidney, *Life of Hill*, p.12.
14 Mathews to Sir R. Hill 12 September 1792, in Sidney, *Life of Hill*, p.13.
15 Army List 1794, TNA, WO 65/44 p.163.
16 Sidney, *Life of Hill*, p14.
17 G. Teffeteller, *The Surpriser* (Newark: University of Delaware Press, 1983) pp.19-20; Sidney, *Life of Hill*, pp.17-9.
18 A.M. Delavoye, *Life of Thomas Graham* (London: Richardson, 1880) p.84.
19 Army List 1795, TNA, WO 65/45, p.194.

The landing of the British troops in Egypt, 8 March 1801, by Philippe-Jacques de Loutherbourg. (Anne S.K. Brown Military Collection)

In the summer of 1795, the 90th was part of force sent to occupy the French island of Île d'Yeu just off the Vendée coast of western France. The operation had little point and was abandoned before the end of the year. In 1796 the 90th sailed to Gibraltar. In 1799 Hill applied for leave and returned home, and was promoted to full colonel at the start of 1800.[20] He was about to travel to Switzerland when he heard that the 90th were going to be joining an expedition to Egypt under Lieutenant General Sir Ralph Abercromby, so he hurried to return to his regiment.

Napoleon Bonaparte had led the French forces that invaded Egypt in 1797 but had then abandoned his men and returned to France in 1799. His army had remained, stranded by Nelson's victory at the Battle of the Nile, and the aim of Abercromby's expedition was to finally expel the French from the country. The fleet carrying the British troops sighted Egypt on 1 March 1801 and on the 8th over 5,000 men were rowed towards the shore at Aboukir Bay. The French were waiting for them but Abercromby's men drove them from the shore and established a beachhead. On 13 March the 90th were leading the British advance when they were surprised by French cavalry. The volleys of the 90th drove off the chasseurs but Hill was wounded. A musket ball struck the peak of the Tarleton helmet he was wearing and he was concussed. He was taken to the British flagship HMS *Foudroyant* and was recovering

---

20   Army List 1800, TNA, WO 65/50, p.318.

when Abercromby was brought into the same cabin, having been mortally wounded at the Battle of Alexandria on 21 March. Hill remained on the *Foudroyrant* until 14 April and then re-joined his regiment.[21]

Cairo fell to the British in June and Alexandria finally surrendered in September. The Treaty of Amiens was signed in March 1802 and brought an end to the war, but the lull in hostilities only lasted until 18 May 1803. The 90th and Hill went to Ireland that summer and shortly afterwards Hill was promoted to brigadier general on the Irish staff, which would mean his leaving the regiment. The officers of the 90th wrote to him:

> On their taking their farewell of an officer who has ever stood so high in their estimation, they feel themselves called upon to declare that the discipline he maintained in the regiment, has ever gained it the distinguished praise and approbation of all the general officers they have ever served with, – a discipline so tempered with mildness that must have endeared him to every individual in the regiment, as well as his general attention to their private interests.[22]

Hill performed well in Ireland and was promoted to major general in October 1805.[23] He was placed in charge of the embarkation of 5,000 troops at Cork for an expedition to Hannover. The convoy stopped briefly at Deal where Hill dined with Major General Sir Arthur Wellesley, who was also commanding a brigade in the expedition. The force arrived off the German coast in December but achieved little and soon returned. Hill had various commands in Britain before he returned to Ireland in early 1807. In 1808 he was assigned to an expedition to Venezuela that was to be commanded by Wellesley. However, the Dos de Mayo uprising in Spain against the French, and the subsequent appeals from the Spanish for aid from Britain, changed their destination to the Iberian Peninsula. Wellesley wrote to Hill on 23 June 1808: 'I rejoice extremely at the prospect I have before me of serving again with you, and I hope we shall have more to do than we had on the last occasion on which we were together.'[24] Wellesley's hopes were certainly realised and the two men would serve together through the Peninsular Campaign to the peace in 1814, and then again at Waterloo.

Hill took charge of embarking the bulk of the expedition at Cork, co-ordinating the movement of troops and supplies, and allocating them to ships. The fleet sailed on 12 July and, since the Spanish were unwilling initially to accept British troops, landed at Mondego Bay on the Atlantic coast of Portugal, in early August. Portugal had been occupied by the French in 1807. After supervising the landing Hill was given the command of the 1st Brigade and led the first column to move inland. The British and their Portuguese allies clashed with the French in the first major action at Roliça. Hill's brigade was part of the British centre and at one point he had to steady the 29th Foot before leading an attack up to the French position.

---

21   Sidney, *Life of Hill*, pp.39-41.
22   Ruthven to Hill 1 September 1803, in Sidney, *Life of Hill*, p.54.
23   Army List 1805, TNA, WO 65/56, p.7.
24   Wellesley to Hill 23 June 1808, BL Add.MS, 35059, p.6.

The Battle of Roliça, 17 August. 1808, by Henri Leveque. (Anne S.K. Brown Military Collection)

At Vimeiro, a few days later, his men were held in reserve and were not significantly engaged. Following the defeat at Vimeiro the French offered terms for their surrender, which were quickly accepted by Lieutenant General Sir Hew Dalrymple, who had arrived to take over command from Wellesley. The 1808 campaign had once again proven Hill's organisational skills, and many of the surviving letters between them show that he and Wellesley worked well together. Hill had handled his brigade skilfully in action and was building a reputation as a commander that cared for his men, who were already calling him 'Daddy Hill'.[25]

Unfortunately, Wellesley was soon forced to return to London to defend himself against the furore that erupted after the lenient terms of the treaty with the French became public. Command of the army passed to Lieutenant General Sir John Moore and Hill commanded a brigade in the winter campaign as Moore led the army into Spain and then, outnumbered and outmanoeuvred by the French under Napoleon, had to retreat in appalling weather to Corunna. There the British fought a hard rearguard action in which Moore was fatally wounded. However, the battle won them enough time to board the remnants of the army onto the ships of the Royal Navy. Hill arrived back in Britain at the end of January, had a brief leave back in Shropshire, and then went to Ireland to take charge of several battalions of reinforcements destined for Portugal. Hill arrived in Lisbon at the start of April 1809 and was again given command of a brigade.

Wellesley arrived soon after Hill and resumed command. The army advanced towards the French held city of Oporto and Hill's brigade was given the task of using boats to cross a coastal lake to get into the French rear. The operation was carried out well, but the French were too numerous for Hill to prevent them falling back to Oporto. The French withdrew across the river

---

25   Teffeteller, *Surpriser*, pp.44-5.

Passage of the Douro, by Henri Leveque. (Anne S.K. Brown Military Collection)

Douro but wine barges were found to ferry troops to the French-held shore and Hill's brigade, being the closest troops, were ferried across. Command of the crossing was given to Lieutenant General Edward Paget but after he was quickly wounded Hill took charge and held a seminary on the far bank against repeated French counter-attacks. Other crossings were made further up and down the river and the French retreated. Hill's part in the battle was not fully acknowledged in Wellesley's dispatch, with most of the acclaim going to Paget.[26] The French were driven out of Portugal and then the allied army shifted southwards and advanced into Spain. Wellesley re-organised his army into four divisions, and gave command of the 2nd Division to Hill.

At Talavera de la Reina in late July a portion of Hill's division was delayed moving into their position when the French launched a surprise evening attack. Hill galloped up the hill his men were meant to be defending and arrived just as the French were reaching the summit. Hill had another close shave when a French soldier grabbed his arm, but his horse shied away. When the Frenchman fired he missed, but one of Hill's aides was killed. Hill led a counter-attack which drove the French back, but the battle resumed the next day. During the action Hill was again shot in the head; a musket ball hitting his hat and grazing his left ear and the back of his head.

Despite the victory at Talavera the allied army was forced to move back to the border with Portugal by the French forces massed against them. In

26   Teffeteller, *Surpriser*, pp.52-3.

August Hill received the news that he had been promoted to the local rank of lieutenant general, at Wellesley's request.[27] In December Wellesley, now Viscount Wellington, wrote to Hill:

> In the arrangements for the defence of Portugal I shall form two principal corps, both consisting of British and Portuguese troops, the largest of which will be to the northward, and I shall command it myself, and the latter will be for the present upon the Tagus, and hereafter it may be moved forward into Alentejo; and I will not make any arrangement either as to the troops that are to comprise it, or as to the officer who is to command it, without offering the command of it to you.
>
> At the same time, I will not separate you from the army, and from my own immediate command, without consulting your wishes; and I shall be glad to hear from you on this subject as soon as possible, as the arrangements for quartering and disposing of the troops depend upon your decision upon this point.[28]

Hill accepted the command. It is probable that whilst Wellington had seen that Hill was brave in battle, able to command with intelligence, and careful to preserve manpower, a large factor in his decision to offer the command to him was Hill's ability to follow instructions diligently, but not slavishly – he could be relied upon to think for himself if the need arose. In short, Wellington trusted Hill in a way that he did few other subordinates. However, that did not stop him issuing strings of detailed directives to Hill.

Whilst Wellington waited for the first nine months of 1810 in the north of Portugal for the expected French attack on the country, Hill guarded the southern route to Lisbon from the Spanish province of Extremadura. Hill and the French commanders facing him would occasionally feint or manoeuvre, and there were minor skirmishes, but Hill's main role was to alert Wellington to any major movements by the enemy. As *Maréchal* André Masséna led the main French effort against Wellington's forces the troops facing Hill also began to move north and he followed, joining Wellington's army massed on the ridge at Bussaco in September. In the subsequent battle the 2nd Division manoeuvred but did not fight. The French attacks were beaten back but in the following days the allied army had to withdraw or risk being cut off. They eventually retreated behind the fortified lines of Torres Vedras, implementing a scorched-earth policy that denied the French supplies. The allied army rested safely behind their redoubts, batteries and forts. The French army slowly starved and eventually withdrew north. Hill's force was again sent across the Tagus river in case French reinforcements came from southern Spain.

In December Hill came down with the fever would force his return to Britain. He wrote to his sister:

> The feverish attack which I had is by no means unusual in the interior of the country, and particularly on the south bank of the Tagus, where we have been lately. The fever is seldom attended with fatal consequences, and a change of air to

---

27   General Orders Spain & Portugal (London: Egerton 1811), Vol.I, p.190.
28   Wellington to Hill, 18 December 1809, in Sidney, *Life of Hill*, p.121.

the neighbourhood of the sea, has almost always an instantaneous effect for the better. I was therefore removed to Lisbon, and since my arrival here have been daily recovering. I have just been out riding for nearly two hours, and do not feel the least fatigued; on the contrary, I feel myself better. I have received your last kind letter. Nothing, I assure you, would give me greater pleasure than to obtain permission to visit Shropshire, which, if I were to ask, I am sure I could procure; but under present circumstances, in my mind, it would not be right to think of it, provided my health will admit of my returning to my post. Surely affairs in this country cannot long remain in a state of uncertainty. I do not, however, think the French have sufficient force in Portugal to drive us out of our strong position, nor do I think Lord W. has sufficient strength to drive them out of the country. It appears as if Massena was waiting either for instructions or reinforcements. It is certain that his adjutant-general was despatched to Paris about three weeks ago; it is also certain that some small reinforcement, about 4,000, which were on the march to Massena, have returned into Spain. I am now living in Lord W.'s house here. He was here about a week ago; he is in high spirits, and seems very confident.[29]

Hill's estimation of the strategic situation was more accurate than his assessment of his own health: 1811 would see attempts by both the French and Wellington to break the developing stalemate. Hill deeply regretted leaving his command. In a letter to a member of his staff written the day he sailed for Britain Hill wrote:

My Physician desires me not to write & I can not at present enter into a detail at what I feel at being obliged to leave the Troops, & I beg you will express to all enquiring friends the regret which this temporary absence gives me, & the sincere pleasure it will afford me to be again at Head of Officers & Men who have so uniformly met my wishes.[30]

---

29   Hill to sister 15 December 1810, in Sidney, *Life of Hill,* pp.153-4.
30   Hill to J.C. Rooke, date illegible, Gloucestershire Archives, D1833/F14.

2

Cáceres

The two main routes from Spain into Portugal were guarded by pairs of fortified towns, one on each side of the frontier. In the north the Portuguese fortress of Almeida was less than 30 miles from Spanish Ciudad Rodrigo, and 180 miles to the south Portuguese Elvas was only a dozen miles from Badajoz, the capital of the Spanish province of Extremadura. In the spring of 1811 Almeida was held by the French but surrounded by Wellington's army. *Maréchal* Masséna's Armée de Portugal, after its expulsion from its eponymous country, was quickly reorganised and replenished. He attempted to relieve Almeida in May but Wellington defeated him at Fuentes de Oñoro. The beleaguered French garrison then managed to escape and the two forces settled into an uneasy stalemate.

Wellington transferred himself, and the bulk of his army, south to besiege Badajoz, but lacking sufficient siege equipment and guns he did little better than Beresford had before Albuera. A strong French relief force approached in June and forced both the lifting of the siege and the withdrawal of Hill's covering force back across the Portuguese border. Once the French succeeded in relieving Badajoz, they turned their attention elsewhere and Wellington returned to the north, leaving Hill to cover the south with his troops among the hills and mountains along the Portuguese border, and across into nearby areas of Extremadura.

Hill's orders were to observe and contain the French, ensure that Elvas and Campo Maior were protected, keep lines of communication open to the north, and to keep Wellington informed of any movements or developments. As well as the 2nd Division Hill also had under his command *Marechal de Campo* John Hamilton's Portuguese division, *Coronel* Charles Ashworth's Portuguese brigade, plus two British and one Portuguese cavalry brigade, with artillery and engineers; a total force of around 16,000 men.[1]

Maréchal Jean-de-Dieu Soult commanded the French Armée du Midi, a force of around 90,000 men spread through the southern provinces of Spain.[2] Hill's immediate opponent in Extremadura was *Général de Division* Jean Baptiste Drouet, Comte d'Erlon, commander of V Corps, composed of

---

1   Oman, *Peninsular War*, Vol.IV, p.649.
2   Oman, *Peninsular War*, Vol.IV, p.639.

A view of Portalegre, from G. Cumberland, *Views in Spain & Portugal, taken during the Campaigns of His Grace the Duke of Wellington*. (London: William Nicol, 1823)

around 16,000 men in two divisions and a cavalry brigade, plus the garrison at Badajoz.[3] Drouet's orders were very similar to Hill's; he was to observe and contain the allied forces in the area, and to maintain communication with the French forces further north.

By the end of the summer, Drouet had his headquarters at Zafra and troops around Merida. Elements of the now optimistically-named Armée de Portugal under the command of Masséna's replacement, *Maréchal* Auguste Marmont, occupied the north of Extremadura around Plasencia and Navalmoral. Hill's force stretched from Castelo Branco in the north, to his headquarters at Portalegre, then to Campo Maior and Elvas in the south. Cavalry detachments occupied villages closest to the frontier with outposts on or across the border.[4] Also in Extremadura was the Spanish 5º Ejército (5th Army) commanded by *Capitán General* Francisco Javier Castaños, consisting of one small infantry division and another of cavalry. Castaños had his headquarters at Valencia de Alcantara, just across the border from Portugal.

Whilst both the French and the allied armies were essentially adopting defensive postures, one cause of both movements and clashes was the necessity for the French and Spanish to raise contributions of food, forage for horses, and taxes from the province. The supply system of Wellington's army was largely based on an extensive network of depots and a supply chain

---

3   Oman, *Peninsular War*, Vol.IV, p.595.
4   S.G.P Ward, *Wellington's Headquarters* (Barnsley: Pen & Sword, 2017), p.115.

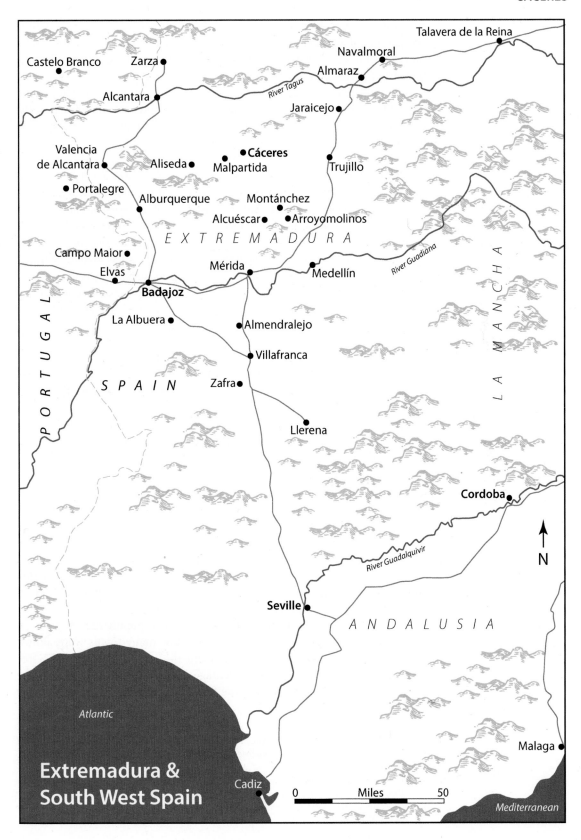

Extremadura &
South West Spain

stretching back to Lisbon, and then to Britain beyond that. Relatively little was gathered locally. However, the French and Spanish armies both relied far more on what could be requisitioned from the immediate area around where their troops were based.

For the French the cost of sustaining an army of over 300,000 men in Spain was one they could scarcely afford. When Soult was appointed to the command of the Armée du Midi in 1810 his instructions from Napoleon included:

> His Majesty's desire is, that you should take the most effectual means of providing for the pay and the requirements of your army. You must act on the principle that war is supported by war. You must push forward the operations on Cadiz, and take measures for getting rid of the banditti. His Majesty supposes that you have occupied and entrenched the most important posts, to keep open your communications, and to prevent their being insulted by the banditti which infest the country. If necessary, M. le Duc, the Emperor authorizes you to … levy extraordinary contributions, to supply the wants of your army. In case the ordinary contributions be not sufficient for the pay, you must raise large contributions, chiefly upon the countries which are yet unsubdued.[5]

The French were demanding one quarter of the harvest.[6] The town of Cáceres, one of the richest in Extremadura, was notionally in the territory of Marmont's Armée de Portugal and had been garrisoned by them, but after Marmont withdrew his troops from nearby Trujillo it left Cáceres dangerously isolated and instead of maintaining a permanent presence he would send expeditions forward from Almaraz to collect contributions. If allied troops moved to attack them then their line of retreat was secure from interception. According to Marmont, Soult saw that the town was not garrisoned and decided to levy contributions there as well.[7] However, a gap created by Marmont's shift north to support Ciudad Rodrigo in September necessitated some presence in the area if communication between the French armies was going to be maintained. Marmont did request that forces from the south move north to help cover his repositioning, but that would mean that Drouet's forces could become dangerously overstretched. Castaños took advantage of the temporary French absence and sent his own men forward to Cáceres before any French arrived from the south.

Paying taxes to what most of the Spanish population saw as an occupying power was obviously unpopular, but many towns were almost as unenthusiastic about the demands from the Juntas that ruled the free parts of Spain. Given the large percentage of the country occupied by the French, the burden of supporting the Spanish army fell disproportionately

---

5   Instructions for the Duke of Dalmatia 14 July 1810, in J. Bonaparte, *The Confidential Correspondence of Napoleon Bonaparte with his Brother Joseph*, Vol.II (New York: Appleton, 1856), pp.129-30.

6   Wellington to Liverpool 28 August 1811, in J. Gurwood, *The Dispatches of Field Marshal the Duke of Wellington, New Edition* (London: John Murray, 1838), Vol. VIII, p.237.

7   A. Marmont, *Mémoires du Marechal Marmont, Duc de Raguse de 1792 a 1841* (Paris: Perrotin, 1857), Vol.4, pp.176-7

on the areas under Spanish control. The unfortunate towns that fell between the two armies, or that were in areas across which the fighting ebbed and flowed, often had to contribute twice. In 1809 a Spanish commander asked the people of Cáceres for shoes, accoutrements and money. The town council initially refused but after some persuasion paid 30,000 reales. A week later 800 French troops plundered the town.[8]

The need for both the French and Spanish to raise contributions from areas not permanently occupied by either could lead to skirmishes if an expedition was caught unawares by the enemy. In August 1811 Castaños reported:

> Obliged of the necessity, for the towns we occupy in this country are already unable to contribute to the daily rations, I raised a vanguard corps that, getting forward between the Tagus and the Guadiana, could make the contribution in rations more bearable since they would be distributed among a larger number of towns.
>
> This vanguard composed of the 2nd Infantry Division, under the command of *Brigadier* Morillo, the Legion Provisional Estremeña, under the command of *Coronel* Downie, and all the cavalry under the command of the *Brigadier* Montemayor, happened to be placed between Alcuéscar, Montánchez and Torremocha.
>
> The troops under the command of *General* Foy that are placed in Trujillo moved on the 22nd at the same time the troops under the command of *General* Girard advanced from Mérida, and both forces headed towards our vanguard. The first warning Montemayor had in Torremocha was the movement of the troops from Trujillo, estimating the force to be about 800 infantrymen and 200 cavalry that were heading against that point. Montemayor decided to wait for them with his cavalry, but soon after he received a second warning that on the path of Benquerencia a second numerous column was also approaching him, and therefore he put his forces into retreat, leaving the *tiradores* of the cavalry and the squadron of the Húsares a Extremadura in the vicinity of Torremocha to cover the retreat of the advanced posts, with instructions not to engage in combat: but despite that they were forced to fight and as a result there were some dead and wounded on both sides, being one of the former the brave *teniente* of the Regimiento a Algarve, Don José Sánchez.
>
> Morillo, being placed in Alcuéscar with the infantry, had the same day warning that Girard's troops were on the move towards that place and therefore, with the agreement of Montemayor, all the vanguard was put into retreat in three columns using three different paths, making the regulated passes through previously indicated towns until the three columns reunited in Aliseda on the 26th where *General* Conde a Penne Villemur took command of the whole force, which occupied an advantageous position with the double object of facing the enemy, covering San Vicente and Valencia de Alcántara, and at the same time securing the retreat of the cadres and depots placed in its vicinity.

---

8   M. McGrigor, *Wellington's Spies* (Barnsley, Leo Cooper, 2005), p.82.

The enemies have reached Cáceres and Arroyo del Puerco; but so far nothing has been undertaken and it seems their aim is to ford the Tagus by Garrovillas according to the reports we have gathered.[9]

In early September the Conde de Penne Villemur led a force including Morillo's infantry and Downie's Legión Extremeña to drive the French out of Cáceres, which they did, taking some prisoners in the process.[10] On the 27th Hill wrote to Castaños regarding a further withdrawal of the French in the area:

Your Excellency will have heard of Girard's departure from Merida. I do however, beg to observe that although I should consider it a fortunate event to fall in with his corps, yet under present circumstance I do not think it advisable to extend my troops more to the right & front than they are at present without Lord Wellington's knowledge.[11]

However, only a few days before, Wellington had written to Hill:

Since I wrote to you yesterday, I have received the inlosed copy of a letter in cypher, from Marmont to Girard, which has been intercepted. Marmont is mistaken, and I do not think that Girard has a force to annoy you.

I reckon that you have about 11,000 men; and he cannot have 6000, of which 11 or 1200 cavalry. If he moves forward, I beg you will fall upon him if you think you can do so with any prospect of success.[12]

At the start of October Hill summed up his view of the strategic situation in a letter to one of his brothers:

Circumstances have a good deal changed since I wrote to Maria on this day week. Lord W. was then in a position covering Ciudad Rodrigo, and Marmont was on his march to relieve it, and the question was, whether Lord Wellington would risk an action to prevent supplies being thrown into C. Rodrigo – The question has now been decided, by his Lordship's declining it, a measure deemed most advisable considering the force of the Enemy. Lord W. has in consequence, fallen back towards Sabugal, & yesterday it was supposed the Enemy were also on their return to the quarters from whence they came, having succeeded in their object of supplying C. Rodrigo. You will perceive from what has happened, that the Enemy is not so weak as we were inclined to suppose him to be last year, when he was running out of Portugal; I am, however, of opinion, that although he probably would have no great objection to meet us in an open country, yet I do not think he is sufficiently strong to undertake offensive Operations against this Country.

---

9   Comunicaciones y oficios de varios realizados en su mayoria por el General en Jefe del 5° Ejército, Francisco Javier Castaños, a cerca de varias actuaciones en Extremadura, Archivo Histórico Nacional (AHN), DIVERSOS-COLECCIONES, 137, N.68

10   Wellington to Liverpool 11 September 1811, TNA, WO 1/250, p.422.

11   Hill to Castaños 27 September 1811, BL Add.MS, 35062, p.74.

12   Wellington to Hill 23rd September 1811, BL Add.MS, 35059, p.390.

Therefore, under all circumstances, it strikes me that Marmont will be perfectly satisfied with having gained his object at C. Rodrigo, and that we shall remain for the winter quiet. Next spring will probably decide the Campaign in favour of England or France according to the reinforcements which may arrive to either army. With respect to my situation, I have been rather on the alert the last ten days. Marmont sent a request to the Commander of the 5th French Corps, Girard, to manoeuvre on this side, while he marched upon C. Rodrigo, at the same time telling him that the English had very few troops in the Alemtejo. Girard (who does not belong to Marmont's force, called the Armée de Portugal) so far complied with the request, & came as far as Merida, and I made a disposition of my troops in hopes of falling upon him if he have come much nearer. He however knew better than M. respecting the force on this side, and is again returned to Zafra.[13]

In early October Morillo marched to Villanueva de la Serena, deep into Extremadura, to gather contributions, and then fell back to the hill town of Montánchez, to the south of Cáceres and only 30 miles from French-held Merida. He reported to the Conde de Penne Villemur that he thought the French were approaching and attempting to surround him, but that he would retain his position for the moment. He also complained that he was having trouble getting the inhabitants of the area to pay the contributions that they owed. Penne Villemur replied that he should tighten the screws and threaten to arrest anyone refusing to pay their taxes. Morillo did not like forcing his compatriots to make contributions and did not get on well with his superior.[14] Reacting to reports of French movements, Hill shifted some of his own brigades to counter any advance towards Portugal. He was receiving reports that Soult had left Seville and it was possible that an attempt was going to be made to resupply Badajoz, but the intelligence was unclear and uncertain.[15]

By 1811, after three years of the peninsular campaign, the allies had developed generally very effective intelligence networks within Spain, which built upon experience gained in the previous two decades of the wars with France. Diplomat Charles Stuart had been appointed to liaise with the Spanish Juntas in 1808. He began to organise a systematic approach to the collection and dissemination of information, work he continued when he was appointed as minister plenipotentiary in Lisbon in 1810. Stuart's network of agents, guerrillas, British officers serving with the various Spanish armies, and other sources, operated mainly in the north while his successor as liaison with the Spanish, Wellington's brother Henry Wellesley, operated a similar network of agents from the besieged city of Cadiz. Both Stuart and Wellesley regularly shared information with each other, with Wellington, with Hill, and with their superiors in London.[16]

---

13   Hill to brother 1 October 1811, BL Add.MS, 35061, pp.83-5.
14   J.A.P. Rubio, Pablo Morillo: Acciones militares y la contribución de los pueblos de las tierras de Montánchez al esfuerzo de guerra (1811-1813), *Revista de Estudios Extremeños*, 2013, Tomo LXIX, Número I, pp.315-8.
15   BL Add.MS, 35062, pp.80-94.
16   H.J. Davies, *Spying for Wellington* (Norman: University of Oklahoma Press, 2018), pp.71-85.

One key advantage that the allies had over the French in terms of intelligence were the numerous bands of guerrillas that operated throughout much of Spain. The quality, reliability, and military effectiveness of the disparate groups varied greatly, both over time and within the different provinces. Some were little more than bandits, and others regular military units in all but name. The mountainous terrain of the Peninsula meant many roads traversed narrow passes ideal for ambushes, and that there were plenty of remote regions the guerrillas could retreat into. French convoys and couriers had to have strong escorts, but even so the capture of dispatches and orders was so common that multiple copies had to be sent from one headquarters to another. Much of the intelligence that Hill received in the late summer and autumn of 1811 came via *Teniente Coronel* de Benito Pelli, a Spanish officer who operated with guerrillas in the mountains to the south and east of Soult's headquarters at Seville.[17]

Many, but not all, of the intercepted dispatches were in cypher and took time to be decrypted by the allies, if they could be read at all. The French introduced a new code in the late summer of 1811, the *Grande Cypher*, and started to encrypt more of their communications. Major George Scovell, on Wellington's staff, led the effort to break the new code, which was far more complex and took longer to break.[18] It could take several days or more for a captured dispatch to reach Wellington's headquarters, then take more time for it to be deciphered, analysed, and the information disseminated and acted upon, by which time the situation may have changed and the information no longer be relevant.

Dispatches between the French armies in the north and those in the south were regularly intercepted and deciphered, even so it could take several such letters to clarify and confirm French intentions. Such interceptions often laid bare the conflicts between the various commanders. In November 1811 Wellington wrote to the Secretary of State for War, Lord Liverpool:

> I likewise enclose a very curious intercepted letter, which was in cipher, from Marmont to Foy, which shows how these gentry are going on; in fact each Marshal is the natural enemy of the King and of his neighbouring Marshal. Pray take care that this letter is not made public, as it would disclose that we have the key of the cipher.[19]

Another letter from Wellington in September illustrates that despite having a great deal of intelligence, from multiple sources, it could still be difficult to divine exactly what the French intended:

> The Plan of operations of the Enemy's Armies or the period of its execution appears to have been altered since the 1st Inst.; as the Generals have not been collected at Salamanca, at least as far as I have heard; and Marshal Marmont

---

17   P. Gennequin, *The Centurions vs the Hydra: French Counterinsurgency in the Peninsular War (1808-1812)* (Fort Leavenworth: U.S. Army Command & General Staff College, 2011), p.102.

18   M. Urban, *The Man Who Broke Napoleon's Codes* (London: Faber & Faber, 2001), pp.107-9.

19   Wellington to Liverpool 13 November 1811, in Gurwood, *Dispatches*, Vol.VIII, p.400.

has undoubtedly removed his Head Quarters back again to Plancetia; and Foy's Division of Infantry of the Army of Portugal which he announced in his letter in Cypher to Girard of the 20th August was to cross the Tagus at Almaraz still remains in lower Estremadura. The Enemy however are actively employed in raising contributions in Castille and Estremadura; and a detachment of the Guards and of the Lanciers de Berg, which arrived at Salamanca on the 1st Inst. drove Don Julian's troops from Ledesma on the 4th – and have since obliged them to retire across the Yeltes. They have however themselves again retired towards the Tormes.

Either these operations or increased vigilance of the Police at Salamanca have prevented my receiving any intelligence from my Correspondents in that town since the 3rd Instant; and I am therefore not fully informed of all that has passed lately, and is passing on the Tormes and the Douro. I am very apprehensive that their silence may be attributed to the latter cause; and even that some of them may have suffered for their attachment to us; as the intelligence which they sent to General Silveira having been constantly published in the Portuguese, and afterwards copied into the English Newspapers, must have attracted the notice of the Enemy; and it is more than probable that if any great operation is in contemplation, particular orders have been sent to increase the vigilance of the Police, and to put an end to all intercourse which I may have had with the interior of Spain.[20]

The letter goes on to discuss Soult's operations against Spanish forces in the south but details the conflicting information Wellington has received, he then says: 'It is so difficult to obtain intelligence in the south of Spain, that I cannot be certain of the truth of this report.'

To add to the information from civilian agents, guerrillas, and intercepted French communications Wellington also sent observing officers, usually with a small escort of cavalry, into French held areas. Their job was to help to record detailed routes and maps, as well as to gather intelligence on French forces in the area. Lieutenant George Hillier of the 29th Foot was employed by Hill to reconnoitre in Extremadura, even as far as Llerena south-east of Zafra and well into French territory. Hillier not only observed the French himself but he also had a confidential correspondent in Córdoba to the south, and his chain of contacts seems to have extended to Madrid.[21] Through men like Hillier, Hill developed his own network of correspondents in his area of operations, stretching all the way to Joseph's headquarters. He was adept at analysing numerous reports and building up a picture of French movements and intentions, then sending reports up to Wellington with his opinions.[22] Through a network of couriers, based in posts spread between the headquarters, letters could leave Portalegre and be with Wellington in Freineda two days later.[23]

20   Wellington to Liverpool 11 September 1811, TNA, WO 1/250, pp.413-22.
21   Ward, *Headquarters*, p.117.
22   Davies, *Spying*, pp.103-4
23   Ward, *Headquarters*, p.125.

On 10 October Wellington wrote to Hill with a somewhat damming assessment of information coming from Castaños:

> It is difficult to give credit to the accounts which we receive from General Castanos of the operations of the enemy's southern armies, as I believe he has very little, if any, intelligence on which he can rely; and I know that the desire to involve us in operations in Estremadura, with a view to cover a certain extent of country, in order to draw provisions from it, gains credit for intelligence very little deserving of any, which is afterwards communicated to us as true.[24]

However, Wellington did add that it was possible that a major French move was coming in Extremadura, to reinforce the garrison at Badajoz, and that it was sensible for Hill to deploy his forces accordingly. Hill, based on his own sources as well as information from Castaños, had also been convinced that Soult was going to advance into Extremadura.[25] However, on the same day, 10 October, Hill wrote to Wellington that he had received new information from de Benito and that there was no collection of French troops at Zafra or to the west of Seville. De Benito knew that Soult had left Seville on the 27 September, but not his destination or objective. Hill told Wellington that he was now almost sure that Soult was not moving in his direction.[26]

On 11 October Girard marched from Merida again. Penne Villemur withdrew Morillo and his other forces in the area back behind Cáceres to the village of Casar de Cáceres, a little to the north. A rearguard of cavalry and light infantry covered his withdrawal, and skirmished with the French on 13 October.[27] The French 27e Chasseurs à Cheval charged the Spanish, driving them back with little loss, but an aide of Penne Villemur was captured, and some of the baggage was lost.[28] The Spanish withdrew to Membrio, close to the Portuguese border. Girard, having the same trouble getting contributions out of the area that the Spanish had, stayed in Cáceres for a fortnight.

On the 15th Hill informed Wellington 'that the French have occupied Caceres, & obliged the Spaniards to fall back. Castanos seems alarmed for the safety of Valencia d'Alcantara, and has applied to me for support, & which I think I can in some degree afford him without risk, or much inconvenience.'[29] Hill proposed sending two battalions to high ground near Valencia d'Alcantara, and also said that having been removed from Cáceres the Spanish would soon be lacking provisions.

Wellington replied:

> I concur entirely in your giving assistance to General Castanos, and should approve of your adopting a measure which should be more effectual, and should drive Girard from Caceres across the Guadiana again, if you think you can do it

---

24   Wellington to Hill 10 October 1811, in Gurwood, *Dispatches*, Vol.VIII, pp.332-4.
25   BL Add.MS. 35062, pp.79-80.
26   Hill to Wellington 10 October 1811, BL Add.MS. 35062, p.89.
27   Hill to unknown 15 October 1811, BL Add.MS. 35062, p.93.
28   G. Van Eeckhoudt, *Les Chevau-Légers Belges du duc d'Arenberg* (Schiltigheim: Le Livre chez Vous, 2002), pp.145-6.
29   Hill to Wellington 10 October 1811, BL Add.MS. 35062, p.92.

without risking the safety of Campo Mayor and Ouguela. It appears to me that you are too strong for Girard in every way, if the other division of the 5th corps have not crossed the Guadiana.

If General Castanos, or his troops, enter the Portuguese frontier, our commissariat must provide for them, keeping a regular account of what they issue to them, but only as long as they remain within the Portuguese frontier.[30]

Wellington explained his thinking in a later letter to Hill's old friend Lieutenant General Thomas Graham, telling him that Girard 'has driven General Castanos' posts beyond the Salor, by which he has distressed him much for provisions and forage, and it was necessary either to prepare to receive these vagabond troops in Portugal, or to replace them at Caceres.'[31]

Hill responded to Wellington:

Having taken into consideration your letter of yesterday I am of opinion that I can move upon Caceres without risking the places of Campo Maior & Ouguela both of which I consider secure from assault. By all accounts I feel satisfied that there is only Girard's Division on this side of the Guadiana, consequently there can be little doubt of obliging him to quit Caceres. It would be very desirable to cut off the whole or part of his division before it could get away or be reinforced and which I shall endeavour to affect. At the same time I am aware this can only be done by promptitude & secrecy.[32]

Hill said that he would keep Wellington informed of his movements and that his cavalry would march on the 21st and the infantry on the 22nd. He also sent an officer to Castaños to ask for some troops for the operation. Whilst he hoped to keep his movements secret from Girard, Hill feared that the French would learn of his approach and retire. Wellington agreed and urged caution, writing: 'I think you had better not pass Caceres with your head quarters and main body. When you have driven off Girard, replace the Conde de Penne Villemur at Caceres, and bring back again your troops towards the frontier.'[33] Getting the Spanish back into Cáceres and avoiding having to supply Castaños' army with rations was the objective. Neither Hill nor Wellington expected an officer of Girard's experience to be foolish enough to allow his division to be outmanoeuvred and brought to battle.

---

30 Wellington to Hill 17 October 1811, BL Add.MS, 35059, p.420.
31 Wellington to Hill 29th October 1811, in Gurwood, *Dispatches*, Vol.VIII, p.362.
32 Hill to Wellington 20 October 1811, BL Add.MS, 35062, p.95.
33 Wellington to Hill 22 October 1811, BL Add.MS, 35059, p.422.

3

The Allies at Arroyomolinos

Hill selected two British and two Portuguese infantry brigades, a cavalry brigade, and Portuguese and British artillery brigades for the operation to dislodge Girard from Cáceres. He left one British and one Portuguese infantry brigade, with two Portuguese cavalry regiments plus artillery, to cover the approaches to Portugal. Castaños contributed Morillo's infantry and Penne Villemur's cavalry.

The Staff

Unlike the French, the allied army had no formal corps level structure bridging the gap between the individual divisions and the field army as a whole, but Hill's command in the south was a corps in all but name. Without a corps headquarters establishment Hill relied on the 2nd Division headquarters and his personal staff. Hill's aides-de-camp (ADCs) were Captain Edward Currie of the 90th Foot, Hill's younger brother Captain Clement Hill of the Royal Horse Guards, and Ensign Chatham Horace Churchill of the 1st Foot Guards.

Currie, who was accompanied on campaign by his wife, had been with Hill's 'family' since 1804 and his first brigade command in Ireland, and before that under his command in the 90th. Clement, ten years Rowland's junior, had been an aide-de-camp to his brother since just after the Battle of Vimeiro and had been wounded at Oporto.[1] One of the primary roles of an ADC was to relay orders, and the job could be a dangerous one in battle. Lieutenant generals were normally only allowed two ADCs but Hill had been allowed an extra aide and Churchill had been appointed in October 1810, after serving two other generals in the same role.[2]

The next most senior officer in Hill's corps was Major General Sir William Erskine, who had held various commands in Wellington's army, none of them particularly successfully. Erskine commanded the 2nd Cavalry Division,

---

1   J.A. Hall, *The Biographical Dictionary of British Officers Killed & Wounded, 1808-1814* (London: Greenhill, 1998), p.279.

2   Anon., *General Orders Spain & Portugal* (London: Egerton, 1811), Vol.II, p.194.

which consisted of only one brigade. He was very near-sighted and prone to bouts of mental instability. When Wellington wrote to Horse Guards querying his appointment to the army in the Peninsula he was told, perhaps with the writer's tongue firmly in his cheek: 'No doubt he is sometimes a little mad, but in his lucid intervals he is an uncommonly clever fellow; and I trust he will have no fit during the campaign, though he looked a little wild as he embarked' and that the commander-in-chief, General Sir David Dundas, thought that 'some of our Generals would not be the worse for a little of his madness'.[3]

Staff roles at the divisional level flowed from those in Wellington's headquarters and were divided between the Adjutant General's department, which dealt mainly with orders, discipline and administration, and the Quarter Master General's department, which largely dealt with equipment, marches and quarters. The 2nd Division's Assistant Adjutant General was Lieutenant Colonel John Charles Rooke, 3rd Foot Guards, and the Deputy Assistant Adjutant General was Lieutenant Charles Bayley, 31st Foot.[4] In a letter to his brother written soon after he took up his post, Rooke was very complimentary about serving in the division's headquarters, writing of Hill: 'He likes to see everything well done, but at the same time makes no fuss, and places the utmost confidence in those under him.'[5]

The Assistant Quarter Master General was Lieutenant Colonel Wilhelm Offeney, King's German Legion, with Captain George Hay, Marquess of Tweeddale, of the 15th Hussars, and Captain Nathaniel Thorn, 3rd Foot, as his deputies. Offeney had been one of the first Hanoverian officers to travel to Britain in 1803 when the Legion was formed and was an experienced staff officer.[6] Also vital to the running of the division was Assistant Commissary General Randolph Isham Routh, with deputies attached to each brigade, responsible for the supply of food for the men and forage for the horses. Robert Grant and Donald McIntosh were the Staff Surgeons assigned to the division, in addition to the regimental surgeons and assistant surgeons, looking after the men's health. Assistant Provost Marshal Sergeant James Stubbs, 31st Foot, was tasked with preventing and punishing crimes by the troops. Captain John Squire was the Royal Engineer with Hill's headquarters. In addition to the officers of the staff there would have been many clerks, orderlies, servants, cooks, and wives with the headquarters.

Lieutenant Robert Blakeney, of the 28th Foot, described life at the headquarters in Portalegre:

> Here we remained some time enjoying all the luxury of campaigning, inviting even to the most refined cockney, keenest sportsman, or most insatiable gourmand. Races were established, partridge-shooting was good, and General

---

3   Torrens to Wellington, in J.W. Fortescue, *A History of the British Army* (London: Macmillan & Co, 1906), Vol.VII, p.419.

4   The details of all the staff of the 2nd Division are taken from the Return of Staff Officers, 25 October 1811, TNA, WO 17/2468.

5   J.C. Rooke to W. Rooke 28 April 1810, Gloucestershire Archives, D1833/F14, p.24.

6   N.L. Beamish, *History of the King's German Legion* (London: Thomas & William Boone, 1837), Vol.I, p.76.

Hill kept a pack of foxhounds, and entertained liberally. He felt equally at home before a smoking round of beef or a red-hot marshal of France, and was as keen at unkennelling a Spanish fox as at starting a French general out of his sleep, and in either amusement was the foremost to cry, 'Tally ho!' or, 'There they go!' As his aide-de-camp, Captain Currie, was married, the amiable Mrs. Currie always dined at the general's table, so that we neither forgot the deference due to beauty nor the polished manners of the drawing room.[7]

Howard's Brigade

Major General Kenneth Alexander Howard's brigade had been transferred from the 1st Division to reinforce the 2nd after the heavy losses at Albuera. Howard had been commissioned into the 2nd Foot Guards in 1786, and

Kenneth Alexander Howard in later life. (Reproduced with the permission of the National Army Museum. NAM 2001-04-355)

had served in the Flanders campaigns, in Ireland during the rebellion, and then in the Helder in 1799. For several years he held various staff positions overseeing the foreign corps and was then appointed as one of the King's ADCs with the rank of colonel. He had been promoted to major general in 1810, and took command of his brigade in January 1811. The brigade fought at the battle of Fuentes de Oñoro and then marched south soon afterwards.

All three infantry battalions in the brigade were relatively recent arrivals to the Peninsula, but all of them had served in the 1808 campaign in Portugal and then had been evacuated with the rest of Moore's army from Corunna. The 1st battalion 50th (West Kent) Regiment of Foot, which landed at Lisbon in September 1810, was known as the 'dirty half-hundred' from the black facings on their redcoats. Lieutenant John Patterson had joined the 50th in 1807 and said of the battalion in his memoir:

In addition to the old hands, they obtained a full supply of young active fellows, who had volunteered from the English Militia,– the whole, officers as well as privates, were in good health and spirits, elated with the prospect of active service, and looking forward to new adventures as well as to encountering the enemy in the field. But it was not alone by numerical strength or physical power that the 50th was likely to be formidable. There was likewise an 'esprit de corps,' a high tone of feeling among them, producing a moral force not easily to be overcome.[8]

---

7   R. Blakeney, *A Boy in the Peninsular War* (London: Murray, 1899), p.214. Cockney at the time was used as a term for a pampered town-dweller.

8   J. Patterson, *The Adventures of Captain John Patterson* (London: T & W Boone, 1837), p.8.

The 1/50th was a conventional line infantry battalion with one light company trained in skirmishing, one grenadier company, formed from the steadiest and often tallest men, and eight centre companies.

The commanding officer of the 1/50th was Lieutenant Colonel Charles Stewart, who had only recently returned from sick leave in Lisbon.[9] Patterson gives an excellent description of his commander, writing that he:

> [W]as an old and very distinguished officer, having encountered the vicissitudes of war, in almost every quarter into which the British arms were carried. In the East Indies, while present at the siege of Seringapatam, as Captain of the 71st Highlanders, he bore a conspicuous part, when leading his company to the assault of that fortress, in which he was severely wounded. He was a hardy Northern, skilled in martial science, and was as eminent in those qualities which are required for training up the young battalion as for those which are displayed in manoeuvring the more experienced in the field. His hoary locks, well blanched by many a hard campaign, indicated the length of service to which his best days had been devoted, while his penetrating expression of countenance indicated the active mind, and the abilities, by which he was so highly distinguished.[10]

The 1st battalion 71st (Highland Light Infantry) Regiment of Foot arrived at the same time as the 50th. The 71st had been trained as specialist light infantry in 1809, after also serving in the early peninsular campaigns. Their conversion from line to light infantry was overseen by Colonel Baron Francis de Rottenburg, the author of the army's manual on light infantry tactics and drill. The training would have taught the whole battalion how to fight in extended order, to skirmish with the enemy's light troops, to select individual targets to fire at, and also to patrol and provide outposts. They would not have lost their ability to fight in close order though, with the ordinary line infantry regiments. The 71st did not wear kilts, except the pipers who wore full highland dress, but did have a type of traditional Scottish blue bonnet with a red and white check band, shaped like the shako-style regimental cap of other redcoat regiments. The 1/71st had been fiercely engaged in the vicious street fighting in the village of Fuentes de Oñoro.

Lieutenant Colonel Henry Cadogan commanded the battalion. He had entered the army in 1797, aged 17, and had purchased his way to lieutenant colonel by 1805. He was one of Wellesley's ADCs in 1809 and was then sent as a liaison to the Spanish armies. He took command of the 1/71st soon after they arrived back in Portugal.[11] Cadogan had attracted some fame for fighting a duel with Lord Paget. Cadogan's sister, Charlotte, had been married to Henry Wellesley, Arthur's brother, but she and Paget had begun an affair which ultimately ended the marriage. Cadogan challenged Paget and the two met on Wimbledon Common. Paget's pistol misfired and Cadogan missed.[12]

---

9   Regimental returns September & October, 1/50th, TNA, WO 17/164.
10   Patterson, *Adventures*, p.5.
11   H.J. Ross, *A New General Biographical Dictionary* (London: Clay, 1848), Vol.V, p.371.
12   *The Edinburgh Annual Register for 1809* (Edinburgh: Balantyne, 1811), Vol.II, pp.151-2.

Lieutenant Colonel John Cameron, 92nd (Gordon Highlanders) Regiment of Foot. (Anne S.K. Brown Military Collection)

The 1st battalion 92nd (Gordon Highlanders) Regiment of Foot had also served in the Corunna campaign and had returned to Portugal in the early autumn of 1810, fighting with the others at Fuentes de Oñoro. Unlike the 71st they did wear kilts, in a dark blue and green tartan with a yellow over-stripe, and they wore traditional Scottish bonnets. The 1/92nd was commanded by Lieutenant Colonel John Cameron, who had been with the regiment since it had been raised in 1794, having abandoned a legal career. Both the 1/50th and 1/71st had received drafts from their second battalions over the summer, but the latest draft for the 92nd had only very recently arrived. Ensign James Hope was one of the 200 officers and men who marched into Portalegre on 6 October: 'Our march was a very dreary one; but the warm reception which we met with from our friends, who on our arrival hastened to welcome us to share their dangers and their glory, soon banished all traces of it from our remembrance.'[13]

All three of the battalions had also served in the disastrous Walcheren campaign of 1809. The British troops, many of whom were still recovering from the retreat to Corunna, had been beset by fever and the Walcheren battalions still suffered higher than average sickness rates in the Peninsula.[14] According to the October regimental returns the 1/50th had 223 men sick, the 1/71st had 328 and the 1/92nd had 170,[15] although Patterson of the 50th blamed their high sick rate on an arduous march in hot weather a few weeks earlier.[16]

Also under Howard's command was No.8 company of the 5th battalion of the 60th (Royal American) Regiment of Foot. The 5/60th had been raised at the end of 1797 as the first rifle battalion in the British Army. Recruited from Germans, Dutch, Swiss, Austrians, Poles, Hungarians and many others, they were one of the numerous foreign corps in the army. Commanded for many years by Baron de Rottenburg, the battalion had provided the majority of the riflemen for Wellesley's 1808 and 1809 campaigns, and he had spread the battalion's 10 companies amongst the army to give most of his brigades specialist rifle-armed light infantry. Wellington had a high opinion of the battalion, referring to them as an 'excellent corps'.[17] No.8 company was led by Captain Peter Blassiere, of whom Patterson wrote a vivid description:

13   J. Hope, *The Military Memoirs of an Infantry Officer 1809-1816* (Edinburgh: Anderson & Bryce, 1833), p.77.
14   A. Bamford, S*ickness, Suffering and the Sword* (Oklahoma: University of Oklahoma Press, 2013), p.226.
15   Regimental returns 25 October 1811, TNA WO 17/164, 17/192 & 17/213.
16   Patterson, *Adventures*, p.157.
17   Wellesley to Donkin 23 June 1809, in Gurwood, *Dispatches*, Vol. IV, p.431.

There was a company of the 60th rifles attached to our Brigade, who were all Germans. They were commanded by Captain Philip [sic] Blassiere, a singularly active and zealous officer. Throughout the whole period of our warfare he never was absent from his station. With unwearied perseverance he braved the hardest weather and the roughest service; his athletic frame and iron constitution enabling him to withstand it all, holding out with stubborn tenacity while hundreds gave way around him. Undergoing all hardships in common with his men, he walked by their side, partook of the same fare, and shared not only with them the dangerous trade of fighting, but all the miseries of cold and famine with their attendant train of horrors. He was foremost on all occasions, where shot and shell abounded, and was at the rendezvous before a man of the brigade was assembled; and long before the march commenced, there was Blassiere ready with his Germans for any thing that might be wanted.

The external appearance of this man was well calculated to excite surprise, and corresponded with his character for self-denial. His wardrobe was of the most scanty nature; the jacket and other parts of his attire, the original colour of which could not be distinguished by the most microscopic eye, were worn out, patched, and threadbare, and were pierced in various places; and the whole of his costume seemed at least for the last seven years to have retained its original situation on the person of its owner. Thus accoutred he trudged along, indifferent about the elements; as fast as he got wet, he got dry again, for he never changed his clothes. His muscular neck was enclosed by a hard leather stock and brass clasp to match, and all his trappings were of the same coarse materials as those worn by his men. The haversack, manufactured of rough canvass, sometimes proved a treacherous friend, for through many rents and breaches, made by the hand of time, the mouldy and crumbling biscuit found its way, leaving but the fragments of his bare allowance. The blue canteen, well clasped with iron hoops, afforded him a source of comfort; its contents being to him a certain panacea for all evils. With habits somewhat eccentric, he was never known to indulge in any thing beyond the rations; and having no desire for the society of others, he discussed his frugal meal in solitude, avoiding even the luxury of a tent. His good humoured though weatherbeaten countenance was the index of his mind, which was cheerful and contented.[18]

The 5/60th wore the green rifleman's jacket, with red collar and cuffs, and blue pantaloons. They were armed with what later became known as the Baker Rifle, and were trained to shoot at targets up to 300 yards range. In battle the riflemen targeted French officers, on marches they frequently formed the advance guard, and they were also often used on outpost duty. Many of their recruits came from foreign deserters or prisoners of war from the French army, so they did suffer more from desertion themselves than the British regiments. No.8 company had joined Howard's Brigade once it had arrived with the 2nd Division, replacing a company of the 95th.

Howard's Brigade was made up experienced battalions led by capable officers, but high sickness rates did reduce its strength. With both the 5/60th

---

18   Patterson, *Adventures*, pp.357-9.

company and 1/71st it also contained more trained light infantry than many other brigades. In total the brigade fielded 1,944 effective rank and file on 25 October; the 1/50th numbered 560, the 1/71st had 595 and the 1/92nd was the strongest at 752. The rifle company mustered only 37.[19]

Wilson's Brigade

The command of the other British infantry brigade that Hill ordered to prepare to march was officially vacant after Major General William Lumley had had to leave the army because of ill health. Wellington appointed temporary command to Brevet Colonel George Wilson of the 39th Foot, whilst he awaited a decision on the vacancy from London.[20] Wilson was the senior of the three battalion commanders. The brigade had fought at Albuera and at that point had been made up of the second battalions of the 28th, 34th and 39th Foot. The 2/28th suffered 32 percent casualties in the battle, the 2/34th lost 21 percent and the 2/39th 20 percent.[21] The British regimental system had been designed with the intention that the second battalions served at home and the first were used for overseas service, drafting men from the second battalions when needed. Pressures on manpower had meant that many second battalions were sent to the peninsula and Wellington was having to fight to keep these experienced units while Horse Guards in London wanted to replace them as their losses mounted and their first battalions became available.

The 2nd battalion 28th (North Gloucestershire) Regiment of Foot had been replaced in the brigade by the first battalion in August, but those soldiers who were still deemed fit for service were transferred from the 2nd battalion to the 1st, as were many of the officers if there were vacancies. Lieutenant Colonel Alexander Abercromby marched the remaining men of the 2nd battalion back to Lisbon to embark for home, but then had to travel back and take command of the 1st battalion after Lieutenant Colonel Charles Belson took sick leave.[22] Abercromby was the youngest son of Lieutenant General Sir Ralph Abercromby, who had been fatally wounded leading the expedition to Egypt in 1801, during which the 28th had to turn its rear rank about to fight French both in front and behind them, winning the right to wear their badge on the back of their regimental caps as well as the front. Alexander had joined the army in 1799, served in various campaigns including as an ADC to Sir John Moore in the Corunna campaign. At Albuera, where Lumley commanded the cavalry, he had commanded the brigade.[23] William Thornton Keep, who joined the 28th in Spain at the end of 1812, wrote of

19 Army in Portugal & Spain by Brigades & Divisions, 25 October 1811, TNA, WO 17/2468.
20 Anon., *General Orders Spain & Portugal*, Vol.III, pp.208-9.
21 Dempsey, *Albuera*, p.273.
22 C. Cadell, *Narrative of the Campaigns of the Twenty-Eighth Regiment* (London: Whittaker, 1835), pp.111-114.
23 Anon., *The Royal Military Calendar*, Vol.IV, pp.188-9.

Abercromby: 'Col. A does everything with such Esprit de Corps that it is the highest gratification to serve under him'.[24]

The 1/28th had served in the early campaigns in the Peninsula, at Walcheren, and then on the eastern coast of Spain, suffering heavy losses at the Battle of Barossa. Blakeney, arriving with the 1st battalion, described the meeting of the two battalions:

> Next morning at dawn we commenced our second campaign in Portugal. Crossing the Tagus, we continued our route through the Alemtejo, and arrived at Villaviciosa on the 10th. Here we joined our 2nd Battalion, commanded by Lieutenant-Colonel Abercrombie. It was the first meeting of the battalions since our separation at the Curragh of Kildare in 1805, and was very interesting. The old veterans of the 1st Battalion with measured phrase recounted their feats in Denmark, Sweden, Holland, Portugal and Spain, cunningly leaving many a space to be filled up by the warm imagination of their excited young auditors. On the other hand the gallant striplings of the 2nd Battalion, with that fervent and frank ingenuousness so inseparable from youth and so rare in advanced man hood, came at once to the bloody fight. They long and often dwelt upon the glorious battle of Albuera; they told of the Spaniards coming late; that Blake would neither lead nor follow; of brigades being cut up through the over-anxiety of their commanders; of colours being taken; in fine, of the battle being all but lost, until their brigade, commanded by their gallant Colonel Abercrombie, in conjunction with the brave Fusiliers, came up and by a combined and overwhelming charge bore down all opposition and tore away the palm of victory already twining round the enemy's standard.[25]

The 1st battalion received 484 men from the 2nd, and then later sent four sergeants and 85, mostly sick, men to the 2nd.[26]

The 2nd battalion of the 34th (Cumberland) Regiment of Foot had arrived in Portugal in July 1809, after the initial campaigns in the Peninsula, and had avoided Walcheren. Like many other regiments one of its main source of recruits had become volunteers from the militia, in its case mainly from northern, eastern and central England.[27] The battalion was commanded by Lieutenant Colonel William Fenwick, who since 1792 had served with the 1st battalion in the West Indies, the Cape of Good Hope and India before joining the 2nd prior to it sailing for Lisbon.[28] In September the battalion had received another draft of 92 men, two thirds of whom were volunteers from the militia. Despite this the battalion was still well below strength with 162 men sick at hospitals in the rear.[29] Illness was the main cause of death for soldiers in the Peninsula, and the prime factor in the need for replacements.

---

24   I. Fletcher (ed), *In the Service of the King. The Letters of William Thornton Keep at Home, Walcheren, and in the Peninsula, 1808-1814* (Staplehurst: Spellmount, 1997), p.128.

25   Blakeney, *Peninsula*, p.213.

26   September & October returns 1/28th, TNA, WO 17/134.

27   Record of the Second Battalion 34th Regiment, Cumberland Museum of Military Life, LIB-843.

28   Anon., *The Royal Military Calendar*, Vol.IV, pp.322-3.

29   September & October returns 2/34th, TNA, WO 17/144.

Lieutenant Moyle Sherer recalled returning to the 2/34th in 1810 after being on sick leave himself:

> Alas! when I came again to stand on the parade, for how many a face did my eye inquire in vain! in the space of four short months, my regiment had buried nearly three hundred men, all in the prime of life, and vigour of their manhood. They had all fallen victims to the sickly season, in Spanish Estremadura. The officers of the army had not suffered in proportion to the men, as they were enabled to live more generously; for, at that time, wine and spirits were never issued regularly to the soldiers; and the wine, which was occasionally procured for them, was very indifferent. There was, moreover, a very great scarcity of bark in the regimental hospitals, and numbers perished for the want of it.[30]

Jesuit's bark, containing quinine, was one of the main treatments for fevers. Ensign George Bell was one of the officers sent to fill a vacancy caused by the losses at Albuera. The 34th were known as 'The Cumberland Gentlemen' because of the high proportion of officers from the aristocracy. In his memoir Bell wrote:

> We had certainly some of the most select and high-caste officers I ever met in the army — such brave and zealous men too; such as Colonels Maister and Fenwick, Willett, Wyat, Fancourt, Egerton, Sherer, Baron, Worsley — Jolliff, the most liberal paymaster, and the clever surgeon, Luscombe; Sullivan and Eccles, bravest of the brave; Norton, Day, cum multis aliis.[31]

Patterson of the 50th noted how well the 28th and 34th worked together:

> The 28th and 34th generally paired off together. The 'slashers,' as the former called themselves, were chiefly Irish, and as a matter of course, were up to every sort of mischief, rushing upon the enemy, when they were unmuzzled, with the fierceness of a tiger. Having the same facings, and a sort of family likeness to the 34th, these regiments matched uncommonly well in harness.[32]

With Wilson commanding the brigade, command of the 2nd battalion 39th (Dorsetshire) Regiment of Foot fell to Major Patrick Lindsay. The battalion had arrived in the Peninsula at the same time as the 34th. They also received a draft in September with 64 men joining from the militia, the depot at Hilsea, or from the recruiting service.[33] The 39th had uncommon pea-green facings, earning them the nickname of the Green Linnets. The 28th and 34th both had more common yellow facings.[34] The battalion was even more severely

---

30 Sherer, *Recollections,* pp.116-7.
31 Cum multis aliis – And many others. G. Bell, *Rough Notes by an Old Soldier* (London: Day, 1867), pp.19-20.
32 J. Patterson, *Camps and Quarters, or Scenes and Impressions, of Military Life,* Vol.II (London: Saunders & Otley, 1840), p.93.
33 September & October returns 2/39th, TNA, WO 17/149.
34 R. Burnham, & R. McGuigan, *The British Army against Napoleon, Facts, Lists, and Trivia 1805-1815* (Barnsley: Frontline Books, 2010), pp.112 & 126.

understrength than the 34th, with the September return showing just 381 effective rank and file, with 182 men sick.[35]

Wilson's Brigade also had a rifle company from the 5/60th attached. No.4 company was commanded by Captain John McMahon. McMahon had joined the 60th after the surrender of the French in Portugal in 1808, and then served with his company in the campaigns afterwards, barring a period of sick leave after he snapped his Achilles tendon dismounting from his horse.

Wilson's Brigade had a total strength of 1,741 effectives in October, with the 1/28th mustering 790, the 2/34th 511, the 2/39th 411 and the rifle company 36.[36] Most of the officers and men had considerable experience but two of the three battalions were significantly understrength.

Long's Cavalry Brigade

The commander of Hill's British cavalry brigade, Major General Robert Ballard Long, was a prickly and controversial character. He did not suffer fools gladly, and seems to have classified most of his superiors as such. He entered the army aged 20 in 1791 as a cornet in the 1st (King's) Dragoon Guards and by 1798 had purchased himself up to the lieutenant colonelcy of the Hompesch Mounted Riflemen, one of the many foreign corps. In 1803 he was lieutenant colonel of the 2nd Dragoon Guards and then moved to the 15th Light Dragoons and oversaw their conversion to Hussars, which amounted to a change of name and uniform rather than of role. He had staff positions for the Corunna and Walcheren campaigns and then sailed in HMS *Victory* for Lisbon in March 1811. As a regimental administrator he seems to have been hardworking and effective. As a commander of cavalry in combat his record was less impressive, with his performance perhaps hampered by a lack of active service command experience. Given a brigade under Beresford he almost immediately garnered criticism over a mishandled action at Campo Maior, for which Long and Beresford blamed each other. Beresford placed another commander over him at Albuera, where the cavalry saw little action, and Long was one of Beresford's main critics after the battle. His command was reduced in size, and when a picquet of the 11th Light Dragoons was surprised by the French in June he again received a portion of the blame.[37]

Long's was a light cavalry brigade, whose primary roles were reconnaissance and outpost duty. The 9th Light Dragoons had only arrived in the Peninsula that summer, and had not seen much active service before then, apart from the controversial and unsuccessful campaigns in Rio de la Plata in South America and on Walcheren.[38] The six troops of the 9th were

35   September return 2/39th, TNA, WO 17/149.
36   Army in Portugal & Spain by Brigades & Divisions, 25 October 1811, TNA, WO 17/2468.
37   T.H. McGuffie, *Peninsular Cavalry General* (London: Harrap, 1951); R. Burnham, & R. McGuigan, *Wellington's Brigade Commanders* (Barnsley: Pen & Sword, 2017), pp.176-83.
38   C.T. Atkinson, 'The Ninth Queen's Royal Lancers, 1715-1936', *Journal of the Society for Army Historical Research*, Vol.18, No. 72, pp.235-8.

Officer of the 9th Light Dragoons, 1809. (Anne S.K. Brown Military Collection)

commanded by the senior captain, Captain George Gore, and they had a total strength of 189 rank and file.[39] Their uniform consisted of an ornately-laced blue jacket with buff facings and breeches, plus a Tarleton helmet. Cavalry regiments on active service would typically be organised into squadrons of two troops each.

The 13th Light Dragoons had arrived in Portugal in 1810 after a long period of home service. They had been involved in several skirmishes with the French, including Campo Maior, and one troop won praise for capturing a French patrol at Ladoera.[40] In command of the 13th's six troops was Brevet Lieutenant Colonel Joseph Muter, and they mustered 262 rank and file.[41] The 13th wore a very similar uniform to the 9th, but with gold lace not silver. The British light cavalry in the Peninsula were often very inexperienced and little-trained in the realities of campaigning. In April 1811 an outpost of the

---

39   October return 9th Light Dragoons, TNA, WO 17/30.

40   Anon., *Historical Record of the 13th Regiment of Light Dragoons* (London: Parker, 1842), pp.35-9.

41   October return 13th Light Dragoons, TNA, WO 17/37.

13th was surprised by the French near Olivenza and over 50 men were captured.[42]

The 2nd KGL Hussars contributed two weak squadrons to the brigade, totalling only 166 effective rank and file,[43] but they were perhaps the most capable cavalry Hill had. The German cavalry were widely respected by their British counterparts. Major Edward Cocks of the 16th Light Dragoons said of them, 'the cavalry are old Hussars, almost all Hanoverians, and many of them men of great respectability. These men are perfectly to be depended on and understand outpost duty better, and take more care of their horses, than British dragoons'.[44]

The 2nd KGL Hussars had been formed in 1805 as light dragoons and then quickly converted to the fashionable Hungarian hussar-derived uniform of heavily laced jacket, fur-lined pelisse worn over one shoulder, barrel sash around the waist, and fur busby cap. The troops with Hill had only arrived early in the summer from the KGL cavalry depot at Ipswich, but they soon proved their worth. On 13 June a patrol came across a party of French dragoons, charged them and took six men prisoner. On the 21 June one of their picquets was attacked by French cavalry, just after being relieved. The relieved hussars returned to help hold the enemy off before the rest of the hussar detachment came up and, with the aid of a nearby British squadron, succeeding in charging and driving off two squadrons of Polish Lancers, capturing several. However, they were then driven back when more French arrived on the scene.[45]

The commander of the hussars with Hill was Major Baron Augustus Frederich von dem Bussche. Many of the KGL had originally been in the defeated and disbanded Hanoverian army but by 1811, with it being impossible to recruit from the French-controlled German states, officers of the Legion, including Bussche, were actively recruiting from Germans amongst the deserters from the French army held by the allies.[46] A field return for the hussars from April 1811 shows that 283 of the men were Hanoverian, 14 were from other German states and 34 from other foreign countries.[47]

Officer of the 2nd Hussars, King's German Legion, by Charles Lyall. (Anne S.K. Brown Military Collection)

42   Anon., *Historical Record of the 13th*, p.47.
43   Army in Portugal & Spain by Brigades & Divisions, 25 October 1811, TNA, WO 17/2468.
44   J. Page, *Intelligence Officer in the Peninsula* (Staplehurst: Spellmount, 1986), p.63.
45   Beamish, *King's German Legion*, Vol.II, pp.3-7.
46   There are references to Bussche recruiting from French deserters in the Foreign Depot muster book, TNA, WO 12/11686.
47   Field Return, 2nd KGL Hussars, TNA, WO 27/105.

Ashworth's Brigade

Coronel Charles Ashworth's brigade had also been dispatched from the north to reinforce Hill in the south after Albuera. Ashworth had been commissioned into the 68th Foot in 1798, rising to major and swapping regiments several times by 1808.[48] In 1809 he opted to be attached to the Portuguese Army, taking a step up in rank. He commanded Regimento de Infantaria n.º 6, before taking over command of the brigade. Beresford had been charged with rebuilding the Portuguese Army from scratch after its defeat and dissolution following the French invasion of 1807. He was a far better administrator than he was a field commander and with the help of a cadre of British officers and NCOs created a very effective fighting force. The Portuguese regiments used translations of British manuals, were equipped with British arms and equipment, and were generally respected by their British comrades in Wellington's army.

Ashworth's brigade consisted of Regimento de Infantaria n.º 6 and n.º 18, both line regiments of two battalions, and Batalhão de Caçadores n.º 6. The line regiments, wearing dark blue, were both raised in the Oporto region: n.º 6 was commanded by *Tenente Coronel* Maxwell Grant and n.º 18 by *Coronel* Manoel Pamplona. Both units were highly rated as effective and well disciplined.[49] N.º 6 had 1,432 effectives across its two battalions, n.º 18 had 1,431, and the caçadores fielded 572.[50]

The Batalhão de Caçadores n.º 6 was a specialist light infantry battalion. Most of the men were armed with muskets but one company of *Atiradores* were armed with rifles. They wore a brown uniform with yellow facings. The regiment was also formed at Oporto and recruited from the mountainous Minho region on the Spanish border, with many of the men being hardy farmers or hunters. It was commanded by *Tenente Coronel* Sebastião Pinto de Araujo.[51] Many of the British officers with the caçadores had previous experience with light infantry or rifle units. Lieutenant Richard Brunton of the 43rd was one such officer. He joined the battalion in March 1811, gained a step up in rank to *Capitão*, and with them made the long march pursing the French out of Portugal, constantly close on their heels and outrunning their own supply lines until they reached Fuentes de Oñoro 'in half starved but tolerably effective state' and then helped to defend the village from repeated attacks in the subsequent battle.[52]

---

48   Anon., *The Royal Military Calendar*, Vol.IV, p.279.

49   A. Halliday, *Observations on the Present State of the Portuguese Army* (London: Murray, 1811), pp.20-1, 29-30 & 146.

50   Return of Portuguese infantry, 20 October 1811, TNA, WO17/2466.

51   Haliday, *Observations*, p.45; S.V. Coelho, *The Portuguese Caçadores, 1808–1814*, at <http://www.academia.edu/3733216/The_Portuguese_Caçadores_1808_1814> (accessed 21 January 2019).

52   Narrative of the Service of Lt. Col. Richard Brunton, National Army Museum (NAM) 1968-07-461.

Campbells's Brigade

One brigade of the Portuguese Division commanded by *Marechal de Campo* John Hamilton was also detailed to take part in the march to Cáceres. Hamilton had entered the East India Company's army in 1773, moving to the King's 87th Foot in 1787, and had spent almost two decades fighting in India before exchanging into the 61st for service in the West Indies. He was promoted to major general in 1809 and appointed as Inspector General of Infantry for the Portuguese Army, and then also to command of a division.[53] The brigade was commanded by *Brigadeiro* Archibald Campbell, of the 46th Foot, and made up of Regimento de Infantaria n.º 4 and Regimento de Infantaria n.º 10, also both line regiments of two battalions each, led by *Tenente Coronel* Allan William Campbell and *Tenente Coronel* Dom Luís Inocêncio Benedito de Castro respectively.[54] N.º 4 was judged 'one of the finest corps in the army,' however n.º 10 was 'not composed of so fine a body of men as the Fourth with which it is brigaded, but it has always been kept in equally good order.'[55] N.º 4 mustered 1,351 men and n.º 10 1,503.[56]

Conde de Penne Villemur's Cavalry

The Spanish contingent consisted of the vanguard of Castaños' 5º Ejército. Nominally consisting of a division each of cavalry and infantry in reality the numbers of troops had more in common with brigades than divisions, and made up most of the troops under Castaños' command. As Captain Squire of the engineers put it: 'This corps is called the vanguard of the 5th army, but it is the whole of it – vanguard, rearguard, & all.'[57] Whereas the Portuguese army was reorganised and equipped with considerable financial and administrative aid from the British government, and had some British officers, the Spanish army was controlled by a series of disparate and fractious Juntas, and found finance, supply and recruitment very difficult with most of the country under occupation. The surprising success against the French at Bailen in 1808 had not often been repeated. The Spanish regular forces were outmatched and outnumbered by the French, but did manage to hold onto some areas, often helped by the activities of the guerrillas tying down large numbers of French troops.

Portuguese line infantryman, by Ribeiro Arthur. (Anne S.K. Brown Military Collection)

53 Anon., *The Royal Military Calendar*, Vol.II, pp.329-30.
54 Hall, *Biographical Dictionary*, pp.103-4 & <http://www.arqnet.pt/exercito/10ri.html> (Accessed 3 July 2019).
55 Haliday, *Observations*, pp.19, 23-24.
56 Return of Portuguese infantry, 20 October 1811, TNA, WO17/2466.
57 Squire to Dickson 18 October 1811, in J.H. Leslie, *The Dickson Manuscripts* (London: Royal Artillery, 1905), Series C, 1811, p.484.

Wellington found co-operation with the Spanish Juntas and commanders difficult, and had low opinions of both their soldiers and their officers.[58] The pervading opinion amongst the British was that the Spanish were poorly drilled, poorly led, and prone to buckle under pressure in battle. However, the Spanish troops at Albuera did stand in the face of concerted, albeit mishandled, French attacks and performed well. In overall command of Hill's Spanish contingent was *Mariscal de Campo* Pedro Agustín Girón, nephew of Castaños and a competent general who Hill seemed to get on well with.

The commander of the cavalry was *Mariscal de Campo* Conde Louis de Penne Villemur, a nobleman from the Hautes-Pyrenees region of France. He had served with one of the foreign regiments of the Spanish Army from 1778, campaigning in Africa, before joining the French army and becoming a lieutenant in the Hussards d'Esterhazy in 1786. He left France in 1791 and became a major in Rohan's Hussars in British service, and fought in the campaigns against the revolutionary army. In 1809 he returned to Spain to fight the French occupation.[59] Penne Villemur's command consisted of squadrons from six different regiments: the 1º Regimiento de la Reina, and the 2º Regimiento de Algarve, were both cavalry of the line; his dragoons came from the 8º Regimiento de Dragones Lusitania and the 6º Regimiento de Dragones Sagunto; and his light cavalry from the 1º Husares de Extremadura and the Cazadores de Sevilla.[60] In total the Spanish cavalry amounted to approximately 600 men.[61]

Morrillo's Infantry

The Spanish infantry was commanded by *General de Brigada* Pablo Morillo. Morillo began his military career in the Regimiento de Infantería Marina. He rose to sergeant and at the Battle of Trafalgar was on board the *San Ildefonso,* where he was wounded and taken prisoner.[62] When the revolt against French rule began, he was commissioned into a volunteer regiment, spent some time leading a band of guerrillas, and then appointed to command his brigade. Lieutenant Andrew Leith-Hay, who spent time liaising with the Spanish army described Morillo's character:

> General Morillo, with all his roughness and his ignorance, was an enthusiastic admirer of every thing English. Throughout the whole course of his various services during the war, he evinced a strong and marked feeling of attachment and respect for the troops of that country. He had raised himself from the lowest ranks by his enterprising courage and cordial exertion in forwarding every

---

58   Wellington to Castlereagh 25 August 1809, in Gurwood, *Dispatches,* Vol.V, pp.82-5.

59   A. Mazaz, *Histoire de l'ordre Royal et militaire de Saint-Louis*, Vol.III (Paris, Firmin Didot, 1861), p.28.

60   J.J. Sañudo Bayón (ed)., *Base de datos sobre las unidades militares en la Guerra de la Independencia Española* (Madrid: Ministerio de Defensa, 2006).

61   Oman, *Peninsular War*, Vol.IV, p.600.

62   A. Rodriguez Villa, *El Teniente General Don Pablo Morillo*, Vol.I, (Madrid: Editorial-America, 1920), p.16.

scheme or measure calculated, as he conceived, to resist French domination. He had obtained considerable authority over the division of Spaniards under his immediate orders; his courage was undoubted, his devotion to Sir Rowland Hill, with whom he had long served, unbounded. Under these circumstances, this officer, in most respects a very ordinary man, became known to the army, and his name identified with some degree of distinction.[63]

The Spanish infantry totalled around 2,000 men.[64] Morillo's troops consisted of one battalion each of the Regimiento de Infanteria Provincial de Unión, the Regimiento de Infanteria de León and the Regimiento de Infanteria Ligera Voluntarios de la Victoria. However, Morillo regarded the Unión regiment as the only one that was properly equipped, trained and disciplined.[65] The Spanish line infantry generally wore blue, but there was a large variety among the volunteer and regionally raised units, and what they actually wore often depended on what they could obtain from the inadequate supply system.

Legión Extremeña

Another part of the Spanish force, contributing both a troop of lancers and a unit of light infantry was the Legión Extremeña. The legion had been formed by John Downie; a Scottish merchant who made and lost a fortune in the West Indies, before becoming involved with the would-be South American liberator Francisco de Miranda in an attempt to free what is now Venezuela from Spanish rule that quickly failed. Back in Britain he was appointed an Assistant Commissary through the influence of his friend, Major General Thomas Picton, and served in the Corunna campaign. However, the mundane life of keeping an army fed did not hold his attention for long and when he heard of a French attack a couple of days ride from where he was stationed, he abandoned his post to get closer to the action. Unofficial reconnaissances into French held Extremadura and further skirmishes, with the French and his superiors, soon followed. He was both praised and censured by Wellington. During the first half of 1810 he badgered the Spanish commanders and Wellington to form a mixed arms unit in Extremadura. Through a mix of effrontery, cajolery, conniving and deception he eventually got his way. He was given the rank of *coronel*, and hoped to build upon regional pride by creating a 16th Century-style uniform that harked back to the days of the conquistadors Pizarro and Cortés, both of whom came from the province. Recruitment was slow, partly due to the poverty of the area, but also perhaps because of the ridiculous uniform. With few modern weapons available the legion was initially armed with cross-bows, swords, slings, lances and anything else they could find. Downie was even given Pizarro's own sword to

---

63   A. Leith-Hay, *Narrative of the Peninsular War* (London: Whittaker, 1832), Vol.I, pp.301-2.
64   Oman, *Peninsular War*, Vol.IV, p.600.
65   Rodriguez Villa, *Morillo*, p.55.

wield against the French and inspire his men.[66] Sherer, of the 34th, described the legion:

> On the line of march this day, I saw a body of the Estremaduran legion; a corps raised, clothed, and commanded by a General Downie, an Englishman, who had formerly been a commissary in our service. Any thing so whimsical or ridiculous as the dress of this corps, I never beheld: it was meant to be an imitation of the ancient costume of Spain. The turned-up hat, slashed doublet, and short mantle, might have figured very well in the play of Pizarro, or at an exhibition of Astley's; but in the rude and ready bivouack, they appeared absurd and ill chosen.[67]

Artillery

Two brigades of artillery were chosen to accompany the expedition: a Portuguese artillery brigade of six-pounders commanded by *Capitão* Sebastião José de Arriaga, and a nine-pounder brigade of the Royal Artillery commanded by Brevet Major James Hawker. An artillery brigade typically contained six guns and their associated ammunition train, stores and baggage. Major George Julius Hartmann of the KGL Artillery was in overall command of the guns.

Byng's Brigade

The brigade of the 2nd Divison left in the rear, commanded by Colonel John Byng, and containing the battalions that had suffered the worst casualties at Albuera, seems to have followed on soon after the rest of the 2nd Division marched. The brigade consisted of the 1st battalions of the 3rd and 57th foot, plus a provisional battalion made up of the remnants of the 2/31st and 2/66th. On 25 October they had marched to the Spanish frontier at La Codosera.[68] They then must have advanced further as in a letter Cameron of the 92nd refers to a British brigade not being present with the rest of the army on the night of the 27th as they had been ordered to take a detour, and that their place in the planned attack was taken by Ashworth's Portuguese brigade.[69] Hill also mentions that Byng's Brigade were a few hours march away on the 28th.[70] In total Hill's force was around 13,000 men,[71] significantly stronger than Girard's division at Cáceres.

---

66 G. Iglesias-Rogers, *British Liberators in the Age of Napoleon* (London: Bloomsbury, 2013), pp.36 & 104-9; C. Esdaile, 'Guerrillas, Bandits, Adventurers and Commissaries: the Story of John Downie', in C.M. Woolgar (ed.), *Wellington Studies IV* (Southhampton: University of Southampton, 2008), pp.94-114.

67 Sherer, *Recollections*, pp.229-30.

68 Army Return, 25 October 1811, TNA, WO 17/2468.

69 Cameron to Hope 2 November 1811, National Records of Scotland (NRS), GD1/736/121.

70 Hill to Hamilton 22 November 1811, BL Add.MS, 35062, p.102.

71 Based on the returns quoted above and the estimate of the Spanish contingent.

4

The French at Arroyomolinos

Général de Division Jean-Baptiste Girard was born in 1776 at Aups, in Provence.[1] He volunteered for the army in 1793 and began a rapid rise through the ranks, initially serving as a *quartier-maître-trésorier* and then in other administrative roles. In 1794 he was with the Armée d'Italie and by 1796 had risen to *sous-lieutenant* and was an ADC to *Général de Brigade* Jean-Charles Monnier. He was wounded for the first time that year when he accompanied Monnier as he led an attack against the Austrians near the Brenta river. Girard was hit in the leg by a musket ball; the ball could not be removed and the wound permanently affected his walking. In 1797 he was promoted to *lieutenant* and then again to *capitaine*. A year later he was a *chef de bataillon*. He still served in various staff roles, but during many of the battles of the Italian campaign he was at the forefront of the action and gained praise for his bravery. By 1799 he was serving as Monnier's adjutant general.

Jean-Baptiste Girard, date and artist unknown. (Public Domain)

In 1804 Girard was deputy chief of staff of a division in Paris. He then moved to a cavalry division and fought at Austerlitz in 1805 and Jena in 1806, after which he was promoted to *général de brigade* and given command of a brigade in V Corps. In 1808 he was made a baron of the Empire and at the end of the year went with his division to Spain. At Arzobispo in 1809 he commanded the infantry division that led the assault across the bridge. He was promoted to *général de division* that year for his conduct at the Battle of Ocaña, where he was again wounded. More action followed in 1810, most notably when Girard's division defeated the Spanish at Villagarcia. Soult, reporting

---

1   R. Du Casse, *Le Volontaire de 1793* (Paris: Dillet, 1880), p.5.

back to his superiors, noted that Girard had fulfilled his orders 'with the highest distinction; he was twenty days in motion, forced the enemy to call back all their detachments and, despite the disproportion of the forces, he gave them a glorious fight'.[2] Soult also praised Girard to *Maréchal* Mortier: 'the good arrangements made by this officer, his talents and his coolness, contributed not a little to the success of this brilliant affair'.[3]

In the spring of 1811 Soult recommended Girard be made a *Grand Officier* of the *Légion d'Honneur*. Girard had been fighting for 18 years, and had proven himself an able and courageous commander. He had won the favour of both his immediate superiors and the Emperor, but he was about to make the first major mistake of his career. At Albuera he was in temporary command of V Corps and requested the honour of leading the attack on the allies, to which Soult agreed. Girard led his men on a complicated march

French line regiment grenadier officer, with uniform details c. 1810-12. (Anne S.K. Brown Military Collection)

---

2   Du Casse, *Volontaire, p.340.*

3   Soult to Mortier 19 August 1810, in A. Du Casse, *Mémoires et Correspondance Politique et Militaire du Roi Joseph* (Paris: Perrotin, 1854), Vol. VIII. p.463.

around the allied flank while a diversionary attack commenced on the village of Albuera. After his first division approached the allied line and crossed a stream, he waited an hour to get his whole formation across and in good order, before advancing in columns against the Spanish troops in his path. A severe squall caused a further delay, but his troops still managed to brush the Spanish aside from a weakly-held small hill. Girard then pressed his men forward, still in column, against the Spanish battalions in line. He expected that the mass of French bayonets would cause the Spanish to break, but they stood and delivered a series of musket volleys, supplemented by cannon fire, that tore into the French ranks. Rather than pressing home the attack over the last few yards, Girard halted his men and ordered them to deploy into line under fire. The result was disastrous; the Spanish kept firing and dozens of French officers fell. Girard had his horse shot from under him and was wounded. The French attack stalled through the weight of firepower against it, and lack of leadership. British brigades replaced the Spanish and continued the murderous musket duel with only a few paces between the armies. Another British brigade attacked the French flank, adding to their casualties. The pressure was only relieved by a French cavalry attack but V Corps was too depleted and disordered, and could not make any progress against the steadfast allies. Soult blamed Girard for his defeat at Albuera, although he stopped short of explicitly saying so in his report to Paris.[4]

Dembowski's Brigade

Girard's troops at Cáceres consisted of the two infantry brigades of his division and elements of two cavalry brigades, plus supporting artillery. *Général de Brigade* Ludwik Mateusz Dembowski commanded one of the two infantry brigades. Dembowski was Polish and had fought against Russia in the Kościuszko Uprising, but after the Poles' defeat he entered French service, first on the staff during the Italian campaign, and then as a *chef de bataillon* in the 2e Légion Polonaise. He sailed to Saint-Domingue in 1803, where the legion was subsequently ravaged by yellow fever and he was one of the few to return. He rose steadily in rank and took on more senior staff roles before travelling to Spain in October 1808 as deputy chief of staff of V Corps. He had been promoted to *général de brigade* in 1809 but had only taken command of his brigade in September.[5] The brigade consisted of three battalions each of the 34e and 40e Ligne. Both had been in Spain for three years and had fought at Albuera; the 34e suffered 44 percent casualties and the 40e lost 43 percent.[6] Swiss-born *Chef de Battalion* Théophile Woiral was the only one of the three battalion commanders of the 40e to survive Albuera.[7] The other

---

4   Dempsey, *Albuera*, pp.103, 109-12, 115-7, & 252-3.

5   G. Six, *Dictionnaire Biographique des Généraux et Amiraux de la Révolution et de l'Empire: 1792-1814* (Paris, Librarie Historique et Nobiliaire, 1934), Vol.I, p.327.

6   Dempsey, *Albuera*, pp.281-2; D. Smith, *Napoleon's Regiments* (London: Greenhill, 2000), pp.90 & 96

7   Dempsey, *Albuera*, p.267.

French infantryman, c.1808. (Anne S.K. Brown Military Collection)

two were both mortally wounded, whereas Woiral's wound was not as severe. Woiral had entered the army in 1799, taking the place of his conscripted brother, and had then risen through the ranks.[8] French line infantry wore blue coats, with red piping, cuffs and epaulettes and white turn backs, with only their buttons and shako plates denoting to which regiment they belonged.

As well as the heavy losses in battle the French units had to cope with the stress of fighting the guerrillas and dealing with a largely hostile populace. All convoys and couriers had to be strongly escorted, blockhouses on the main supply routes had to be garrisoned, and any stragglers ran the risk of being murdered. Ambushes were a constant danger and troops were often sent on gruelling expeditions to root out the guerrillas and conduct reprisals. In 1810 the 40e had been part of a force sent to the Serranía de Ronda to hunt down a guerrilla chief called Romero. *Capitaine* Ballue de la Haye-Descartes of the 40e recalled: 'On April 28, 1810, the 40e and 103e Regiments left Seville under the orders of General Maransin to enter the mountains of Ronda, or rather into hell, because if there is one it is not alone, since these mountains can be viewed as being another.'[9] As the French approached Romero retreated from his village, leaving a few sharpshooters to harass the enemy. The French set fire to his house and many others. Ballue goes on to say the column eventually trapped Romero in Algodanales, burnt most of the town and killed 700 men, women and children.

Remond's Brigade

Général de Brigade Charles-François Remond had, until August, been commander of the 34e Ligne. He was also born in Switzerland and joined a volunteer battalion as an officer in 1792, served through the campaigns of the 1790s defending France, and then later in Prussia and Poland, becoming commander of the 34e in 1806 and entering Spain with his regiment in 1808. He was made a baron of the Empire and a *commandant de la Légion*

---

8   'Un général né à Tavannes:Théophile Voirol' <https://docplayer.fr/6196352-Les-dossiers-de-memoires-d-ici-un-general-ne-a-tavannes-theophile-voirol-de-tavannes-a-besancon-une-carriere-militaire-d-exception.html> (accessed July 2019).

9   A. Goupille, 'Mémoires du Capitaine Ballue de la Haye-Descartes', *Bulletin Trimestriel de la Société Archéologique de Touraine*, V.XXXIII, pp.351-65.

d'honneur in 1809.[10] Remond's brigade consisted of three battalions each of the 64e and 88e Ligne, but one battalion of the 88e was detached at Seville.[11] At Albuera the regiments had taken 41 percent and 45 percent casualties respectively, and of the seven regimental and battalion commanders present, one had been killed and four wounded.[12]

The Cavalry

Girard's cavalry came from *Général de Brigade* André-François Bron de Bailly's brigade of dragoons and from *Général de Brigade* André-Louis-Elisabeth-Marie Briche's brigade of light cavalry. Bron had enlisted as a dragoon in 1777, becoming an officer after the revolution. He defended France in the early 1790s and then served with the Armée d'Italie. He was commanding the cavalry brigade that attacked the 90th Foot in Egypt in 1801, when Hill was wounded. Bron did not advance again in rank but held various posts across the Empire before taking up a command in Spain. His brigade had suffered heavy casualties at Usagre in May 1811 when they were routed by British and Portuguese cavalry. The majority of Bron's brigade was dispersed around Seville on other duties and only four squadrons of the 20e Dragons were present with Girard.[13] Squadrons of the 20e had been in Spain since 1808 and had fought at Bailen and Albuera. The 20e Dragons wore green with yellow turnbacks and cuffs, a brass helmet with a brass crest and black mane, with white breeches and waistcoat.

Briche had enlisted in the cavalry in 1790, quickly became an officer and then also served in many of Napoleon's early campaigns, distinguishing himself at Marengo and Saalfeld. He had been operating in Estremadura for well over a year.[14] His light cavalry brigade was made up of three squadrons from the 27e Chasseurs à Cheval and three from 10e Hussards, with two other regiments detached near Seville. Both the chasseurs and hussars had been in Spain for at least two years and had been engaged in numerous skirmishes and battles, including the clash with the Spanish at Cáceres on 13 October. The 10e Hussars wore a light blue pelisse, dolman and breeches with red facings and white lace.

The 27e Chasseurs had been raised as the Cheavau-Legers Belges du Duc d'Arenberg in 1806 at Liege, and recruited from local volunteers. The D'Arenberg family estates were near Brussels, and 21-year-old Prosper-Louis, 7th Duc d'Arenberg, had no military experience but became colonel of the regiment. The regiment first saw action in 1807 in the Germans states. In 1808 the regiment became the 27e Chasseurs à Cheval and d'Arenberg

10 Six, *Dictionnaire Biographique*, Vol.II, p.355.
11 A. Grasset, *Malaga Province Français (1811-12)* (Paris: Lavauzelle, 1910), p.584. Grasset lists the states of the Armée du Midi for October and November, but transposes Remond and Dembowski when he lists the brigades in Girard's division.
12 Dempsey, *Albuera*, pp.282 & 268.
13 R. Burnham, *Charging Against Wellington: Napoleon's Cavalry in the Peninsula 1807-1814* (Barnsley: Frontline, 2011), p.63.
14 Six, *Dictionnaire Biographique*, Vol.I, pp.158-61.

Trooper of 27e Chasseurs
à Cheval, by Pierre Albert
Leroux. (Anne S.K. Brown
Military Collection)

married a niece of the then Empress Joséphine. At the end of the year he took his regiment to Spain, where, over the next three years it was heavily engaged in anti-guerrilla operations as well as several major battles.[15] D'Arenberg had made his regiment deviate from the normal chasseurs à cheval simple green uniform by adding a braided hussar-style dolman, and yellow stripe with a row of buttons down the outside of the leg.

In total Girard's division numbered around 5,000 infantry and 1,000 cavalry, with one battery of foot artillery made up of one 8-pounder, one 4-pounder and 6-inch howitzer.[16] His commanders were all very experienced, many far more so than their opponents in the allied armies. The regiments too had been fighting long and hard in Spain, and were familiar with both their enemy and the terrain in Extremadura.

15   Daniel Clarke, 'The Chevau-Legers du Duc d'Arenberg and the 27th Chasseurs-aCheval, 1806-1814' <https://www.napoleon-series.org/military/organization/Arenberg/ArenbergChasseurs.pdf> (accessed July 2019).

16   Oman, *Peninsular War*, Vol.IV, p.599; Robert Burnham, 'The Battle of Arroyos dos Molinos 28 October, 1811', *The Napoleon Series* < https://www.napoleon-series.org/military-info/virtual/c_molinos.html> (accessed November 2020).

5

Hill's Advance

The allied troops left Portalegre and the surrounding area before dawn on 22 October and headed for the Spanish border. For at least some of the troops the order to move had come as a surprise. Lieutenant Benjamin Ball, of the 39th Foot, wrote to his mother:

> General Hill formed his plans for surprising them [the French] with such secrecy & decision that no one for a moment suspected he had any intention of the kind, so much so that we were extremely astonished on 21st October, to see the 71st Regt marching into Alegrete from Castelo de Vide without our having in any manner been apprized of their coming, or being ordered to make way for them. We of course concluded it was some mistake, & sent into Portalegre for orders; when we were soon set to rights by an express from the General ordering both the Regts to march the following morning to Codosera, where we were joined by the whole Division & encamped.[1]

The women and most of the baggage were left behind so the troops could travel faster over the poor roads. Hill's men marched the 23 miles to the village of La Codosera through the mountains of the Serra de São Mamede.[2] The Conde de Penne Villemur, with the Spanish troops, pushed forward from Salorino and reoccupied Aliseda, 19 miles from Cáceres, without loss, as the French cavalry outposts withdrew to Arroyo del Puerco.

For Ensign George Bell of the 34th the march was his first experience of campaigning:

> The rainy season had commenced, and the weather was dreadful. We marched all the day, and lay down on the wet sod by night, which rather surprised and alarmed me, expecting to be under cover in some civilized way after our day's work, instead of herding with the beasts of the field. I had an old boat cloak and a blanket for my bed and bedding. I never had more, but sometimes less, for the

---

1   Ball to mother, 15 November 1811, Hampshire Archives 20M62/11B/5.
2   The distances quoted in this chapter are derived from modern mapping software and may not exactly match the routes taken. They are given as an indication only. However, the region is still sparsely populated and many of the routes will have changed very little.

next three years. 'We have made a raw and rainy beginning of our campaign,' said Richardson, my chum 'how did you sleep?' 'Slept like a fish,' I said; 'I believe they sleep best in water.' 'Bravo!' said he; 'you'll do.' I thought in my own mind I might *do* for a night or two more, but I would soon be done in a bivouac in such weather; however, I kept that secret to myself.[3]

Lieutenant John Patterson of the 50th, a more seasoned campaigner, also recalled the difficult conditions encountered on the march:

When the clouds and mist had cleared away, the ancient castle of Alegrete, placed on the summit of a barren chain of mountains was discernible. To our left extended a long range of heights, in some parts clothed with wood, and in others with verdant pasture, the brightness of which gave the prospect a lively effect. The road was broken and uneven, and, in general, so bad, that our baggage animals could scarcely make their way. Towards noon the heaviest rain we had ever experienced set in, increasing as we pushed onwards against the storm, pelting most furiously, and blown into our faces through the clefts and openings of the mountain sides close to which we travelled. We were thoroughly wet to the skin, benumbed by the intense coldness of the cutting blast, and well nigh deprived of life and motion. However, supporting each other with hopes of better times, we jogged on amidst the ceaseless war of hail, wind and rain.[4]

However, Patterson was luckier than Bell in finding accommodation for the night:

We halted at the village of Codiceira, just within the Spanish frontier, where a few of us darted into one of the best looking habitations we could see. There, after taking up without ceremony a good position in the chimney corner, and before a blazing pile of fagots, we got rid of our well drenched garments; in exchange for which, cloaks and mantillas were supplied by the hands of a benevolent old dame, whose exertions to administer comfort to our exhausted frames deserve to be recorded in the annals of her country.[5]

Unfortunately, his good fortune was not to last as he and his comrades were soon rudely ejected from their billet to make room for a colonel of light dragoons. Ensign James Hope of the 92nd was also suffering from the rain and cold as the troops occupied the olive groves around the village:

The arms of our poor fellows were no sooner in pile, than they set about felling trees, constructing huts, and making fires in several parts of our gloomy and cheerless encampment. Frost having succeeded the rain during the night, our situation had become, by the dawn, one of the most miserable you can possibly imagine. Never, while I breathe, shall I forget the miserable night I spent in the

---

3   Bell, *Rough Notes*, p.13.
4   Patterson, *Adventures*, p.162.
5   Patterson, *Adventures*, pp.162-3.

bivouac at Codeceira, where, wet and weary, I laid myself down to sleep, — the cold clay earth my bed, and the canopy of heaven my only covering.[6]

The recruits who had arrived with the recent drafts did not know the basics of camp life and, whilst the old hands went off in search of firewood and materials to make shelters, the new arrivals sat and shivered.[7]

Hill wrote to Wellington on the morning of the 23rd from La Codosera:

Colonel Offeney yesterday explained to Gen. Murray the arrangements I had made with regard to the advance of the troops and also mentioned the broken and uncomfortable appearance of the weather. The latter part of the day was wet, however the night was dry but cold – the appearance of the weather is still unsettled and I hope I shall not have occasion to expose the troops again for so uncertain a object as that of cutting the enemy off from Merida – indeed I am inclined to think my showing a force at Albuquerque and St Vicente this day will determine his retreat, as the Count de Penne seems to think that he was inclined to move towards Montanches yesterday after driving him without loss from Aliseda.[8]

The troops at La Codosera formed up before dawn. Mercifully, the day was fine and clear. Many of the men were probably very glad that the uncomfortable night was over. James Hope certainly was:

Never did I listen with so much pleasure to the hoarse murmurs of the bagpipes, as on the morning of the 23d, when they called us to arms. At their sound I attempted to rise, but my limbs were stiff, and for some time refused to perform their ordinary functions; having, after many attempts, succeeded in rising, I prepared to march to where I knew not, but fondly hoped we were going to a more comfortable quarter.[9]

The weather may have improved but roads did not and Major Hawker's Brigade of 9-pounders had to be left behind as one column marched the 12 miles direct to Alburquerque, whilst another marched via San Vicente de Alcántara. Alburquerque was a prosperous town on a hill, surrounded by high walls and would have afforded some of the officers and men a more comfortable billet for the night.

Hill had been worried about reports that Soult was advancing from the south but he received other intelligence that reassured him that this was not the case and he told Wellington that he would advance towards Aliseda.[10] This meant that on the 24th the men would have another long march of over 20 miles. They moved in two columns, one commanded by Erskine and

6   J. Hope, *Letters from Portugal, Spain and France* (London, Underwood, 1819), p.80.
7   C. Greenhill Gardyne, *The Life of a Regiment – The History of the Gordon Highlanders* (Edinburgh: Douglas, 1929), Vol.I, p.220.
8   Hill to Wellington 23 October 1811, BL Add.MS, 35059, pp.424-5.
9   Hope, *Letters*, p.18.
10   Hill to Wellington 24 October 1811, BL Add.MS, 35059, p.442.

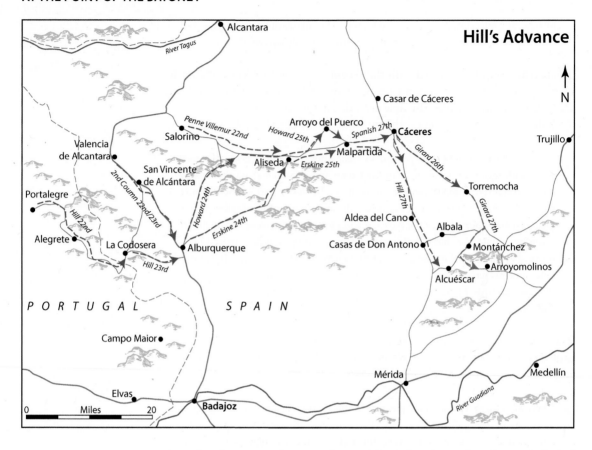

the other by Howard. Somewhat confusingly, Howard's column included Wilson's Brigade and Erksine's included Howard's Brigade. Erskine reached Aliseda that evening with Howard stopping at nearby Casa de Cantillana. The Spanish had already occupied the town and positioned picquets along the nearby river Salor. The French had picquets on the other side of the river. Two regiments of cavalry and a battalion of infantry commanded by *Général de Brigade* Briche occupied Arroyo del Puerco.

The march that day may have been another long one but Patterson indicates that the conditions had improved:

> Marching again on the 24th we passed through the thick woods bounding the Sierra, our route lying over a wide and level plain. It was late in the afternoon when we halted in a valley of broom, interspersed with cork and chestnut trees, beneath the spreading branches of which we took shelter for the night, and, wrapped up in warm cloaks and blankets, around huge bundles of burning cork, solaced our weary limbs after the labours of the day.[11]

The final stretch of road approaching Aliseda was very poor and steep and the guns of the Portuguese 6-pounder brigade had to be dismantled and

---

11   Patterson, *Adventures*, p.170.

carried with the help of the infantry.[12] Despite this, the speed of advance was beginning to outpace that of the commissariat and a soldier of the 71st notes in his memoir:

> The velocity of our advance soon leaving the provision waggons far behind, we were at one time obliged to make an attack on a large cabbage-field along with the starving horses and mules: however, we put the cabbages through the operation of boiling before feeding on them, – and miserable cheer they were, after all.[13]

On 25 October 400 Spanish cavalry probed towards Arroyo del Puerco and Girard's outposts retired to Malpartida. Hill ordered Erskine's column directly to Malpartida and Howard's via Arroyo del Puerco.[14] Hill was now in striking distance of the French and made plans to attack them at Malpartida. The 92nd paused briefly at Aliseda, as James Hope recalled:

> On arriving at Aleseda, we were ordered to cook with all expedition. This we subsequently found to be rather an ominous order, being generally the precursor of a long march, or a sharp battle and not unfrequently of both. At this time, the bullocks on which we were to dine, were running and jumping around us, as free as the air of heaven, but in less than an hour, they were amusing us with more interesting leaps in our camp-kettles. The soup, just removed from the fire, having been placed before us, at the same time that the bugle called us to arms, we were compelled by dire necessity to despatch it into the regions of the stomach, in a state little colder than boiling lead.[15]

Erskine's column marched on to Malpartida late in the afternoon, as the sun set the rain returned. Battling torrents of rain and stumbling on the muddy, rutted and uneven roads the troops halted for a short time on a brush covered hilltop before continuing on to Malpartida.[16]

The journal entry Captain James Gubbins, 13th Light Dragoons, for 25 October gives a good impression of the pace and privations of the advance:

> Friday 25th La Aliseda
> Marched at half past five, fine roads, beautiful country. 1 league cross the River Salor; a bridge of 15 or 16 arches. Soon after cross a sierra, a large stone house outside the sierra, very strong pass through the sierra, bad road, the town on the other side. 5 leagues, overtook 2nd Hussars. In the pass found the Conde de [Penne], Morillo with his legion about 50 men badly mounted and shabbily dressed; like mountebanks with lances. General Hill, W. Erskine, Howard and Long. Halted and fed and got our men refreshed, marched again at 4 p.m. 2 leagues on the road to Malpartida, the French corps of Gerard within a league.

---

12   J. Hope, *The Military Memoirs of an Infantry Officer 1809-1816* (Edinburgh: Anderson & Bryce, 1833), p.81.
13   Anon., *Vicissitudes in the Life of a Scottish Soldier* (London: Colburn, 1827), p.187.
14   Hill to Wellington 25 October 1811, BL Add.MS, 35059, pp.428-31.
15   Hope, *Memoirs*, p.81.
16   Patterson, *Adventures*, pp.170-1; Hope, *Memoirs*, p.82.

Halted and killed oxen and dressed two days provisions for the troops, not a tree, linked our horses. Got a tent up and took refreshment laid down for a couple of hours. Found a large tarantula on my blanket. Sounded to horse at half past two and marched off immediately. 9th Light Dragoons, 2 squadrons 2nd Hussars, 13th Light Dragoons, 2 brigades of infantry, a company of Portuguese artillery and a Brigade of Spaniards. Very dark coming on to rain hard, passed the fires the French had left at Nine o'clock the evening before, formed in two columns of squadrons to the right of Malpartida, learnt that the French made off at one o'clock in the morning, marched into the Town between 7 and 8 on the 26th, very cold and wet, very poor village, got ourselves to rights with some difficulty, a poor town and wretched inhabitants, half a mile off an old ruined castle. Tonight orders to march at 6 on the morrow.[17]

Alerted to their approach, Briche had withdrawn from Malpartida in the middle of the night, at the same time Girard marched out from Cáceres, south-east towards Torremocha. Girard's immediate superior, Drouet, had been warned by Spanish officers defecting from the allied army that Hill intended to advance on his isolated division and sent a staff officer with orders for Girard to withdraw back to Merida. Girard replied to Drouet that he had no concerns and was confident that Hill's troops remained in their cantonments. Drouet, who had by then received other reports of Hill's movements sent one of his ADCs to Girard with an order to move without any further delay.[18] It is not clear if this second order is what made Girard move, or if it was the appearance of the allied troops so close to his headquarters.

After covering around 70 miles in four days over poor roads and in terrible weather, Hill let his Portuguese and British infantry rest at Malpartida on the 26th. A small party of the 2nd KGL Hussars reconnoitred towards Cáceres and skirmished briefly with the French rearguard, and had one man wounded. It was confirmed that Girard had left Cáceres but his destination was unclear. The Spanish troops re-occupied Cáceres whilst Hill decided what do next. He had completed his immediate objective of removing the French from Cáceres. He wrote to Wellington, updating him on his progress:

If the Enemy continues his march by Torremocha towards the Guadiana I consider it unnecessary for me to go to Caceres, but in order to hasten his retreat & to prevent my Troops from being exposed to the Weather longer than is necessary I shall most likely march tomorrow on Aldea del Cano & the Count will follow Girard on to Torremocha road.[19]

Hill planned to keep the pressure on Girard until the French crossed the Guadiana river at Merida or Medellín, two or three days' march south of Cáceres, and then return his men back to their cantonments. However,

17   Transcripts made by Rev. E.E. Gubbins of letters and journal written by Captain James Gubbins, 13th Light Dragoons, NAM, 1992-12-138, pp.150-1.

18   J.B. Drouet, *Le Maréchal Drouet, Comte d'Erlon, Vie Militaire* (Paris: Barba, 1844) p.69.

19   Hill to Wellington 26 October 1811, BL Add.MS, 35059, pp.432-3.

Benjamin Ball, recounting the pursuit of Girard to his mother in November, credits Hill with a bolder plan:

> General Hill was no sooner informed of the Route they had taken than he resolved on one effort more to come up with them, though a day's march ahead of us. The more effectually to accomplish this he had to recourse to a Ruse de Guerre, which was sending into Caceres, to prepare Quarters & Rations for his Army which was to be there the following day, & of which he well knew the French would be Duly apprized. Instead however of going to Caceres, the next morning as we also expected we set out for Aldea de Cano, escorted by the same Guide who had conducted the French the preceding day.[20]

On the 27th, before daylight, the British and Portuguese troops began the march to Aldea del Cano, which from Malpartida effectively cut the corner off the route the French had taken when withdrawing from Cáceres. Hill received intelligence whilst on the march that Girard had only left Torremocha that morning and had halted at Arroyomolinos, with a rearguard at Albalá. He came to the conclusion that Girard was unaware both of his strength and how close on his heels he was. There was suddenly the realistic prospect that the allies could close with the French and attack. After reaching Aldea del Cano, where the Spanish joined the British and Portuguese troops, the allies continued on to Casas de Don Antonio. The routes of the allied and French marches were now separated by around eight miles and a heavily wooded ridge. A patrol of the 2nd KGL Hussars, led by Major Bussche, confirmed that the enemy had marched less than a dozen miles and was at the small village of Arroyomolinos.[21] Hill decided to press on to Alcuéscar in the hope of surprising Girard the following morning.

By the time they reached Alcuéscar, nestled on the side of a hill, the allied troops had covered over 30 miles that day, George Bell, already becoming more used to campaigning, recalled:

> On the evening of the 27th of October we got close to their heels; it rained all the day, and in the dusk we halted on ploughed ground. 'Pile arms; keep perfectly quiet; light no fires; no drum to beat; no bugle to sound,' were the orders passed through the ranks. I was very tired; threw myself up against the side of a bank ditch, dived into my haversack, where I had in reserve a piece of cold bullock's liver and salt, some biscuit, and a very small allowance of rum, so I was not so badly off.[22]

Major General Long's cavalry had encountered no French patrols or vedettes around Alcuéscar, despite it being only three miles from Arroyomolinos.[23] *Marechal de Campo* John Hamilton had been left with Campbell's Portuguese brigade at Casas de Don Antonio to cover any attempt by the French to

---

20 Ball to mother, 15 November 1811, Hampshire Archives 20M62/11B/5.
21 Beamish, *History of the KGL*, Vol.II, p.21.
22 Bell, *Rough Notes*, p.14.
23 McGuffie, *Peninsular Cavalry General*, p.138.

Alcuéscar, seen from the road to Arroyomolinos. (Author's photo)

march westwards and threaten Hill's line of retreat. Hamilton was ordered to barricade the streets and to hold long enough for Hill to come up with the rest of the troops, should he be attacked. Lieutenant Robert Blakeney of the 28th was selected by Hill to carry the orders to Hamilton:

> The despatch was read to me with the view that, should I be pursued by any French cavalry patrols, I should tear it, and if I fortunately escaped, deliver its contents verbally, or if I were driven out of my road, communicate its import in Spanish to any peasant I might meet, who could perhaps creep his way to San Antonio, although I should not be able to get there.[24]

Blakeney was accompanied by a Spanish dragoon as a guide and set off through the bleak night. On his return he got lost as the dragoon did not actually know the area, and in the dark forest during a storm it was not easy to find even an army without campfires to guide them. Blakeney eventually reported to Hill's headquarters and was given some cold roast beef and port to revive him.

Captain Peter Blassiere of the 5/60th had a much more dangerous mission that night. He was sent into Arroyomolinos to get details of the French positions. No account of his nocturnal adventures has survived but he evidently entered the village, learned where the French troops were billeted, that French cavalry were bivouacked in the olive groves, and then reported back to Hill.

The rain was relentless, heavy and cold. Without shelter, without fires, and with few rations, the men spent another miserable night warmed only by an extra ration of rum. Most of the troops camped to the rear of the Alcuéscar, but the 71st occupied the village, and they, and some of the light companies from other regiments, placed picquets to stop any spy or informer alerting the French to the allied presence. The 71st were luckier than most, being able to cook hot food in the hearths of the village houses:

> It was now nigh ten o'clock, the enemy were in Arroyo del Molino, only three miles distant. We got half a pound of rice served out to each man, to be cooked immediately. Hunger made little cooking necessary. The officers had orders to

---

24   Blakeney, *Peninsula*, p.217.

Arroyomolinos, seen from the road from Alcuéscar. The church is at the centre of the village and much of the area on the left is more recent development. (Author's photo)

keep their men silent. We were placed in the houses, but our wet and heavy accoutrements were, on no account, to be taken off. At twelve o'clock we received our allowance of rum, and shortly after the Serjeants tapped at the doors, calling not above their breath. We turned out, and at slow time continued our march. The whole night was one continued pour of rain. Weary and wet to the skin, we trudged on without exchanging a word; nothing breaking the silence of the night save the howling of the wolves. The tread of the men was drowned by the pattering of the rain. When day at length broke, we were close upon the town. The French posts had been withdrawn into it, but the embers still glowed in their fires.[25]

Ashworth's Portuguese brigade bivouacked about two miles to the rear of Alcuéscar, at the junction of the road from Casas de Don Antonio. The Regimento de Infantaria n.º 6 and Batalhão de Caçadores n.º 6 moved up during the night, with the Regimento de Infantaria n.º 18 following on later.

At around 2:00 a.m. the word was passed quietly to the infantry to stand to and form up. The route to Arroyomolinos was only three miles long, but the road was very rough and went through a forest. It took the men four hours to get into position, behind a ridge, out of sight of the enemy. *Subteniente* Don Diego Hernández Pacheco, who came from Alcuéscar, gathered a group of guides to lead the columns forward.[26]

Captain Gubbins of the 13th Light Dragoons wrote in his journal:

Bivouac before Alcuesca Sunday 27th
Marched from Malpartida at 6 o'clock, wet weather, crossed very fertile and extensive plain, halted to feed before the village of Casa de Antonio, marched

---

25   Anon., *Soldier of the 71st*, pp.144-5.
26   Historia de Arroyomolinos <http://historiarroyomolinos.blogspot.com/2008/06/guerra-de-la-independencia-batalla-de.html> (accessed July 2019).

The Sierra de Montánchez seen from the south-west. Arroyomolinos is hidden but lies at the foot of the foremost spur on the left. (Author's photo)

on with the advanced squadron to within a mile of Alcuesca. The whole division encamped there came on to rain hard at 9 o'clock at night, very dark. Orders to bridle up and mount at 12 at night, pitch dark & torrents of rain, marched immediately. Some difficulty in getting the half squadron in column and men and horses drenched and benumbed. Very bad and deep road, delayed two hours by the oversetting of a Portuguese gun. Learnt that the French were in the village of Arroyo Molinos, 2 leagues off.[27]

Capitão Richard Brunton with the Caçadores later summed up the advance:

Nothing could exceed our suffering on this short march, nor nothing but the hope of success would have enabled us to keep the men up. We marched on one Day 7 leagues, and on another 6, over most dreadful roads and the rain falling in torrents during nearly the whole time. After the latter march being close to the enemy we passed the night lying in a ploughed field, in a heavy rain, and were not permitted to have a light or fire of any kind.[28]

The village of Arroyomolinos lies at the foot of the Sierra de Montánchez, a small mountain range that rises to 995 metres. The lower slopes rise steeply behind the village to the north and extend in an arc to the east. The population in 1811 was just under 2,000 and the village consisted of around 500 houses, some of which were little more than huts spread over the lower slopes of the hills. The sixteenth-century church was the heart of the village, and the streets were narrow and winding. Much of the area surrounding the village was covered with groves of olive, fig and cork trees. The ground was stony, with occasional rocky outcrops. Drystone walls criss-crossed the gently rolling landscape. The flatter area to the south-west of the village was given over to flax, which was woven into linen locally. A stream ran through the centre, powering the 20 flour mills in the area, and gave the village its name, which translates as 'stream with mills'. In many of the contemporary accounts the village is referred to variously as Arroyo dos Molinos or Arroyo de Molinos, and today it is differentiated from a similarly named community in Madrid as Arroyomolinos de Montánchez. The road from the larger settlement of Montánchez came around the hills from the north. The road from Alcuéscar came from the west and three roads led from the town. The Trujillo road went east and around the hills. The Merida road went south and the one to Medellín south-east.

---

27   Journal written by Capt James Gubbins, NAM 1992-12-138, p.151.
28   Narrative of the Service of Lt. Col. Richard Brunton, NAM, 1968-07-461.

The shallow valley of the river Aljucén on the road from Alcuéscar, showing the rise towards Arroyomolinos behind which Hill gathered his troops prior to the attack. (Author's photo)

Hill's plan was to attack in three columns. The left column commanded by Lieutenant Colonel Stewart, consisting of the 1/50th, 1/71st, 1/92nd and the rifle company from the 5/60th supported by three 6-pounders and Morillo's infantry, would assault the village. The right column commanded by Major General Howard, consisting of the 1/28th, 2/34th, 2/39th, 5/60th rifle company, the Portuguese Regimento de Infantaria n.º 6 and Batalhão de Caçadores n.º 6, two 6-pounders and a howitzer, would move around the right of the village to cut off any attempt by the French to escape. The cavalry would advance between the two infantry columns.

By 7:00 a.m. the troops were in position in the shallow valley of the river Aljucén, out of sight of Arroyomolinos and about a mile from the village. Bell, who as senior ensign was to carry the King's Colour, recalled that Hill had time to say a few words to the men as they prepared themselves:

It was just the dawn of day, with a drizzling rain. We could just see our men to call the roll.
The regiment now was mustered,
And ready on parade,
Every man was present,
And none of them afraid.
Our gallant and worthy general, riding along our front, said, 'Are you all ready?' 'Yes, sir.' 'Uncase your colours, and prime and load.'[29]

---

29   Bell, *Rough Notes*, p.15.

6

The Surprise

Hill's men had marched over 100 miles in six days, through appalling weather and over rough terrain. They had outpaced the commissariat and what little they had to eat they had not been able to cook due to the ban on fires. After six nights without much sleep or shelter, they must have been tired, cold, hungry and soaked to the skin. The French had not marched as far and many had been billeted in the houses of Arroyomolinos overnight. By 7 o'clock on the morning of 28 October Remond's brigade had already left and was well on its way to towards Medellín. Dembowski's brigade and the cavalry rear-guard were beginning the process of forming up on the southern edge of the village, between the roads to Merida and Medellín. Their baggage crowded the narrow streets, and many of the officers and men were still in their quarters. Girard was in his bed at the mayor's house. The heavy black clouds that enveloped the sierra behind the village meant the morning was far darker than it should have been. Lieutenant Colonel Cameron of the 92nd described the state of the weather as 'one of the most dreadful mornings for wind and rain I ever remembered'[1] – which is quite something coming from a Scot.

Stewart's advance was led by the 1/71st and the rifles of the 5/60th. Behind them came the 1/92nd, with the 1/50th and the Portuguese artillery as a reserve.[2] Morillo's Spanish infantry remained further back, ready to support the attack if required. The light company of the 1/92nd had been left in the rear, possibly occupying Alcuéscar.[3] The scots and the riflemen marched at the double across the 1,000 yards of the cork-oak dotted plain towards Arroyomolinos. The light infantrymen were to loop around the north-eastern edge of the village, through an area of olive groves, while the 1/92nd headed up the road from Alcuéscar and aimed for the central square.

The 1/71st and the rifles advanced quickly and silently. The adjutant of the 1/71st, Lieutenant Robert Law, was sent ahead to reconnoitre a chapel on a hill. He rode forward and found a picquet of French cavalry, dismounted

---

1   Cameron to Hope, 2 November 1811, NRS, GD1/736/121.
2   Hope, *Memoirs*, p.85.
3   Cameron to Hope, 2 November 1811, NRS, GD1/736/121.

and huddled around a fire made from the doors and window frames of the chapel. As the day lightened the picquet mounted and retired.[4] One of soldiers of the 71st recalled that Hill had spoken to them just before they marched off:

> Presently, the busy sound of examining flints and tying down chin-straps was heard – the certain indications of an approaching brush. All these necessary preparations being accomplished, General Hill gave the word of command, – 'Shoulder arms'. When that was done, he said, 'Move on, my lads, and God be with you!' Just at the time, a tremendous shower of rain came on, which, although it wet our skins, did not damp out courage – the secrecy of the enterprise being rather favoured than otherwise by the cloudy discharge. When we reached the outskirts of the place, a picket of French cavalry was discovered in an olive wood, squatting round some fires, with their horses tied to the trees: – they had apparently retired to this shelter in consequence of the shower, perhaps not many minutes before our arrival, – so much, as some folks would say, had Providence favoured us. Fearful of disturbing the cavalry, lest they should escape, and spread the alarm of our approach, we marched cautiously by, while they were lulled into such security that not one of them perceived us. Leaving a company to surprise them, we pushed on, and entered the town without opposition.[5]

The French cavalry, probably the 27e Chasseurs, were finishing feeding their horses when the detachment of the 1/71st subsequently rushed into the bivouac and took them prisoner.[6]

As Hope of the 92nd succinctly puts it: 'The 71st and 92d regiments entered the village at a quick pace, and, at the point of the bayonet, soon cleared it of the enemy, who were quite unprepared for such an unceremonious visit'.[7] The highlanders had orders to push through the village as fast as possible and not to slow themselves down by securing prisoners. That task fell to one wing of the 1/50th, the other moved around the south-west of the village with the artillery.

According to a *Capitaine* Margen of the 34e the first warning that the French had of the approach of the British was a surgeon running through the streets shouting *'Chargez vos armes'*.[8] As the 92nd entered the town, probably along what is now Calle Hernán Cortes, their pipers played 'Hey Johnnie Cope are ye waukin' yet'. The choice of tune by the pipers was both an amusing and a curious one as it celebrated a morning surprise attack by Jacobite rebels on British government forces at Prestonpans in 1745. The men of the regiment later came up with their own words to the tune:

---

4   John Patterson, writing in W.H. Maxwell, *Peninsular Sketches* (London: Colburn, 1845), Vol. II, pp.315-7.

5   Anon., *Vicissitudes in the Life of a Scottish Soldier* (London: Colburn, 1827), pp.189-90.

6   J. Wyld, *Maps and Plans*, p.21; G. Glover (ed.), *The Journal of Sergeant David Robertson* (Godmanchester: Kent Trotman, 2018), p.113.

7   Hope, *Memoirs*, p.85.

8   Quoted in the Journal of Capt James Gubbins, NAM 1992-12-138, p.156.

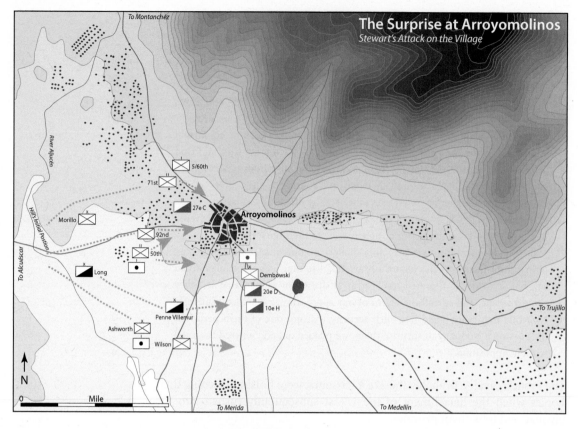

Go and tell Napoleon, go,
While Freedom's laws he tramples low,
That Highland boys will be his foe.
And meet them all in the morning.
Hey, Monsieur Gerard, are ye waukin' yet?[9]

As the highlanders stormed into the village French troops, many half-dressed, ran this way and that in confusion. The skirl of the pipes, the shouts and shots, echoed in the narrow streets. The villagers called out '*viva los ingleses*'.[10]

Benjamin Ball of the 39th was later told that Girard's two orderlies had brought the general's horse to the door when a volley from the 1/71st killed both them.[11] Girard, only half-dressed and still inside, grabbed his sword, ran out, mounted and then fought his way out of the village to the men of Dembowski's brigade forming up on the road.[12] Dembowski ordered the 2/34e Ligne to cover the rest of the infantry as they formed up, and to stop the British as they emerged from the village.[13]

9   A. Clerk, *Memoir of Colonel John Cameron* (Glasgow: Murray, 1858), p.52.
10   Anon., *Journal*, p.146.
11   Ball to mother, 15 November 1811, Hampshire Archives 20M62/11B/5.
12   Du Casse, *Le Volontaire*, p.357.
13   Girard to d'Erlon 2 November 1811, in Wellington, *Supplementary Despatches,* Vol.XIII, p.729.

As the surprise wore off some of the French began to rally, Sergeant David Donaldson recalled:

> By this time a number of the French assembled and threw themselves across the head of the street along which we were marching and commenced firing upon us. Owing to the narrowness of the street, and the compact way in which we were at the time, their shot told with deadly effect. Our front section dashed forward at a rapid pace and quickly dislodged them. The greatest uproar and confusion now prevailed in the town, and the work of death was going on at a fearful rate.[14]

The streets of Arroyomolinos are narrow and winding, many not really wide enough for a modern car. (Author's photo)

The 1/50th came up behind the highlanders and secured the prisoners. Girard rallied his men on the edge of the village and formed two squares on a field between the Merida and Medellín roads. One square was about a hundred yards from the village, the other slightly more distant with its left flank covered by cavalry. The 1/71st lined the stone walls on the edge of the village and began to shoot at the French. The Portuguese artillery came up and also began to fire at the enemy, to great effect.

Lieutenant James Ker Ross, with the grenadier company of the 1/92nd, wrote his account of the battle, his first, in a letter to his brother:

> Just as were getting into the town we saw all their cavalry mounting in the greatest confusion possible in a small wood a little to the left of the end of the town one or two companies of the 71st went out to skirmish at them, which I am certain every shot must have told, they were in such confusion, scampering off in dozens, we moved on through the town as fast as possible.[15]

The French cavalry, eager to escape, rode through the village and Lieutenant Colonel Cadogan, commander of the 1/71st, was wounded; as one of his men recollected:

---

14   Glover, *Robertson*, p.113.
15   Ross to brother, 5 November 1811, NAM – 1980-02-66.

The north-eastern approach to Arroyomolinos along the CC-60 road that leads into Calle Real, where the 71st advanced into the village. (Author's photo)

Continuing our course through the town, we met the body of French cavalry direct in the teeth, who had been dislodged from the wood at the first outset of the affair; they had fled by a circuitous route, and thus came unexpectedly upon us. Seeing no other means of escape but that of forcing through us, they charged with the fury of despair: unfortunately, our muskets were in such a state, on account of the late rains, that few or none of them would give fire this encouraged the horsemen, they being now intermixed with us, hewing and cutting on all sides; some of them penetrated to the place where Colonel Cadogan was: a blow aimed at him divided his cap in two, but, happily, the sword glanced off without doing any real injury. The Marquess of Tweeddale, and a Major [sic.] Churchill, perceiving the colonel's imminent danger, immediately rode up and cut down the assailant, at the same time completely dispersing the others. We had ere this betaken ourselves to the trusty bayonet; one of the men had driven his with such force into the body of a horse, that the animal, writhing with pain, made a sudden jerk, and ran off a good distance, with both musket and bayonet sticking in its side, the rider being unable to stop its furious course: the owner of the arms soon afterwards recovered them.[16]

---

16   Anon. *Vicissitudes*, pp.192-3, & Hope, *Memoirs*, pp.97-8.

Lieutenant Colonel Cameron, leading the 1/92nd, was also injured, as he recounted when writing to the colonel of his regiment:

> The 71st and 92nd soon drove those they did not Bayonet out of the Village, and upon the Merida road. On my getting to the Merida end of the Village I found a considerable opening between two Vineyards, which admitted about one half of the 92nd in Column. The walls of the Vineyards were occupied by the 71st on both sides as Light Infantry.
>
> The French Infantry had formed in a Square on a plain immediately opposite. The 71st were firing at the French Square and a Small Corps of Light Infantry extended beyond them, which Corps was returning the fire most briskly. The fire of the French Rifle Men [sic] annoyed the head of the Column of the 92nd Regiment considerably, nor could we advance without being exposed to the fire of the 71st also, however we got the 71st to cease firing, and to allow us to advance, as each Company had cleared the opening I caused them to deploy to the right keeping them under cover of the left hand wall as much as possible, directing them to pass to the right into Line with the utmost rapidity, as we were then in the presence of the French Square of five Battns. Which I proposed charging the moment my line was formed. Three Companies were scarcely in Line when the French Square moved off throwing out a Cloud of Sharp Shooters to impede our advance, by this time the other British Brigade Composed of the 28th, 34th & 39th, the British Cavalry and Portuguese Artillery having got round the Town, were coming up upon their left Flank and the whole followed in pursuit. The result you will know by the Public Accounts which we here think very highly of. Your Regiment conducted themselves much to my satisfaction during the whole time, and under the trying circumstances of not one Firelock in Ten giving Fire when attempted to be used. – As I was carrying on the deployment a Ball struck my right hand passing through my middle finger and afterwards through the hilt of the Sword which I held in my hand, and striking me in the breast.[17]

Cameron fell out, thinking himself seriously wounded, but quickly returned to his unit, with his finger hanging on by a small piece of skin and bleeding profusely. After the battle he found a surgeon and had the finger amputated. Captain Clement Hill was riding through the village when he had his horse shot from under him. Law, of the 71st, rode to help him, cutting at the nearest Frenchman with his sabre until the arrival of some British infantry persuaded the French to withdraw.[18]

The fire of the 1/71st and 1/92nd, despite the many the misfires on account of the rain, and the bombardment by the guns of *Capitão* de Arriaga's battery broke the French will to stand. Some threw down their muskets and fled:

> [T]he rest, keeping up as much appearance of order as their situation would admit, immediately commenced a precipitate retreat, but this was promptly baulked by the appearance of General Howard's troops in the path: the enemy were thus nearly enclosed on all sides; terror and surprise caused every restraint

17   Cameron to Hope, 2 November 1811, NRS, GD1/736/121.
18   Maxwell, *Sketches*, p.317.

A view back to the centre of the village along Calle Cervantes, the road down which the bulk of the French retreated. (Author's photo)

to be abandoned, and irretrievable confusion took place amongst them: 'save himself who can,' was the order of the day, and happy was he who gained the summit of the neighbouring lofty hills.[19]

The men of the 1/71st jumped over the walls they had been positioned behind and joined the 1/92nd in pursing the French away from the village, having quickly and completely achieved their objectives.

One soldier of the 1/92nd had marched into the battle without even a musket to defend himself:

> A few days previous to the battle of Arroyo-del-Molinos, a private soldier of very weak intellect, named Brown, lost his firelock, but where, or in what manner, he could give no proper account. On the circumstance being reported to the commanding officer, he was so enraged, that he ordered Brown to be taken into the first action without arms. The captain of his company, however, feeling for the

---

19   Anon, *Vissitudes*, p.194.

situation of the poor fellow, ordered him to fall out when close to the village of Arroyo. But no: the proud spirit of the half-witted creature would not permit him to accept of the kind indulgence tendered him. Brown continued in his proper place in the ranks, during the whole of the engagement. Seeing some firelocks without owners, Captain D_ desired Brown to arm himself with one of them, but the latter replied, 'Colonel Cameron having been pleased. Sir, to order me into action without arms, here I will remain unarmed until the action is over, or poor Jack Brown is sent into another world;' which resolution the heroic simpleton faithfully kept.[20]

There are several accounts of the capture of senior French officers in the village, mostly concerning the Duc d'Arenberg, colonel of the 27e Chasseurs, because of his connection to Napoleon through his wife being the niece of the former empress Josephine. An account from 92nd claims the capture of the Duc d'Arenberg for their own regiment:

Aroused by the sound of the bagpipes, the Duke de Armburgo came out in a half-naked state, when a sergeant of the 92nd seized him by the arms and made him prisoner. The Duke made some resistance, but the sergeant applying the point of his sword, compelled him to move forward.[21]

The episode is also recounted in a memoir from the 71st:

An interesting object now drew our attention, – it was one of the French commanders, Prince d'Aremberg, running out with a coffee cup in his hand,- alarm and astonishment strongly depicted on his countenance, at the arrival of such uninvited visitors, and at the joyous shouts with which we made the welkin ring. Little time was allowed for his amazement to subside; scarce an instant elapsed till the epaulets and other frippery were plucked from his person by some of the men; he was also rather roughly treated, being shoved about from side to side, in order to compel him to join in the noisy cheering: this request was at length complied with by the poor man, but with great reluctance, and endeavours to let it be known that he was a 'principe'. To save himself from further ill usage, he then threw himself into the arms of an officer, in hopes of protection, – but was rudely thrust away by this gentleman, who should have known better: however, men in the heat of a confusion such as this, may be hurried into actions which they will blush for at a cooler moment.[22]

Another memoir from the 71st may concern d'Arenberg, or possibly a different senior officer:

As we advanced, I saw the French General come out of a house, frantic with rage. Never will I forget the grotesque figure he made, as he threw his cocked hat upon the ground and stamped upon it, gnashing his teeth. When I got the first glance

20 Hope, *Memoirs*, pp.99-100.
21 Glover, *Robertson*, p.113.
22 Anon, *Vissitudes*, pp.191-2.

of him he had many medals on his breast. In a minute his coat was as bare as a private's.[23]

However, Patterson of the 50th gives a slightly different account of the duke's capture:

Prince d'Aremberg, commanding the 27th regiment of chasseurs à cheval, (a corps that was raised in Brussels,) was endeavouring to make his escape during the *melée* which took place before the enemy left the village, when Corporal Dogherty, of the 71st, perceiving his manoeuvre charged his bayonet, and stopped the prince in his career. Muffled up in a large green cloak, which almost extinguished him, (for he was a very little personage,) he was but indifferently prepared for an encounter with the stalwart Irishman, who, suddenly reining back the Frenchman's horse, the force of the bit, which was very powerful, threw the animal upon his haunches, the rider at the same time falling on the pavement.

Dogherty, at once perceiving the advantage of his own position, resolved to profit by it, when, presenting his weapon he called out to the prince for his surrender. The latter, prostrate on the ground, and therefore in no condition for a contest, sung out, 'Peccavi!' when, throwing the ample folds of his cloak aside, he exposed the honours and decorations by which his breast was covered, which he thought would protect him (and he judged rightly) from being transfixed by the corporal's bayonet. Making signs to him to rise, Dogherty marched him in a prisoner to Captain Clements, of the 71st, into whose charge he was delivered. The corporal was a fellow remarkable for his bravery in many battles, where, being often wounded, he was discharged with a liberal pension.[24]

In the *Narrative of the Campaigns of the Twenty-Eighth Regiment* Charles Cadell, a captain with regiment at the time and present at the battle, claims that Lieutenant Robert Blakeney captured the duke. However, Blakeney makes no such claim in his own memoir, even though he did escort the duke to Lisbon. The incident that Cadell alludes to was in fact Blakeney's capture of *Chef de Battalion* Théophile Woiral of the 40e Ligne.[25] In his history of the 27e Chasseurs, Guy van Eeckhoudt relates another very different account of the duke's capture and that claims that he was at the head of his regiment and charged the British and Spanish cavalry, had his horse killed under him and was then captured by Spanish infantry. Van Eeckhoudt gives a German newspaper from December 1811 as his source.[26] A similar account is given in the British press which published Soult's letter to *Maréchal* Berthier. Soult wrote: 'The Duke d'Aremberg was also dismounted in a charge, and in falling, received two bayonet wounds. It is said they are not dangerous'.[27] Blakeney makes no mention of the duke being wounded, but does say that the duke

---

23   Anon. *Journal*, p.147.

24   Maxwell, *Sketches*, pp.318-9.

25   Cadell, *Narrative*, p.119; Blakeney, *Peninsula*, p.361.

26   G. Van Eeckhoudt, *Les Chevau-Légers Belges du duc d'Arenberg* (Schiltigheim: Le Livre chez Vous, 2002), pp.146-7.

27   Soult to Berthier, 12 November 1811, in Wellington, *Supplementary Despatches*, Vol.XIII, p.731.

told him that he was with Girard when the attack started and was ordered to gather the cavalry and form on the plain outside of the village. Captain Squire of the Royal Engineers, in a letter written soon after the battle, states only that the duke was captured in the village.[28] All other British accounts were published years after the events, and given the duke's connection to Napoleon there may have been a temptation to claim the honour of capturing him for their regiment, but likewise many French accounts seem to be more interested in avoiding, or placing, blame for the disaster, and attempting to regain some credit by emphasising the bravery of French resistance.

With Girard leading his men away from the village it fell to the cavalry and Howard's column to stop as many of the enemy escaping as possible, and to turn a victory into a rout.

---

28   Squire to Dickson 6 November 1811, in J.H. Leslie, *The Dickson Manuscripts*, Series C 1809-11 (London: Royal Artillery, 1905) pp.495-7.

7

Girard's Retreat

Whilst Long's British cavalry brigade were delayed by an upset Portuguese cannon, the Spanish cavalry of the Conde de Penne Villemur found a route around the obstruction and were the first allied horsemen on the field. He later wrote:

> At two in the morning I was placed across the roads to Alcuescar and Arroyomolinos to wait for the cavalry of the division I commanded which, according to General Hill's orders, must be the last one to march on, but inevitably, in a night of the darkest and the most abundant rain, the British cavalry lost the way and I saw that the columns of infantry and artillery had long since passed, and calculating that without the support of the cavalry they, and especially the artillery, could be in real danger in the case of being charged by the enemy, I took it upon myself to go forward to make up for the lack of English cavalry. For mine had had the good fortune to find a good way. In this state of affairs the columns arrived half a league from the village of Arroyomolinos, which I reconnoitred to the right and left using a small detachment of my *tiradores*.[1]

Penne Villemur's scouts discovered the French forming a column just outside Arroyomolinos on the road to Merida, with the escorting cavalry to the front. He dispatched the Cazadores de Sevilla to the Merida road to cut off that line of retreat. The arrival of the Spanish cavalry added to the confusion of the French caused by the sounds of Stewart's men charging into the village behind them. The remaining Spanish cavalry formed two lines and rode forward to charge the French cavalry at the head of the column. They scattered the French horsemen and took many of them prisoner. *Général de Brigade* André-François Bron had already left the village with 150 of the 20e Dragons when he heard the firing. He turned his men about and charged back to attack the allied horsemen.

---

1   Dispatch published in *El Patriota Compostelano* newspaper, in J.A.P. Rubio, 'Pablo Morillo: Acciones militares y la contribución de los pueblos de las tierras de Montánchez al esfuerzo de guerra (1811-1813)', *Revista de Estudios Extremeños,* 2013, Tomo LXIX, Número I, p.320.

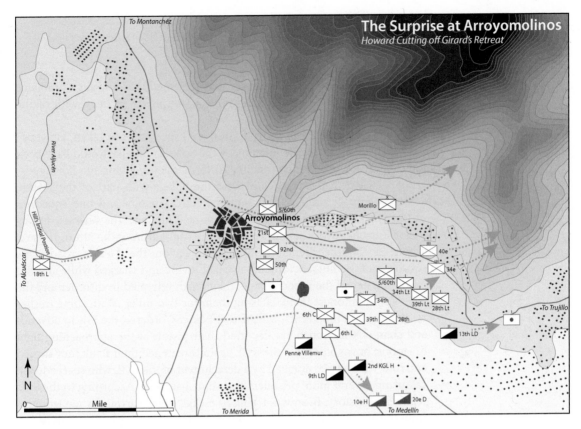

The Surprise at Arroyomolinos
Howard Cutting off Girard's Retreat

The British cavalry had, by now, come up and advanced on the left of Howard's column whilst the Spanish moved to the right. Gìron's dispatch to Castaños states:

> Thus disposed, and in the finest order imaginable, our troops marched upon the place, and in a few moments saw the enemy who had got out of it, by the road of Merida. To see, attack, defeat, and completely disperse them, without firing a shot, was but the work of an instant; nothing could equal the boldness and valour of the Spanish allied troops employed on this occasion, and to this is owing that the enemy was so completely surprised, though formed and in march, that they could make no disposition, nor do any thing else than fly, surrender, or die.[2]

Blakeney, of the 28th, was less complimentary about some of the Spanish cavalry; specifically, the lancers of the Legión Extremeña:

> There was also an equestrian Spanish band, clothed like harlequins and commanded by a person once rational, but now bent on charging with his motley crew the hardy and steadily disciplined cavalry of France; and yet, however personally brave their commander, Mr. Commissary Downy, little could be expected from this fantastic and unruly squadron, who displayed neither order

---

2   Giron to Castaños, 30 October 1811, quoted in *The Globe*, 3 December 1811.

nor discipline. Intractable as swine, obstinate as mules and unmanageable as bullocks, they were cut up like rations or dispersed in all directions like a flock of scared sheep.[3]

Blakeney's seems to be the only account that mentions any such problems with the legion that morning, and other accounts credit them with taking 200 prisoners.[4]

Long's cavalry did not arrive until the village had been taken. However, their arrival and the earlier actions by the Spanish cavalry would have been the catalyst for the French infantry to form square, giving the Portuguese artillery, which had advanced around the village with part of the 1/50th, a more compact target. Long sent the KGL Hussars and one squadron of the 9th Light Dragoons to assist Penne Villemur. The hussars, led by Major Bussche, with Captain George Gore's squadron of the 9th in reserve, advanced towards French cavalry gathered on the Merida road. One squadron of the hussars forded a flooded ravine and charged while another party threatened the French flank. The French retreated in disorder and the KGL got in amongst them, chasing them for two miles. With some fresher reinforcements the French rallied and Bussche ordered the 9th to advance and charge. The French cavalry fired their pistols at the approaching light dragoons, but as a party of the KGL again threatened their flank they turned and rode for Merida, pursued by a detachment of the KGL who succeeded in capturing several more prisoners and some baggage.[5] According to the 9th's regimental history, Bron was trying to escape in his carriage when troopers from the 9th caught up with him. The general shot two with his pistols before surrendering.[6] However, historian Charles Oman places Bron's capture in the village.[7] Blakeney recalls:

> When after the action the officers made prisoners were required to sign their parole, Le Brun refused, saying that the word of a general of the French was sufficient. Our quartermaster-general, Colonel Offley, a gallant and determined soldier, a German by birth, soon settled the affair in a summary way by giving orders that if the general refused to sign his parole, he was to be marched with the bulk of the prisoners. This order cooled the general's hauteur: he subscribed.[8]

Girard retreated eastwards with his infantry, away from the village, hoping to skirt the end of the sierra and make their escape along the Trujillo road. The area on their left was covered by cork and olive groves, bounded by drystone walls. Beyond the groves rose the steep slopes of the sierra, along which Morillo's infantry was advancing after having looped around the back of the village. The more open area on their right, near the road, was dotted with

---

3   Blakeney, *Peninsula*, p.226.
4   Rubio, *Revista de Estudios Extremeños*, 2013, Tomo LXIX, Número I, pp.321.
5   Beamish, *History of the KGL*, Vol.II, p.22.
6   R. Cannon, *Historical Record of the 9th or the Queen's Royal Regiment of Light Dragoons; Lancers* (London: Parker, 1841), pp.42-3.
7   Oman, *Peninsular War*, Vol.IV, p.603.
8   Blakeney, *Peninsula*, p.248.

The area near the small lake, showing the ground over which the French retreated from the village, moving left to right, hoping to get around the end of the line of hills. (Author's photo)

rocky outcrops and trees, with a few low rises. The French were now moving in column. The distance they had to cover before reaching the end of the arc of hills was over a mile and half. The 1/92nd, 1/71st and a portion of the 1/50th were still behind them and Howard's column was advancing rapidly on their flank. Patterson, of the 50th, recalled the speed of the French retreat:

> Retiring across the plain, into the depth of the forest, they flung away knapsacks, accoutrements, and other trappings, by which they were encumbered, making, as they vanished among the trees, such very good use of their legs, that we found it no easy matter to keep them within hail, or within the range of those missiles that were despatched to bring them to.[9]

Howard's column of the 1/28th and 2/34th, with the 2/39th and Ashworth's Portuguese in reserve plus more of the Portuguese artillery, was preceded by the light companies of Wilson's brigade commanded by Major Roger Parke of the 39th. The whereabouts or actions of Captain McMahon's company of the 5/60th are not specifically mentioned in any of the accounts but they would normally have been with the light companies. The light companies were ordered to try and capture the French guns, but they were slowed down by the heavy mud of a ploughed field. They were then told that the cavalry would be given the task instead. Blakeney, with the 1/28th's light company, recalled in his memoir:

> We now brought up our right shoulders and faced the enemy's column, the head of which was by this time close at hand. A low ridge or rising ground was between us, and, the 28th Light Company leading, I galloped up the ascent, urged by the ambition natural to youth to be the first to meet the foe. In this however I was disappointed; for on gaining the summit I discovered immediately on my left General Hill with his aide-de-camp, the late Colonel Curry, attended by one sole dragoon. The light company came quickly up and commenced firing (the

---

9   Patterson, *Adventures*, p.174.

enemy not above a hundred yards distant), upon which the general showed his ·disapprobation in as marked a manner as a person could do who never, under any excitement whatsoever, forgot that he was a gentleman; at this moment he felt highly excited. The enemy perceived it impossible to pass by us, and as our left column were moving up in their rear every eye was casting a woeful look up the side of the dark and stubborn Montanchez, which forbade access; they saw no mode of escape. Becoming desperate, and arriving at where the mountain began to dip, they made a rush at the broad and high stone wall which ran along its base, and tearing open a breach, the head of their column, led by General Gerard, entered the opening at the very moment that the light company topped the rising ground and saw them. Thus did Gerard make his escape, which he could not have effected had we not been sent trotting after the guns, by which we lost upwards of twenty minutes' time.

But there was still a remedy left, had it been taken advantage of, as will afterwards be shown. I observed the displeasure which our men's firing gave the general, who at the moment used the remarkable words, 'Soldiers, I have done my duty in showing you the enemy; do you yours by closing on them'. Upon this truly eloquent and inspiring appeal, which must have fired the breast of the most phlegmatic, I instantly placed my cap on the point of my sword, and waving it over my head I rode between the contending troops to prevent the light company from firing, exhorting them to come on with the bayonet, a weapon which they well knew from experience the enemy could never resist.[10]

Girard had placed a rearguard of elite companies, commanded by *Chef de Battalion* Woiral of the 40e Ligne, to cover his retreat. The light companies were heavily outnumbered but succeeded in forcing the breach in the wall, and taking dozens of the French prisoners. Blakeney jumped over the wall on his horse, in pursuit of Woiral:

We met face to face and instantly commenced a martial duet. We were both superbly mounted, but the rocky nature of the ground was such that our horses were totally unmanageable. We soon fell, or rather dragged each other to the ground, when, true to the immutable laws of nature, I as the lighter and more trivial remained uppermost. On falling, I must instantly have been forked to death by the many Frenchmen around me; but all were too intent on flight to look to others, and immediately after Voirol and I came to the ground the most advanced soldiers of the 28th and 34th Light Companies charged through the opening in the wall…[11]

Woiral was secured and the light companies continued the pursuit up the slopes of the sierra.

Long and the 13th Light Dragoons supported Howard's advance and had tried to get between the French and the hills, Long wrote:

10 Blakeney, *Peninsula*, pp.227-8.
11 Blakeney, *Peninsula*, p.361.

Whilst in motion for this purpose I received an order from General Hill to press upon them. I thought the doing so injudicious, but immediately formed a Column of Squadrons and advanced, as if to attack upon their rear. They halted – what I wanted. I did the same – they then got in motion. I repeated the feint, they halted a second time.[12]

Towards the end of the arc of the sierra. The saddle on the left is where Morillo's infantry crossed the hills. The slopes on the right are where Girard and the bulk of the French ascended. (Author's photo)

Long was then told Howard was about to charge and repositioned his squadrons to support the infantry, but the French fell back and the redcoats did not charge. So Long again sought to get between the French and the slopes but Hill rode up and ordered him to pursue and capture the French artillery which was escaping along the road towards Trujillo:

I therefore left one squadron to pursue my original intention, and with the other I made after the guns, which I overtook and secured. This accomplished, I returned back to the scene of deeper interest, and to my mortification observed the Enemy had passed the road and gained the Sierra. Had I been here sooner, I could certainly, by charging them in the act of passing the road, have checked their advance, and given time to General Howard's Brigade to close upon their rear. This was neglected, and General Hill lamented the circumstance as much as I did, but I could not be everywhere at once.[13]

Captain James Gubbins of the 13th remembered events slightly differently from his brigade commander:

General Hill came up and took our Centre Squadron with him to charge the Enemy's guns, the General in high spirits, showed us the direction of the French artillery, charged obliquely, the right Squadron first up with them took the guns, 2 guns and a howitzer 6 pounder. General Howard's Brigade cheered us

---

12   McGuffie, *Cavalry General*, p.138.
13   McGuffie, *Cavalry General*, p.139.

A closer look at the slopes up which the French fled. With such good terrain for defence it is perhaps surprising that allied casualties were not higher. (Author's photo)

on passing, rode forward and pursued the fugitives. Sullivan only up with me. Took four prisoners and the horse and baggage of the French Colonel of the 4th Regiment, sent them to the rear, went with my troops only 15 rank and file with Lord Tweeddale, crossed the Sierra of Montanches.[14]

The rest of the 1/28th and 2/34th joined the pursuit up the rocky slopes of the sierra; scrambling over the boulders, through the brush, and amongst the discarded French equipment, taking prisoners those French that gave up or were overtaken. Captain William Irvine of the 28th passed out from sheer exhaustion and Lieutenant William Irwin of the same regiment brought down two Frenchmen by throwing stones at them.[15] Sherer of the 34th recalled:

The French sustained some loss from the fire of the first brigade, and some from the guns, which accompanied that column; but our share of the business, among the rocks, was a scene of laughter and diversion, rather than of bloodshed and peril; for though some of the enemy's grenadiers discharged their muskets at us before they broke them, still our loss was very trifling, and the danger too inconsiderable to be thought or spoken of. We had here a most amusing specimen

---

14   Journal written by Capt James Gubbins, NAM 1992-12-138, pp.151-2.
15   Cadel, *Narrative*, p.118.

of French character: in the French column one of the regiments was numbered thirty-four; in the British column also the thirty-fourth regiment led the pursuit, and got quite mixed with the enemy. Several of the French officers, as they tendered their swords, embraced the officers of the English thirty-fourth, saying – 'Ah, Messieurs, nous sommes des frères, nous sommes du trente-quatrième régiment tous deux'.[16]

Capitaine Ballue, commanding one of the 40e Ligne's grenadier companies, was bayoneted by one of his pursuers and then surrounded by an officer and six redcoats who called upon him to surrender. He broke his sword and threw it into the rocks. Of his 60 men, only six or seven managed to escape.[17] Jean-Michel Richers of the 40e wrote in a letter to his parents 'We had to retreat fast and, after a fight lasting at least three hours, only 350 men of the 40e and 34e regiments came back'.[18]

Morillo had found a path up the sierra to the left, across a saddle in the hills, and took up the pursuit from the exhausted and scattered 1/28th and 2/34th. The light companies of Wilson's Brigade had been chasing and firing at the French, up and then down the sierra, for four hours before they were ordered to halt. The Spanish infantry chased the enemy down the other side of the hill. Morillo detached the Voluntarios de la Victoria and Legion Extremeña to follow some of the French over the hills while he took the rest of his force to tackle the French in the La Quebrada pass. The Spanish were accompanied by the 2/39th Foot, the Batalhão de Caçadores n.º 6 and some of the 13th Light Dragoons, who had come around the base of the hills.

Benjamin Ball with the 39th wrote:

> We kept to the foot of the hill along the plain, while the other Regts drove them up the Mountain which was composed entirely of craggy rocks, at the point of the bayonet, making great numbers of Prisoners. After winding round the Mountains about a League we ascended a stupendous hill which we expected would command the Road they had to pass, but how great was our disappointment on gaining its summit to find they were not within musquet-shot. A great part of our men were so completely knocked up by the fatigues they had undergone, that they were unable to proceed any further.[19]

Girard began to rally his men and defend each rocky outcrop or choke point. One position, near Montánchez, they defended vigorously for 30 minutes until the allies outflanked them on higher ground.

Ball continued:

16 'Gentlemen, we are brothers, we are from the thirty-fourth regiment both'. Sherer, *Recollections*, pp.237-8.
17 A. Goupille, Mémoires du Capitaine Ballue de la Haye-Descartes, *Bulletin Trimestriel de la Société Archéologique de Touraine*, V.XXXIII, pp.365.
18 Richers to parents, 2 February 1812, in B & R Wilkin, *Fighting the British* (Barnsley: Pen & Sword, 2018), p.105.
19 Ball to mother, 15 November 1811, Hampshire Archives 20M62/11B/5.

Determining however, to strain every nerve to cut them off we descended the plain, & following our former course gained a road which led into that by which they were retiring – but too late, we came within reach of them across a Vineyard, when we commenced a very brisk fire on them which they returned for half an hour. Suddenly they all made off as hard as they could run, & gained a very high ascent where they made a second stand. From this position they opened a very heavy fire completely enfilading the road we were in, we pushed directly for some rocks which commanded their position, but in this manoeuvre so much time was lost, they gained a full league, & returned without much further molestation from us tho we followed them as close as we could the whole way, having been informed that the cavalry was waiting to cut them off as soon as they reached the plain, & indeed about 20 Dragoons did show themselves when the French collecting, formed the square & kept them at a very reasonable distance.

On arriving at the foot of the Mountain tho we had but a few men up, Lt Col Lindesay who commanded the Regt, resolved on demanding them to surrender & fixing his handkerchief on a Stick by way of Flag of Truce, rode up to their Column & was met by Girard himself who had conducted the Retreat the whole time & was wounded in the Arm. Col. Lindesay desired him in order to spare any further effusion of blood, to lay down his Arms. Girard with tears in his eyes answered he would rather die – but several of the Men calling out 'yes we will surrender', Lindesay desired them to follow him when 15 Men & an Officer came out of the Column, & returned to us with him. The whole of these Men were wounded. The wretched Remains of the Enemy retired into a wood, whither they were followed by the Guerrillas who took about 50 of them. We were then at the end of our chase of 3 Leagues from Aroyo de Molino, & finding a small village called Val de Fuentes we halted in it for the night. It was unfortunate our Men were so severely fatigued, as had they been fresh as their Antagonists every man would have been taken.[20]

Blakeney saw Girard as he descended the other side of the sierra to the road beyond, and witnessed an earlier occasion when Girard could have been captured:

But my astonishment was caused at seeing a squadron of British cavalry drawn up on the road who moved not at all, although within a hundred yards of where Gerard and the enemy descended in these small bodies from the mountain. Some time afterwards I asked the officer who commanded the squadron how it was he did not charge the fugitives, remarking that he lost an opportunity which most probably would never again present itself, that of taking prisoner the enemy's commanding general. He replied with perfect seriousness that his orders were to halt on that road, and that therefore the escape of the enemy was no affair of his; that had he been ordered to charge, he would have done so willingly. This I firmly believe; and he was not very long afterwards killed while gallantly charging with his regiment.[21]

---

20   Ball to mother, 15 November 1811, Hampshire Archives 20M62/11B/5.
21   Blakeney, *Peninsula*, p.230.

Long claims that he placed the cavalry on the road to intercept Girard but that they were then withdrawn in order to ride to Merida and wrote: 'Had the pursuit continued, and the Cavalry remained where I had posted them, his escape was impossible'.[22]

Captain Richard Brunton with the Caçadores recalled their part in the battle and the continued pursuit:

> Day break on the morning of the 28th repaid us for all our hardships. We followed close on the heels of the Enemy's Picquets as they retired, and came upon them quite unprepared to see us. Tho they were ready formed in close column to commence their march, which they immediately did on perceiving us, but our movements had been too rapid, we marched for some time in open column parallel with them and within Pistol shot without a shot being fired on either side, they having the Sierra de Montanches on their left flank and we striving to reach the Merida road before them; at length finding we were heading them, they broke and pushed up the Sierra to their left. After this the warfare became very irregular, my Battalion exerted themselves in the pursuit, but they had the advantage of us, as every few yards of the Sierra presented a defensible position and they having thrown off their Knapsacks and all incumbrances got away from us the moment there was a chance of our getting at them. We however continued following them all day taking many Prisoners, and where we arrived at the extreme point of the Sierra nearest Truxillo, had the mortification of seeing the remnant of them under the command of General Gerard at a very short distance formed in mass, and retiring across the plain to Truxillo. – I was with General Ashworth and we used our utmost exertions to collect a few men to follow them, but in vain. We could only get together a few stragglers, and they so completely knocked up that they could go no further. – At this time the Marquis of Tweeddale came up to us, and said he could muster (I think it was) 16 Dragoons with which he would attack them, if we could support him. We made fresh exertions but it was all in vain, and we reluctantly saw about 500 men who by that time must have expended nearly all their ammunition walk unmolested away from us.[23]

James Gubbins also recorded the moment that Girard slipped away:

> A league from Arroyo, found the 39th Regt. driving the French fugitives from the Sierra. Morillo's men dispersed in all directions, much firing on both sides. Persuaded by Tweeddale to go up the mountain against my judgement, in the direction of the village of Santa Maria, the French making rapid progress along the Sierra and began to descend. [Girard] endeavoured to form his troops in the plain but in vain, very anxious myself to support him, the 39th quite exhausted and could not bring up a company. The Enemy in the plains formed in close column and retiring with astonishing quickness covered by their skirmishes. – About 500 of the Enemy the Spaniards dispersed in tens and twelves all over the plain, and firing to no effect the enemy still retiring in a masterly manner, very anxious to check him being upon his flank. Constantly showing him my front. He gave me

22   McGuffie, *Cavalry General*, p.139.
23   Narrative of the Service of Lt. Col. Richard Brunton, NAM, 1968-07-461.

The other side of the hills that Girard retreated over. The French marched right, up the valley towards Montánchez. (Author's photo)

some shots, offered Tweeddale to charge him rather than allow him to gain the wood if he would take share in the responsibility, however he said it would be madness, (an indeed I now think it would) – 30 to 500 – The French gained the wood. [Girard] wounded his men very turbulent, took road to Salvatierra. The Spaniards still following him in disorder. Dismounted my troop at half past three p.m. Tweeddale left me. Lt. Colonel Luke, Major of the 39th came up to me to know my intentions which I informed him of. I accordingly took my troop into the village of Valdefuentes and got my men a little bread and the horses some straw. Got a chicken killed, dressed and eaten in ten minutes. Placed my vedette and learnt from Col. Luke that he would keep sentries and strong guard. The 39th quite exhausted. Got a little wine and bread which we divided with difficulty. Got straw for the horses and only one bushel of barley. A prisoner brought in said that the Enemy had halted 3 leagues off. Offered Col. Lindsay to march in 3 hours if he would bring 200 men which he said he would not do, nor had he orders. Very anxious that they should but in vain. Vexed and disappointed. Changed my linen and got my clothes dried, gave orders to march in the morning at daylight.[24]

Morillo carried on the pursuit for nearly 20 miles, first to Torre de Santa María and then the village of Santa Ana, until his men could go no further.[25] Girard headed for Ibahernando with between 350 and 500 of his men, many of them wounded. Morillo thought that if the British cavalry had been more

---

24 Journal written by Capt James Gubbins, NAM 1992-12-138, pp.152-3.
25 A. Rodriguez Villa, *El Teniente General Don Pablo Morillo* (Madrid: Editorial-America, 1920), Vol.I, p.57.

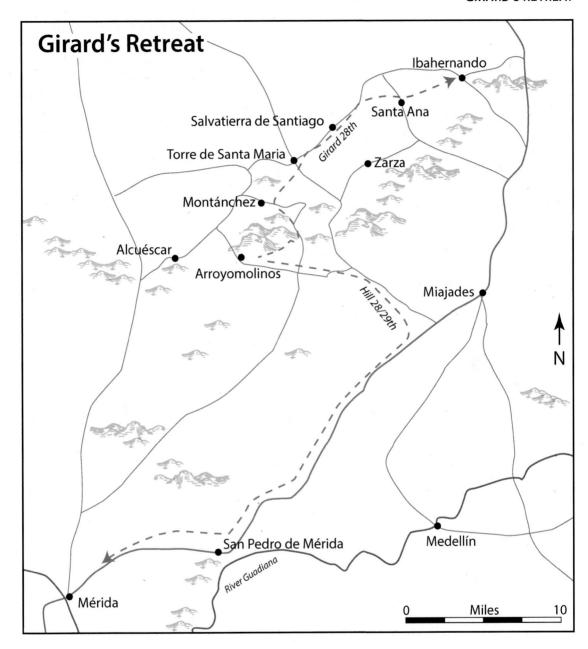

Girard's Retreat

active then Girard could have been captured.[26] After a long trek through the mountains Girard and his men eventually crossed the Guadiana at Orellana la Vieja, 20 miles to the east of Medellín, and re-joined Drouet's corps two days later.[27]

Penne Villemur followed the French cavalry for the rest of the day as they looped south towards San Pedro de Mérida and then onto Almendralejo,

---

26   Rubio, *Revista de Estudios Extremeños, 2013*, Tomo LXIX, Número I, pp.322-3.
27   Oman, *Peninsular War*, Vol.IV, p.604, & Du Casse, *Volontaire*, p.361.

but while they took some prisoners they could not catch up with them or Remond's brigade. The Spanish entered Merida around noon on the 29th. Long also headed south with his cavalry and some foot, but his advance was slow because of the fatigue of the infantry. He placed a picquet at a crossroads and succeed in taking over 30 French prisoners as small groups tried to flee south. Long entered Merida five hours after the Spanish.

8

Praise and Blame

At Arroyomolinos, once the sounds of battle had faded as the French were pursued over the hills, the commissaries bought flour from one of the mills that gave the town its name and baked fresh bread for the troops, who also got an extra rum ration.[1] The French prisoners were secured and the surgeons got to work and did what they could for the wounded. Many would have had been hit by musket balls or canister shot but, given the nature of the fighting, there would also have been those injured in hand-to-hand combat. For example, the allied surgeons treated *Maréchal de Logis* Francois Bouvier, of the 20e Dragons, for a bayonet wound to his lower right arm and severe swelling after being hit in the testicles by a musket butt.[2]

There was also a lot of French baggage to be seized, either officially or more informally. The French property taken included Bron's carriage and a chest containing 5,000 Dollars which Girard had raised from Cáceres. Benjamin Ball told his mother that the 28th Foot had between them netted around £10,000, with some individual soldiers making as much as £400, whilst lamenting the fact that his own regiment had missed out on all the plunder because of their part in the pursuit.[3] The return of ordnance captured listed one 6-inch howitzer, one 8-pounder cannon, one 4-pounder cannon, five ammunition caissons for the artillery and one for small arms, and one store waggon.[4]

Gíron also noted in his dispatch:

One stand of colours were taken by the British troops, and by those under my command, the flag of the 40th Regt. of the Infantry of the Line, which I have the honour of transmitting to your Excellency, and an immense number of muskets, swords, knapsacks, and horses, together with the whole of the baggage and equipage of the division. The enemy likewise lost an Eagle, but we have not yet been able to find it.[5]

---

1   Bell, *Rough Notes*, p.17.
2   Statement of the service of Francois Bouvier, 1817, <http://www2.culture.gouv.fr/LH/LH027/PG/FRDAFAN83_OL0342090v011.htm> (accessed October 2019).
3   Ball to mother, 15 November 1811, Hampshire Archives 20M62/11B/5.
4   Return of Ordnance and Stores taken from the Enemy, TNA, WO 1/251.
5   Giron's dispatch, reproduced in *The Globe*, 3 December 1811.

The drums and drum-major's staff of the 34e Ligne. (Cumbria's Museum of Military Life, Carlisle Castle)

The eagle seems never to have been found and metal detectorists still search the sierra near the village in the hopes of locating it. The Spanish had also captured Dembowski's papers and other correspondence regarding French officers in Spain.[6] Hill proposed giving the Spanish the 5,000 Dollars and the guns, and Wellington agreed.[7] At Merida Hill organised an auction of the captured French horses for the benefit of his men. One soldier of the 71st received 2s 6d as his share.[8] A sergeant of the 92nd also mentions the capture of 'a chest belonging to a mason lodge with all the jewels and paraphernalia belonging to the order of masonry'.[9]

---

6   Hill to Wellington 13 November 1811, BL Add.MS, 35059, p.462.
7   Wellington to Hill 8 November 1811, BL Add.MS, 35059, pp.450-3.
8   Anon. *Journal of a Soldier of the 71st*, p.148.
9   Glover, *Journal*, p.114.

The 2/34th Foot captured the drums and drum-major's staff of the 34e Ligne. Sergeant Moses Simpson of the grenadier company, who seized the staff from the drum-major, was later given a medal by the officers of the regiment.[10] The drums remained in the possession of the regiment through subsequent amalgamations until 2007, when they were placed in the regimental museum at Cumbria's Museum of Military Life. They were played on the anniversary of the battle and from the 1920s the regiment's band dressed in replica uniforms from the period.[11] In the Crimea the drums were white-washed to disguise them from the French units fighting alongside the British.[12] In 1845 the 34th were granted the battle honour 'Arroyo dos Molinos'. They were the only regiment to be so honoured, despite not having the most prominent role in the victory. In 1836, whilst Hill was general commanding-in-chief of the army, William IV had authorised the 34th to commemorate the battle by wearing a red and white pom-pom on their shakos, the same colours as the centre companies of the 34e. When the rest of the army changed to red and white pom-poms it prompted the regiment to request the battle honour instead. The request was granted but when in 1890 General Sir John Alexander Ewart, Colonel of the 2nd Battalion Gordon Highlanders, requested that 'Arroyo dos Molinos' be added to their colours the request was refused as the decision to grant it to the 34th had only been due to the exceptional circumstance of the pom-pom and the 13th Hussars (formerly the 13th Light Dragoons) had been refused when they had asked for the same battle honour.[13] When the Military General Service medal was eventually issued by the British government in 1847 Arroyomolinos was not considered significant enough to merit a clasp but in 1817 the Spanish awarded the Cross of Arroyo-Molinos to the troops who were present under Gíron.[14]

A total of 1,032 prisoners of war were marched to Portalegre on the 29th.[15] George Bell noted the acceptance of many of the French to their new circumstances:

> The 34th now took charge of all the French prisoners, officers and men. The former accepted parole; the latter we locked up in the church, a goodly congregation for the old padre. Yesterday, perhaps, they were robbing his hen-roost, and to-day certainly teasing his church-toggery – indeed, before the day was closed, they had arranged a theatrical troop, and were performing a play, all rejoicing in the expectation and hope of being escorted to their future banishment by British

10 R. Cannon, *Historical Record of the 34th, Or the Cumberland Regiment of Foot* (London: Parker, Furnivall, and Parker, 1844), p.52.
11 Pathé Newsreel from 1934, <https://www.youtube.com/watch?v=erT4LNlQB54> (accessed August 2019).
12 *The Lion and the Dragon, The Newsletter of the Friends of Cumbria's Military Museum*, Autumn 2011, & email from Cumbria's Museum of Military Life March 2019.
13 Correspondence between Ewart and Adjutant General's office, TNA, WO 32/6867.
14 H.E. Gillingham, 'Spanish Orders Of Chivalry And Decorations Of Honour', *Numismatic Notes and Monographs*, no. 31 (1926), pp.1-165.
15 Hartmann to Framingham 30 October 1811, in Leslie, *The Dickson Manuscripts*, Series C 1809-11, p.493.

troops, being under bodily fear of the Spaniards, who would, as they well knew, have bayoneted every man of them that fell out of the ranks; for they had a long account to settle with these French marauders. The following day we had a rest, and the prisoners opened a bazaar in the church to dispose of, 'perhaps,' all their unlawful gains. It was a great day for the church and for the priests when these fellows departed; every one of them seemed to have a watch for sale, gold or silver, and a great variety of bijouterie; there were some great bargains going, but I had not a dollar to get a single kind remembrance of those dear departing friends! My regiment escorted them down to Portugal. By the way they were very cheery, and went to church every night for safety![16]

However, Moyle Sherer recalled that some were not quite so contented:

I should lose sight, however, of the French military character, if I omitted to notice, that several of the serjeants and old soldiers who were decorated and wore the chevrons of service, appeared exceedingly sulky, and vented their anger in a sort of muttering smothered swearing. Those who have seen a ferocious Frenchman utter from between his closed teeth his favourite oath of 'Sacré Dieu!' will agree that there are few things more savage and offensive.[17]

James Gubbins rode back through Arroyomolinos on the 29th and wrote in his journal: 'passed the field of battle, several bodies laying naked, the limbs swelled and stiffened with cold, showed the human form in horrid grandeur'.[18] Captain Charles Cadell of the 28th Foot noted with regret:

Many of the unfortunate French were so badly wounded that they could not be moved; we were therefore obliged to leave them in the village, when we marched. It was truly heart-rending to hear their cries, and many requested, we would shoot them, rather than leave them to the mercy of the Spaniards. No doubt, after our departure, the stiletto put an end to their sufferings.[19]

The only French officers killed during the battle were *Capitane* Tailleur and *Sous-Lieutenant* Deweyle de Romans of the 27e Chasseurs; that regiment also had one other officer wounded, *Capitane* Larchier, besides their commander, the Duc d'Arenberg. The 20e Dragons had just one officer, *Sous-Lieutenant* Poulin wounded. Amongst the infantry the 34e had *Capitanes* Heurtaud and Secretin wounded, and the 40e had four officers injured: *Chef de Battalion* Woiral, *Capitanes* Bourdon and Ballue, and one of their medical staff *Chirurgien Aide-Major* Bounin. One of Girard's ADCs, *Lieutenant* Barreu-Duborg, was also wounded.[20]

---

16   Bell, *Rough Notes*, p.18.
17   Sherer, *Recollections*, p.240.
18   Journal of Capt James Gubbins, NAM 1992-12-138, p.153.
19   Cadell, *Narrative*, p.123.
20   A. Martinien, *Tableaux, par Corps et par Batailles, des Officiers Tués et Blessés Pendant les Guerres de l'Empire (1805-1815)* (Paris, Charles-La Vauzelle, undated), pp.48, 199, 212, 560, 612, & 806.

Lieut. General Lord Hill, K.B. (1814), by William Heath. (Anne S.K. Brown Military Collection)

Portrait of Pablo Morillo by Horace Vernet (painted between 1820-22). (The State Hermitage Museum, St. Petersburg. Photograph © The State Hermitage Museum. Photo by Natalia Antonova, Inna Regentova)

Sir John Downie, unknown artist. (The Stirling Smith Art Gallery & Museum)

Arroyomolinos, seen from the road from Alcuéscar. (Author's photo)

The 92nd Foot, the Gordon Highlanders, charge into Arroyomolinos on the morning of 28 October 1811 as the Duc d'Arenberg and other officers of 27e Chasseurs à Cheval emerge from their quarters. (Original artwork by Christa Hook (www.christahook.co.uk) © Helion & Co.)

The slopes where Girard and the bulk of the French ascended on their retreat from Arroyomolinos. (Author's photo)

The view from Fort Napoleon, above the bridge near Almaraz, towards Fort Miravete on the peak just left of centre. (Author's photo)

The view downstream from the Albalat Bridge, near Almaraz, towards the site of the French pontoon bridge. The Tagus is wider than it was in 1811, due to a series of dams further down the river. (Author's photo)

On the allied side the casualties had been mercifully light. The British regiments lost seven rank and file killed and 47 wounded, according to the post-battle casualty return. Also wounded were one lieutenant colonel, two majors, four captains and four sergeants. The Portuguese regiments present had six men wounded. One staff officer was listed as missing. Five horses were killed, 11 wounded and four listed as missing.[21]

The individual regimental casualty reports allow most of the soldiers killed to be identified. The 9th Light Dragoons lost Privates John Gahagan and John McDole from Captain Benjamin Handley's Troop. Both were Irishmen; Gahagan was a labourer from Kildare and McDole a weaver from Monahan. Gahagan was married and the £1 13s 3d pay that he was owed was paid to his wife. McDole's £1 10s 3d was paid to his brother. Both the wife and the brother were probably with the regiment as there is no note in the return as to when the payments were made, as is the case when payments were made to next of kin back in Britain.[22] The 2/34th's only fatality was Private John Hutton, a labourer from West Lowden in Scotland. The 10s 3d of pay that he was owed was not paid out to his next of kin until April 1818.[23] The 1/92nd had two men killed: Private William McDonald, a labourer from Perth whose £1 11s 3d and prize money from the Walcheren expedition was paid to his brother in 1815; Private John Denoon, a weaver from Elgin, was owed only 2s 4¼d but his father still had to wait four years to receive it.[24] Casualty reports have survived for all the British regiments present so it is unclear who the other two men killed in action were, if the figure of seven killed is correct. Lieutenant Colonel Cameron, in his letter to the 92nd's colonel dated 2 November, claims that three of his men were killed but only two are listed in the return he signed on the 24th. Sergeant David Robertson mentions Private William Campbell as the third casualty.[25]

Only those killed in action, missing, taken prisoner or deserted are listed in the regimental casualty returns. The wounds of ordinary soldiers are not recorded but lists of wounded officers were included with the dispatches after a battle. Captain Hardress Saunderson, 39th Foot, was severely wounded in the head. He was granted a pension of £100 per annum in 1812 and the wound was still troubling him as late as 1827 when he listed it as a reason for him retiring on half-pay.[26] Benjamin Ball also states that the 2/39th had one sergeant and three rank and file wounded.[27]

Captain Donald McDonald, 92nd Foot, was also severely wounded. One shot went through his right knee and another caused a compound fracture of his left leg. It was the third time he had been wounded, but he survived to command the regiment at Waterloo.[28] Captain John McPherson, also of the 92nd, was severely wounded in the left wrist. He would be severely wounded

21   Return of Killed, Wounded and Missing, TNA, WO1/251.
22   25 October to 24 November 1811 Casualty Return, TNA, WO 25/1423.
23   25 October to 24 November 1811 Casualty Return, TNA, WO 25/1722.
24   25 October to 24 November 1811 Casualty Return, TNA, WO 25/2119.
25   Glover, *Journal*, p.115.
26   Hall, *Biographical Dictionary*, p.507.
27   Ball to mother, 15 November 1811, Hampshire Archives 20M62/11B/5.
28   Hall, *Biographical Dictionary*, pp.363-4; Anon., *The Royal Military Calendar*, Vol.V, p.94.

again, twice, in July and December 1813 and died of his final wound at the start of 1814.[29] The 92nd's commander, Lieutenant Colonel Cameron, was the most senior officer wounded, but his lost finger only entitled him to be listed as slightly wounded, as was Brevet Major Robert Dunbar, of the same regiment. Major Bussche, leading the 2nd KGL Hussars, was also slightly wounded and so was one of his troop commanders, Captain George Lewis Schultze.[30]

Exact figures for Spanish and French casualties are harder to find. In his dispatch to Castaños, Gíron estimated that: 'Our loss in all does not exceed 20 killed and 100 wounded,'[31] but it is unclear if he means only the Spanish, or all of the allies. If just the Spanish then it would intimate that the Spanish suffered much heavier losses that the British and Portuguese. One estimate of French losses claims that, out of the approximately 3,000 men Girard had with him when the allies attacked, he lost 2,000, with 1,400 being taken prisoner.[32] This tallies with Hill's estimate of the number of prisoners taken. Major Hartmann put the number of French dead and wounded at around 300.[33] Other estimates put the number of French dead as high as 800, which seems unlikely.[34] Morillo did claim that he found 600 French dead in the woods and mountains.[35] Many of the French who escaped could have been separated and scattered for some time before finally re-joining their units.

After the action had concluded on the 28th Campbell's Brigade and the Regimento de Infantaria n.º 18 came up from the rear, and then were sent with Howard's Brigade to follow Penne Villemur's and Long's cavalry to Merida in the faint hope of catching up with Remond, but they had far too long a lead. The allies reached San Pedro de Mérida that night, where James Hope witnessed a minor postscript to the battle:

> We had not been long in camp, before a party of twenty-three French dragoons were observed scampering across the plain in our front, in the direction of Medellin. As no time was to be lost, one of our cavalry piquets, consisting of seventeen men, dashed across the plain to intercept them. In a few minutes the two parties stood in the presence of each other, and without much ceremony, proceeded to business. The action, however, was of short duration, for the enemy, after a feebler resistance than was anticipated, agreed to accompany our dragoons into camp, where they were received with three hearty cheers. Both parties being in full view the whole time, the scene was altogether extremely interesting.[36]

---

29 Hall, *Biographical Dictionary*, p.387 & NRS, GD1/736/121.
30 Names of Officers Wounded & Missing on the 28th of October, TNA, WO 1/251.
31 *The Globe*, 6 December 1811.
32 J. Sarrazin, *Histoire de la guerre d'Espagne et de Portugal de 1807 à 1814* (Paris: J.G. Dentu, 1814), pp.232-3.
33 Hartmann to Framingham 30 October 1811, quoted in Leslie, *The Dickson Manuscripts*, Series C 1809-11, p.493.
34 Teffeteller, *The Surpriser*, p.111.
35 Hill to Wellington 30 October 1811, TNA, WO 1/251, p.129.
36 Hope, *Military Memoirs*, pp.89-90.

The troops rose at 3:00 a.m. the next morning to continue their wet and weary march to Merida, arriving late in the day on the 29th. Drouet had been waiting at Merida for Girard but once he got word of the battle he withdrew to Almendralejo, ordering Remond to meet him there.[37] Hill found the time to write his post-battle dispatch to Wellington from Merida on the 30th.[38] Soon after the battle Hill had sent his brother, Clement, to carry the news north to Wellington, who had not received any word from Hill for several days. The ride would have been a difficult one; the heavy rain had swollen the rivers and made crossings hazardous. Wellington was not expecting to hear of a battle, confident that Girard would have withdrawn south and Hill would have seen to it that the Spanish were secure in Cáceres before pulling back to the Portuguese border.[39] In the report Hill outlined the course of events and singled out his subordinate commanders and staff for praise. Clement arrived at Wellington's headquarters on 1 November and Ensign Chatham Churchill, carrying Hill's official dispatch, arrived on the 6th.[40] Wellington wrote back to Hill on the 7th:

> I have had the honor of receiving your letter of the 30th October from Merida; and I congratulate you upon the success of your Expedition into Estremadura.
>
> I beg leave at the same time to return you my thanks for the zeal and ability which you have manifested in carrying into execution the measures which I had recommended to your attention in that Province; and I request you to take an opportunity of assuring the General Officers and Troops under your Command, that I have perused with the greatest satisfaction your report of the patience, perseverance, gallantry, and discipline, of their conduct throughout the late expedition; and that I have not failed to make my sense of these qualities known to His Royal Highness the Prince Regent, and to His Royal Highness the Commr. in Chief, as well as to the Portuguese Government.[41]

Brigadier General George Murray, Wellington's quartermaster general, also wrote to Hill to offer his congratulations:

> I will not refuse myself the pleasure of expressing to you how much I am gratified by your successful affair at Arroyo Molinos. It gives me the more satisfaction from my having entertained very little hope of Girard being unwise enough to allow you to come up with him – and in saying that I feel a peculiar pleasure in this fortunate affair, as it concerns yourself personally, and assure you that I only repeat the sentiments which are in the mouth of every one whom I have heard speak upon the subject.[42]

---

37 Drouet, *Vie Militaire*, p.70.
38 See the appendix to this work.
39 Wellington to Liverpool 30 October 1811, in Gurwood, *Dispatches*, Vol.VIII, p.373.
40 Wellington to Graham 3 November 1811, in Gurwood, *Dispatches*, Vol.VIII, pp.376-7 & Wellington to Hill 7th & 8th November, p.389.
41 Wellington to Hill 7 November 1811, BL Add.MS, 35059, pp.446-7.
42 Murray to Hill 1 November 1811, BL Add.MS, 35059, p.443.

Wellington quickly forwarded Hill's report to Lord Liverpool, the Secretary of State for War. In his covering letter he wrote:

> I have frequently had the pleasure to report to your Lordship the zeal and ability with which Lt. General Hill had carried into execution the operations intrusted to his charge; and I have great satisfaction in repeating my Commendations of him, and of the brave troops under his Command, upon the present occasion, in which the ability of the General, and the gallantry and discipline of the Officers and Troops, have been conspicuous.[43]

Wellington sent Clement on to London, via Lisbon, with the dispatch. He had a rough passage of 18 days and the news had already arrived by the time he delivered it to Lord Liverpool on 1 December. He quickly wrote a letter back to his brother:

> I got here yesterday with the despatch. Lord Liverpool was at his country house at Coomb, where I went to him. He read the contents of it, and then sent me on with it to Oatlands for the Prince to see. His Royal Highness is still confined to his bed, and I did not see him. I saw the Duke of York and a great many other of the great people there, and every one spoke in the highest terms of the business. I returned to Lord Liverpool's at night, and dined there: he was uncommonly kind, and, like every body else, pleased. In short, I am sure – nothing that has been done during the war has given so much satisfaction.[44]

Lord Liverpool's response to Wellington was fulsome in its praise of Hill and his men:

> Few enterprises of this nature have been so judiciously planned or so ably carried into execution as the surprise of the French column under General Girard, on the morning of the 28th of October; and the Prince Regent has felt particular pleasure in observing the complete success which has attended this operation, and which the ability displayed by General Hill, and the good conduct of the allied troops under his command, have so fully deserved.
>
> I am commanded to desire that your Lordship would take the earliest opportunity of conveying to Lieut. General Hill, and the Officers and soldiers of the British and Portuguese forces who have served under his command in the late expedition, the high approbation which His Royal Highness the Prince Regent has been pleased to bestow upon their exemplary conduct; as I am to request you would take such a course as you may see proper for making known, in the most public and marked manner, these gracious sentiments of the Prince Regent.
>
> His Royal Highness has also been gratified to remark the zealous and active co-operation of the Spanish troops serving with Lord Hill's corps upon this occasion, as well as the fidelity and steady attachment to the cause of their country evinced

---

43   Wellington to Liverpool 6 November 1811, in Gurwood, *Dispatches,* Vol. VIII, p379.
44   C. Hill to R. Hill 2 December 1811, in Sidney, *Life of Hill,* p.174.

by the inhabitants of the province in which these operations have been carried on.[45]

Hill's friend Lieutenant General Graham wrote to Hill to add his congratulations:

> I rejoiced most truly on hearing of your success, but I delayed writing to congratulate you on it, till I should see your despatch with the particulars.
>
> Ld. Wellington sent me your letters two days ago at the same time expressing his high approbation of your conduct, a testimony more valuable than any other, but one which in every body's opinion is most justly deserved by the judgement, activity, & admirable arrangements which produced so brilliant a result with so trifling a loss – Currie has been good enough to send me a sketch of the ground and disposition of the troops, which I prize much & which perfectly explains the movements described in your report. I beg you will make him my best thanks, & pray remember me too to Squire, who, I am happy to see is such a favourite with you – I hope your health has not suffered by the fatigue and bad weather – Adieu.[46]

In his reply to Graham, Hill noted the factors that had led to the victory, and also made a veiled criticism of one of his subordinates, mostly probably Long:

> With respect to the result of the business at Arroyo del Molino, it certainly proved more fortunate that I had reason to calculate upon. I was always confident that there could be no difficulty in dislodging Girard from Caceres, but I feared that as I advanced he would walk off. The secrecy and good conduct, however, of all concerned enabled me to come up with him, and where there was so much good fortune, I ought not to complain of a partial failure; but between ourselves, to the eye of an infantry officer some part of our force did not appear to be very well managed.[47]

For his part Long seems to have anticipated the reproval. In his journal for 30 October he wrote:

> I fear I shall not have the credit I might have gained had I let my dogs loose and charged them vigorously, which in the state their musquets were in I could have done without risk or loss, but I foresaw the doing so would only tend to accelerate their dispersion and more rapid flight to the mountains and thereby defeat the object proposed to be gained by General Howard's column.
>
> I regret that I was not present at the time they gained the Sierra, for a charge at that moment could have done no injury, and must have produced some degree of delay which would have favoured the closing of our Infantry upon them.

---

45   Liverpool to Wellington 2 December 1811, in Anon., *General Orders Spain & Portugal*, Vol. IV, pp.1-2.

46   Graham to Hill 12 November 1811, BL Add.MS, 35059, pp.458-9.

47   Hill to Graham 17 November 1811, in Teffeteller, *Surpriser*, p.112.

> But above all I lament the message which counteracted my first intentions, the prosecution of which would in my opinion have been decisive.[48]

So it would seem that Hill apportioned some blame to Long, probably for not exhibiting the dash and elan typical of a light cavalry commander and which Bussche seems to have displayed in his handling of the KGL hussars. Conversely, Long blamed Hill for making him chase down the French artillery rather than get between Girard's troops and the sierra.

Others were also writing their accounts, letters and journals at Merida. Major Hartmann, of the KGL Artillery, wrote an account of the operation and brought his letter to a close with:

> Our provisions [sic. possibly meant to be privations] moving this expedition are not trifling having left all our baggage at Portalegre. I am now sitting in wet clothes and not entirely so well as I could wish. I beg therefore you will excuse my scrawl. Upon the whole I think that this has been one of the best conducted expeditions of that kind and I am the more glad of it as it is Lieut. General Hill who has conducted it. Some of our troops have made immence bouty.[49]

Benjamin Ball also outlined the rigours of the campaign to his mother:

> The day before the action we marched at six in the morning & continued on the Road till Eight at night, halted in a new ploughed filed till two while the Rain almost beat us into the Ground, & being forbidden to make fires, could get nothing to eat, marched again at two, came up with the Enemy at five, & continued our pursuit over Mountains till four in the evening having had nothing to eat or drink from 5 o'clock in the evening of 26th till 9 at night of 28th, incessantly on the move, & constantly wet through. To add to my comfort, my baggage was carried back to Portalegre during the fight, & I was left with only the clothes on my back, & these in no very Catholic condition, until a few days ago when it was restored to me in a most melancholy plight, one half of my things having been stolen, & these which remained, utterly destroyed by the wet, & my horse almost dead from ill-usage & starvation, so you see I am no great gainer from these wars.[50]

Hill let his men have one day's rest at Merida before commencing the march back to the Portuguese border and letting them return to their winter cantonments. The expedition had not only resulted in the near-destruction of a French division but had achieved its aim of putting the Spanish back into Cáceres, and, for a time, it disrupted the communication between Soult in the south and the French armies further north. Only in early December did Dembowski's brigade reoccupy Merida and secure the route to Marmont.[51]

Once back at Portalegre, Hill wrote to his sister back in Shropshire:

48 McGuffie, *Cavalry General*, p.140.
49 Hartmann to Framingham 30 October 1811, in Leslie, *The Dickson Manuscripts*, Series C 1809-11, p.493.
50 Ball to mother, 15 November 1811, Hampshire Archives 20M62/11B/5.
51 Oman, *Peninsular War*, Vol.IV, p.606.

I am sure my dear Friends at Hawkstone will rejoice to hear of my good fortune, & share with me the satisfaction I feel in having, under the will of Divine Providence, given a severe blow to the Common Enemy & thank God almost without loss on our side. My Official report on the business which I dare say Clement will carry to England in the same ship which will take this will give you a detailed account of what has happened but in case it should not I have time merely to inform you that on the morning of the 28th at day break I succeeded in surprising, attacking, and annihilating the French Corps under Genl Girard at Arroyo del Molino. The Enemy's Force when attacked consisted of about 3,000 Infantry, & 600 Cavalry, & artillery. The result is the capture of one General, Brun, one Colonel, the Prince D'Aremberg, 35 Lt. Col. and inferior Officers, 1400 prisoners probably 500 killed. The others dispersed having thrown away their arms. We have also got all the Enemy's Artillery, Baggage, Magazines in short, every thing that belonged to the Corps.

Clement I am pretty certain will go in the ship that carries this otherwise I would give you a more detailed account although I should lose my dinner, which is now going on the table. The Prince and most of the French Officers dine with me. The British here have been very kind to French since they have been in our possession and they seem very grateful for it. Clement behaved very gallantly, as indeed did all.[52]

The number and seniority of French officers taken prisoner at Arroyomolinos was impressive: As well as d'Arenberg and Bron, there was Girard's chief of staff *Colonel* Hudry, *Chefs de Bataillon* Veiten and Woirol of the 34e and 40e respectively, plus an aide-de-camp of Girard's, a *commissaire de guerre*, and around 30 other officers.[53] Some were almost immediately exchanged for British prisoners of equal rank but Wellington recognised the value of holding on to d'Arenberg:

The Prince d'Aremberg is a great card, being a member of the Confederation of the Rhine, and a Prince of the Imperial family; that is to say, married to Mlle Tascher, Josephine's niece, who was to have been married to Ferdinand the 7th. You should take care, therefore, that in any communications he has with his Brother, or other Officers, he has the attendance of a sharp English Officer, and the sooner he is sent off the better.[54]

The exchange system relied on good faith and trust; the rest of Wellington's letter indicates that he had serious doubts as to the fidelity of the French and their treatment of British prisoners and he urged Hill to take precautions against being tricked.

Robert Blakeney escorted d'Arenberg to Lisbon with a corporal and six men of the 2/34th. The duke had with him his secretary, two cooks, his coachman and three servants. The party also included the captured commissary and a captain of the duke's regiment. Blakeney was confident

52   Hill to sister 5 November 1811, BL Add.MS. 35061, p.87.
53   Hill to Wellington 30 October 1811, TNA, WO 1/251, pp.122.
54   Wellington to Hill 8 November 1811, BL Add.MS 35059, pp.450-3.

they would not escape as they feared the Spanish peasants more than captivity in Britain, and the duke had given his parole.[55] On the journey Blakeney and the duke dined with the senior officers in the towns that they passed through. Once in Lisbon the duke regularly hosted dinners for both allied officers and fellow prisoners. Blakeney recalled:

> One officer alone, a lieutenant of artillery, was never invited. It was alleged that when we attacked on the morning of the action, this unfortunate young man, who commanded the artillery, had no matches lit, and that had he been prepared we must have lost more men in killed and wounded while filing through the town; in consequence, he was cut by every French officer in Lisbon. I felt much for him, and mentioned to the prince that where they were all alike unfortunate, it appeared invidious to single out one for neglect; for whatever his fault might have been, it could not have had the slightest effect in changing the result of the action. The prince, although a stern soldier, somewhat relented; but there was such a person as Napoleon to be taken into consideration. However, he mentioned the circumstance to General Le Brun, expressing an inclination to become reconciled to the artillery officer. Le Brun would not listen to it, alleging that it would be setting a dangerous example to look over or in any way countenance gross neglect of duty, at the same time casting a scowling look at me, knowing that it was I who spoke to the prince on the subject. Annoyed at his obduracy and a little nettled by his indignant look, I asked him if he did not think that, had there been mounted patrols on the look-out to give alarm in proper time, the artillery officer, thus warned, would have had his guns in battle array; instead of which, we came absolutely into the town without encountering a single French dragoon. The general treated my observation with haughty silence; but the French adjutant-general, also a prisoner, being present, darted a fiery glance at Le Brun, and would no doubt have applied his censure of the artillery officer to himself, had he not been restrained out of consideration for the prince, who was second in command of the cavalry. Le Brun was disliked by all from his haughty and overbearing manner.[56]

Entertaining French officers in Lisbon often revealed useful information. Major William Warre, scion of the wine-merchant family, who served on Beresford's staff and often undertook intelligence duties, wrote to his father about meeting the duke and the two *chefs de batallion* taken at Arroyomolinos:

> The Prince d'Aremberg, Colonel of the 27th Chasseurs à Cheval, and married to the Empress Josephine's niece, is arrived here, and 1400 prisoners taken at Arroio del Molino by Hill. He is an insignificant looking creature, and not reckoned a great Officer. Genl. Bron is not yet arrived. I have dined with the Lt.-Col. of their 40th Regt. He is a fine intelligent young man, but quite a Frenchman. He lies without the least hesitation. He half cries at times at his misfortune, but, when he has drank a little wine, sings and dances, and seems to forget entirely that he is a Prisoner. I am going this morning to take the Lt.-Col. of 34th F.A. to make some

---

55   Blakeney, *Peninsula*, pp.233-4.
56   Blakeney, *Peninsula*, pp.247-8.

purchases he wants, and then to dine at Hardinge's. I think him steadier a good deal than the other, who is a most amusing companion, and less of a soldier. This man is reserved, but I know what he says is true, and therefore we intend to try what the bon vin de Bordeaux will do towards opening his heart, for we often get very interesting information in this way, and, though I hate and despise the fellows, I am rather amused by them now and then.[57]

D'Arenberg sailed to Britain and, like many other French officers on parole, was housed in one of a number of towns designated for the purpose, in his case Oswestry in Shropshire. Bron was at nearby Welshpool and in December 1812 broke his parole and attempted to reach the Kent coast, but was quickly apprehended at Shrewsbury.[58] The duke balked at reporting to the representative of the Transport Board, as officers on parole were required to, and in August 1812 he was sent to the Norman Cross prisoner of war camp until a compromise was reached where the representative would call upon the duke instead.[59] The British newspapers reported his views on the war and the battle at Arroyomolinos:

The Prince has a very youthful appearance, is extremely affable, speaks very lightly of his present condition, and much more so of politics. The war in Spain he considers at an end, but for the enterprising Guerrillas and the presence of the British army; of the latter, however, he says that it is at the option of Bonaparte to annihilate the whole, by the sacrifice of 50,000 men in carrying the lines of Torres Vedras – which he acknowledges to be almost incredibly strong fortified. In this opinion Gen. Brune, who is a most intelligent man, vehemently coincides; and further states that the Emperor's purpose against England is better answered by far in the present state of things in Spain and Portugal, by keeping a British army there, which creates so enormous an expense to the British nation – and, in his opinion, 'without having any important object in view'. They acknowledge their surprise to be unequalled when rising from their pillows and seeing the Highlanders in the streets of Arroyo Molina, rushing in with bayonets fixed, and carrying all before them, when the very Spaniards, who but the night before had declared to assist them, were throwing their hats, and crying 'Vive Engliterre'. Gen Brune had two horses killed under him in this affair, while endeavouring to disengage the troops. Although Gen. Girard escaped the English, they state it as their opinion, that he will be immediately put under arrest by the Emperor. They speak in very contemptible terms of the Spanish soldiery – but say that the boldness and courage of the Guerrillas is truly astonishing, a boldness which all the regular armies of Europe will never be able finally to subdue. They wish that the British soldiers were deprived of their bayonets, and in that case alone they expect success in a general engagement, where there is any thing like equality of numbers – while the British troops are commanded by such a very superior office as Lord Wellington, which they acknowledge, though with regret, to be the case to

---

57   W. Warre, *Letters from the Peninsula* (London: Murray, 1909), pp.210-1.
58   *The Shrewsbury Chronicle*, 11 December 1812.
59   *Northampton Mercury*, 15 August 1812 & *Cheltenham Chronicle*, 27 August 1812.

a degree. Gen. Brune asserts that Girard's Division was the finest, best appointed, and stood highest with respect to courage, of all the French army.[60]

Some of the French prisoners had more important concerns than the course of the war. Major General Long received a note from an officer of the 27e Chasseurs whom his cavalry had captured after the battle, and in a letter to his brother Long wrote:

> The poor creature has lost half his senses, and the first thing he shewed me on being taken was his wife's picture hanging around his neck, stating at the same time that her existence and that of six children depended solely on his exertions, and that their ruin would be consummated by his detention.[61]

Long tried to get the officer exchanged quickly, but without success. The Spanish wanted to exchange d'Arenberg for a Spanish grandee captured in 1808 but Wellington thought him 'too great a card to be so thrown away'.[62] *Chef de Battalion* Woiral was exchanged a year after the battle, and continued to serve in the French army into the 1840s.

The exchange of *Capitaine* Margen, of the 34e Ligne, for Captain Brinsley Nixon, of the 85th Foot, who had been captured during the siege of Badajoz in June, took place on 21 November. Margen was escorted towards Badajoz by Lieutenant Samuel Dikes King, 13th Light Dragoons, under a flag of truce. The British met the French escort and the exchange took place. King then asked the French officer if he could see Badajoz and both parties rode towards the town. Some Spanish guerrillas were spotted on a nearby hill and the French officer warned that they would not abide by the flag of truce and they should keep their distance. The French officer galloped away but King thought that if they knew he was British he would be in no danger. King rode up to the Spaniards with his trumpeter who was carrying the flag to explain, but they opened fire and he was killed by a shot to the chest. The trumpeter fled to the safety of the French advanced posts.[63] Hill later wrote of King: 'I fear he has lost his life in consequence of his own disobedience of orders relating to Flags of Truce'.[64]

The exchange of *Lieutenant* Barreu-Duborg, one of Girard's ADCs, for Lieutenant Anthony Strenuwitz, 21st Light Dragoons, faced complications of a different kind. Strenuwitz was Austrian and had been in French service before joining first the Spanish guerrillas and then entering British service, and so he could have been treated as a deserter. He was an ADC of Major General Sir William Erskine. He had been shadowing Girard's movements during the expedition and was the staff officer listed in the return after the battle as missing in action. The exchange for Dubourg was arranged but

60   *Hereford Journal*, 8 January 1812.
61   Long to C.B. Long 12 November 1811, quoted in McGuffie, *Cavalry General*, p.143.
62   Wellington to Liverpool 20 November 1811, in Gurwood, *Dispatches*, Vol.VIII, p.413.
63   Hall, *Biographical Dictionary*, pp.327-8, Journal of Capt Gubbins, NAM 1992-12-138, p.158, & C.R.B. Barret, *History of the XIII Hussars*, (London: Blackwood, 1911), Vol.I, p.163.
64   Hill to Stewart 24 November 1811, BL Add.MS, 35062, pp.105-6.

The death of Lieutenant King by Harry Payne, from C.R.B Barret, History of the XIII Hussars, Vol.I. (Reproduced with the permission of The Light Dragoons Regimental Association)

before it could take place Strenuwitz took matters into his own hands and escaped from his guards, making his own way back to allied lines. Wellington ordered Hill to send Dubourg over to the French anyway as there was some question as to whether Strenuwitz had been under parole at the time of his escape.[65]

Hill's dispatch of 30 October included extensive praise for his subordinate commanders and his Spanish allies. In a follow-up letter, he brought other officers to Wellington's attention, including his aide Currie, Squire of the engineers, the Marquis of Tweeddale, Hillier of the 29th for his intelligence duties, and Blassiere of the 5/60th. He also again praised the troops under

---

65   BL Add.MS 35062, p.99, 35059, pp.396-7, & Bell, *Rough Notes*, pp.17-8.

his command, the Spanish, and the local population for their support.[66] Hill wrote to Castaños to thank him for the part the Spanish troops played in the victory:

> As General Girón, Chief of Staff to your Excellency, witnessed the operations recently executed in Extremadura and is well instructed in all my movements and in all of my dispositions as well I consider it not necessary to disturb Your Excellency with further details as I am sure that General can produce a complete report for Your Excellency about this business.
>
> Nevertheless I can not resist the desire I have to express to your Excellency my gratitude for all the services of General Girón, whose advice and support essentially contributed to the happy success of the combined arms, and added to the energy he used to fulfil all my wishes, give him the incontestable right to my recognition and expressive thanks.
>
> I also want to have the satisfaction of expressing to your Excellency the admiration with which I have seen the zeal, good conduct and gallantry with which the Spanish troops that acted jointly with those under my command behaved; and I beg you in the same manner to kindly thank in my name General Count de Penne-Villemur, Brigadier General Morillo, Colonel Downie, and other Officers for their good conduct on this occasion adding to them my most sincere wishes that in the future they will achieve the same success against the enemies of their country.
>
> I must also show my gratitude to Brigadier General Josef de Ezpeleta, and to all the Staff officers under General Girón command, omitted no opportunity of supporting me with their advice and exertions. I at the same time return your Excellency many thanks for the letter in which I was honoured to receive your congratulations for this happy success that I view just as the first of a chain of even greater successes.[67]

Girón also wrote to Castaños, his uncle, even more effusively:

> My aide-de-camp, Don Manuel Bretón, comes to congratulate Your Excellency for the memorable victory that the vanguard of this army, together with the British troops, have achieved on the 28th in the vicinity of Arroyo-Molinos, surprising, beating and destroying the best division the French had, commanded by one of their most accredited and fortunate generals. The bonds of blood and friendship that so closely unite me with your Excellency prevent me from paying tribute to the prudence, talent and gallantry you are creditor to, but none more proper than your Excellency to express to *General* Conde de Penne-Villemur, to *Brigadier* Don Pablo Morillo, to the senior and junior officers and troops of the vanguard my satisfaction for the glory they have acquired on this day, due to the perseverance and heroism that they displayed in the previous ones, suffering

---

66   Hill to Wellington 30 October 1811, TNA, WO 1/251 pp.141-6.
67   Hill to Castaños 6 November 1811, AHN, ES.28079.AHN/5.1.24.1.1.7.8.4.3//DIVERSOS-COLECCIONES, 137, N.68.

from hunger, lack of uniform, and fatigue capable of robbing those who are not Spaniards who defend their religion, independence and homeland.[68]

Girard's dispatch about the battle necessarily contained less self-congratulation and rather more self-justification.[69] In the dispatch Girard claims he was not still in his quarters when the attack commenced but already on the march, and that only a small portion of the rear-guard occupied the village. There are other points where Girard's narrative differs from the allied accounts but the flow of the action is substantially the same and Girard does deserve the credit he gives himself for extracting as many men as he did after the initial surprise, and for keeping them together on the extended retreat. He is critical of the cavalry but he does frequently praise Dembowski for his handling of the infantry. His covering letter to *Maréchal* Soult also emphasised his efforts to save his men:

> Your Excellency will see that I was in march, that I could have retired and avoided fighting with my rear guard, but the cavalry had compromised themselves, and it would have been requisite to have abandoned them.
>
> The enemy was numerous; I considered but the honour of his Majesty – the duty of a devoted soldier. I marched upon the English, and by drawing upon myself all the forces of the enemy, disengaged the light cavalry.
>
> We have suffered sensible losses, but disengaged ourselves with honour from a difficult situation. Three times surrounded, three times we opened ourselves a passage with the bayonet.
>
> Marshal – I shall be in despair if the results of the unfortunate affair should make me forfeit the confidence of his Majesty. I merit it by the sentiments which directed me – by those which animate me.[70]

Even before he had received Girard's official dispatch Soult had written to *Maréchal* Berthier, Napoleon's chief of staff, in Paris:

> The event reported to me by General Comte d'Erlon, commanding the 5th Corps in his reports of the 28th, 29th and 30th of October, is so shameful that I do not know how to describe it...
>
> On the 28th of October, the first brigade, commanded by General Remond, was already on its way, and more than an hour and a half from Arroyo del Molinos, when General Hill arrived with his troops at the quarters of General Girard, without a shot being fired. A battalion of the 34th and one of the 40th were in town with three pieces of light artillery, and were thus surprised by the negligence of their leaders...

---

68   Rodriguez, *Morillo*, p.58.

69   See the Appendix to this work.

70   Girard to Soult 4 November 1811, this English translation in *The Caledonian Mercury*, Thursday 9 January 1812. The original French of this and the subsequently quoted letters between the French commanders can be found in Wellington, *Supplementary Despatches*, Vol.XIII, pp.728-32.

General Girard had with him elite troops, he has shamefully let himself be surprised by an excess of presumption and confidence. At the time he was in danger, no guard was established. Officers and soldiers were in the houses, as in full peace. I will order an investigation and a severe example.[71]

Drouet, in his letter to Soult which accompanied Girard's report, tried to salvage what credit he could for his subordinate:

There was throughout a reprehensible security; but the Honour of the French arms has been saved, by the firmness and valour of Gens. Girard and Dembrowski; and this affair, which might have been attended with fatal, even dishonourable, consequences, ought now to be ranked in the number of those which are not unfrequent in war.[72]

On 15 November, after reading Girard's dispatch and Drouet's letter, Soult wrote again to Berthier with further details, attempting to paint a more positive picture of the action:

The honour of our arms has been saved – the eagles have not fallen to the power of the enemy. The remains of the two battalions have joined the 5th Corps, with Gen. Girard and Dombrouski, and the staff of our army which was with this rear-guard.

According to the reports that have reached me, our loss consists of 400 infantry, 120 cavalry, 200 horse and 25 artillerymen, who belonged to the three pieces taken.

Gen. Bron was in march from Arroyo de Molinos, at the head of 150 horse from the 20th Dragoons, when the enemy attacked the village. He instantly retraced his steps, and executed, with much valour, three charges, but the forces were too disproportionate; his horse were overthrown, and he had the misfortune to fall in to the enemy's power. The Duke d'Aremberg was also dismounted in a charge, and in falling, received two bayonet wounds. It is said they are not dangerous.[73]

However, later in the letter Soult continued:

The Conduct of the General of Division is too reprehensible, not to give room for a strongly-marked disapprobation.

I informed your Excellency, that if General Girard should return, I would displace him from the command of his division, and have him brought to a Court Martial. Considering notwithstanding, what he has done, since his surprise, to bring back the remains of the two battalions, and save the eagles – considering, likewise, that the light cavalry had not established a guard to discover the defile by which the enemy penetrated, I have thought that, waiting for further instructions from your Excellency, to confine myself to depriving him of his command,

---

71 Soult to Berthier 2 November 1811, in Wellington, *Supplementary Despatches*, Vol.XIII, p.728.
72 Drouet to Soult 4 November 1811, in *The Caledonian Mercury*, Thursday 9 January 1812.
73 Soult to Berthier, 12 November 1811, in *The Caledonian Mercury*, Thursday 9 January 1812.

and sending him to Cordonne, where he will remain unemployed, till a new disposition.[74]

It took until 12 November for the first news of Girard's defeat to reach King Joseph in Madrid, and once the news had got as far as Paris Joseph received orders to send Girard and Briche back to France.[75] In December Napoleon instructed Berthier to write to Soult, the Duke of Dalmatia:

> Express to the Duke of Dalmatia my disapprobation of the flank movement performed by General Girard in the presence of the enemy, a march which lasted for three days, and was so ill managed that the enemy might have cut him off at any time: he should have been supported by a strong detachment. It is unfortunate that, with an army of 80,000 men, they could not make the dispositions which prudence demanded to avoid being beaten by a troop of 6000 English. Remind him that, when one has to fight, particularly against the English, one must not divide one's forces, but collect them and present imposing numbers: all the troops which are left behind run the risk of being beaten in detail or forced to abandon their positions.[76]

On 2 January 1812 the emperor wrote again to his chief of staff:

> My Cousin, I wish you to write for me a report, which will be printed, on the correspondence respecting General Girard's affair. It seems that General Britche was posted on the side by which the enemy attacked; that he was completely surprised, not in his bivouac, but in bed in a comfortable house, while the horses of his hussars were unsaddled. I will dictate this report to you. My object is to impress on the colonels and generals of light troops the general principle that a colonel of chasseurs or hussars who goes to bed, instead of spending the nights in bivouac and in constant communication with his main-guard, deserves death. I think that Marshal Mortier has some information on the subject. As my object is not merely to punish General Britche, but to excite the zeal of the whole light cavalry, this report must be vigorously drawn up.[77]

Girard reached Paris on 21 January and immediately had an audience with Napoleon. Whilst it may have been a difficult interview Girard emerged with his career intact and was given command of a division of Polish troops. In a letter to his brother-in-law Girard blamed a 'general of the cavalry' both for being negligent before the action and for subsequently attempting to place the blame on to him, and it seems likely that he was referring to Briche.[78]

---

74   Soult to Berthier, 15 November 1811, reproduced in *The Caledonian Mercury,* Thursday 9 January 1812.

75   A. Du Casse, *Mémoires et Correspondance Politique et Militaire du Roi Joseph,* (Paris: Perrotin, 1854), Vol.VIII, pp.106, 146.

76   Napoleon to Berthier 6 December 1811, in J. Bonaparte, *The Confidential Correspondence of Napoleon Bonaparte with his Brother Joseph* (New York: Appleton, 1856), Vol.II, p.196.

77   Bonaparte, *Confidential Correspondence,* Vol.II, p.203.

78   Du Casse, *Le Volontaire,* pp.369-71.

Girard may have been successful in avoiding disgrace but in a conversation with his escort, Blakeney, d'Arenberg claimed that Girard had been told of the allied presence near Arroyomolinos. Blakeney wrote:

> In allusion to the late action and the movements which led to that event, I warmly expatiated on the praiseworthy fidelity of the Spaniards, particularly those of Arroyo Molinos and Alcuescar, in never having communicated our near approach to the French army. The prince replied that they did not use such fidelity as I imagined, for the night previous to the action two Spaniards came to his quarters in Arroyo Molinos and informed him that we were much nearer than the French general seemed to be aware of; that upon this he immediately imparted the information to Gerard, who replied; 'Prince, you are a good and active soldier, but you always see the English in your front, rear and flank. I tell you they are eight leagues distant, for I know to a certainty that they were seen in the morning marching hastily towards Caceres, thinking to find us there; and so confident do I feel as to the certainty of what I tell you that I shall delay the march to-morrow an hour later to give the men more time for repose'. Much hurt at the general's remark, which had the appearance of insinuating that he entertained a dread of encountering the English, the prince returned to his quarters.[79]

Capitaine Margen repeated a similar story to James Gubbins, saying that both Bron and Spanish peasants had warned Girard that the allies were close and that he had said that it was not possible.[80]

With all their efforts to avoid or to place blame the only one of the French senior commanders to come out of the action with his reputation intact was Ludwik Dembowski, who was unfortunately killed in a duel in July 1812.[81] Girard went on to serve in the Russian campaign in 1812 and the campaigns in Germany in 1813, when he was wounded and captured. In 1815, when Napoleon returned to the throne, Girard was again given command of a division and was fatally wounded at the Battle of Ligny. He died in Paris on 27 June, a few days after Napoleon had issued a decree granting him the title of Duc de Ligny. Bron and d'Arenberg both remained prisoners for the rest of the war and opted not to serve Napoleon again in 1815. Briche rose to command a division before Napoleon's first abdication, and then served King Louis XVIII. He also chose not to serve during the Hundred Days.

The news of the victory at Arroyomolinos was very well received in Britain. The year had been a mixed one for the army in the Peninsula. Wellington's success at Fuentes de Oñoro had been followed by the appalling losses and controversy surrounding Albuera. The accounts of Arroyomolinos lifted morale, both in the army and at home, and helped to maintain political support for the campaign. It also greatly enhanced Hill's reputation. In December the Duke of York, commander in chief of the army, wrote to

---

79   Blakeney, *Peninsula*, pp.235-6.
80   Journal of Capt James Gubbins, NAM 1992-12-138, p.156.
81   El General Polaco Dembowski y la Iglesia de Santiago de Valladolid, <http://www. batalladetrafalgar.com/2012/05/el-general-polaco-dembowski-y-la.html> (accessed October 2019).

Wellington to pass on the gratitude of his brother, the Prince Regent, for the efforts of Hill and his men and to assure Wellington that Currie and Squire would be promoted to major immediately, that Clement Hill would also be promoted as soon as he had served sufficient time in the rank of captain, and that the service of the other officers Hill had singled out had been noted and they would receive advantage when and where possible.[82] Hill also received notification from Lord Liverpool that the Prince Regent had honoured him with a knighthood:

> I have had particular satisfaction in transmitting to Lord Wellington, by the mail of this day, the Prince Regent's most cordial and decided approbation of your conduct in the late operations against the French force under General Girard. His Royal Highness does the fullest justice to the distinguished ability with which you have conducted this important service, and I can assure you, that his Majesty's confidential servants, and the public in general, most entirely participate in the Prince Regent's feelings upon this occasion. I have great pleasure in being enabled further to add that the Prince Regent has authorised me to assure you that as soon as the restrictions upon the regency have expired, it is his intention to confer upon you the Order of the Bath, as a proof of the sense which his Royal Highness entertains of your services.[83]

Hill replied:

> I have the honour to acknowledge receipt of your Lordship's letter conveying the gracious Intention of the Prince Regent to confer upon me the honor of the Red Ribbon a mark of his Royal Highness' approbation which I shall ever endeavour to merit and which I shall receive with the most heartfelt gratitude.
>
> Permit me to return your Lordship my warmest thanks for the flattering report which you have been pleased to make of my services to the Prince Regent and for the very friendly and handsome manner in which you have conveyed His Royal Highnesses Gracious Intentions towards me.[84]

The Prince Regent also mentioned the success at Arroyomolinos in his speech at the opening of Parliament in 1812, praising both Hill and his men.[85] Arroyomolinos also earned Hill's 2nd Division the nickname of 'the surprisers'.[86] Many of the memoirs and journals of the division relate how pleased the officers and men that he led were at the praise heaped upon their well-loved commander. Moyle Sherer wrote:

> One thing in our success at Arroyo de Molinos gratified our division highly; it was a triumph for our General, a triumph *all his own*. He gained great credit for

---

82 York to Wellington 6 December 1811, in Anon., *General Orders Spain & Portugal*, Vol.IV, pp.3-4.

83 Liverpool to Hill December 4 1811, in Sidney, *Life of Hill,* pp.176-7.

84 Hill to Liverpool 5 December 1811, BL Add.MS, 35059, p.498.

85 Anon., *Royal Military Panorama* Vol.III, January 1814, p.317.

86 Bell, *Rough Notes*, p.19.

this well conducted enterprise, and he gained what, to one of his mild, kind, and humane character, was still more valuable, a solid and a bloodless victory; for it is certainly the truest maxim in war, 'that conquest is twice achieved, where the achiever brings home full numbers'.[87]

---

87   Sherer, *Recollections*, pp.241-2.

9

Breaking the Stalemate

During the winter of 1811 into 1812 the French besieged the Spanish held city of Valencia on the east coast. Napoleon, managing the war from Paris and frequently working with out of date information, continued to press his commanders in Spain to take the offensive and ordered the transfer of resources between the various French armies to suit the situation as he saw it. He ordered Marmont to send reinforcements to Valencia, weakening the troops facing Wellington. Both Napoleon and Marmont believed that the Anglo-Portuguese army, suffering from a high rate of sickness, would wait for the better weather of spring to take the offensive.

The failed sieges of Badajoz during 1811 had led Wellington to ask for a proper siege train of heavy artillery, associated engineering equipment, and stores. This had arrived from Britain and was in place near Ciudad Rodrigo. Reinforcements of both cavalry and infantry had also bolstered Wellington's army, which was now stronger and more experienced than it had ever been. The fortresses of Ciudad Rodrigo and Badajoz guarded the approaches into Spain and Wellington now had the means to take them; all he needed was an opportunity. Receiving reports of French troops moving north Wellington decided to act, on 6 January he wrote to Hill:

> I am about to attack Ciudad Rodrigo; in which enterprise I shall succeed, or I shall bring back towards this frontier the whole army which had marched towards Valencia & Aragon. By these means I hope to save Valencia, even if I should not succeed in getting this place. If I should get this place, we shall, I hope, make a fine campaign in the spring.[1]

Still in the south, Hill had also been tasked with relieving pressure on the Spanish armies by advancing back into Extremadura and driving Dembowski from Merida. Hill then threatened Drouet at Almendralejo, who withdrew and let the allies enter the town after brief contact between the advance and rear guards on 1 January. Hill kept the pressure on by sending Lieutenant Colonel Abercromby with the 1/28th, the 2nd KGL Hussars, and

---

1   Wellington to Hill 6 January 1812, BL Add. MS, 35059, pp.500-1.

the Portuguese Regimento de Cavalaria nº 10 further south to Fuente del Maestre. Abercromby's force clashed with a party French cavalry near Los Santos and routed them. Hill's advance alarmed Soult and had the desired effect of relieving some of the pressure on the Spanish at Tarifa. With the weather and the roads worsening Hill withdrew rather than take any further risks. On 9 January Wellington ordered Hill back to the Portuguese border and asked him to position his forces at Portalegre, Niza, and Castello Branco, so that he could intercept any French attempt to relieve Ciudad Rodrigo from the south.

For Hill's men the advances and retreats along rough roads in bad weather became somewhat tiresome. Ensign George Bell of the 34th wrote:

> Monsieur le General Drouet gave us a great deal of bother at this time, marching and counter-marching across that great plain to Almandraleho, a little town some five leagues distant. There he assembled his army, took up position, inviting a quarrel, but always declining to fight. When we got within reach of a nine-pounder gun, he was off in retreat, leaving no chance of giving him a checkmate. Here we halted, generally for a couple of days, and returned to Merida. This game was played so often, I was thoroughly acquainted with every big tuft of grass and swampy pool over that dreary plain ploughed up by wheels, cavalry, and baggage animals. The object of the French was to harass our troops as much as possible, and to keep us away from Ciudad Rodrigo, a great fortress, which he knew would be attacked by Wellington before we could advance up country.[2]

In the same letter by which Wellington informed Hill of his intention to besiege Ciudad Rodrigo he had also written:

> It is very desirable that you should endeavour to discover the state of the Enemy's works, & their force, at the Ponte d'Almaraz. It would aid all my plans very much, if we could destroy their bridge, & Works at that Point. You'll recollect that the top of the Sierra de Mirabete, where there is a tower commands the ground the whole way down to the river.[3]

The bridge near Almaraz was the main crossing point for the French on the river Tagus, to the west of Toledo. It was a vital route for troops coming from Soult's forces in the south to support Marmont in the north, or for those in the north to march south. The original stone Albalat Bridge had been destroyed by the Spanish early in the Peninsular War and the French had subsequently constructed a temporary pontoon-bridge nearby. Other crossings across the Tagus west of Toledo, at Arzobispo and Talavera de le Reina, were unsuitable for mass troop movements due to the mountains south of the river.

Despite being reinforced, Wellington's army was still vastly outnumbered by the French. If the French commanders could unite against him then he would be forced to abandon the siege of Ciudad Rodrigo and retire back

---

2   Bell, *Rough Notes*, p.22.
3   Wellington to Hill 6 January 1812, BL Add. MS, 35059, pp.500-1.

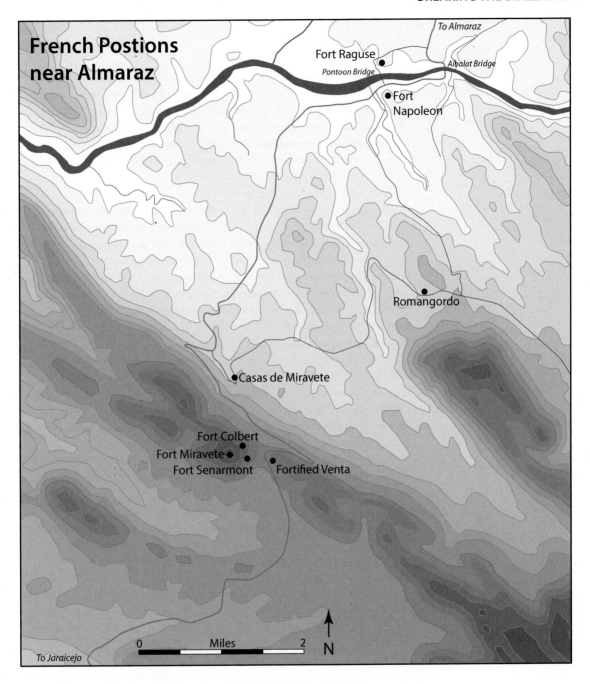

French Postions near Almaraz

To Almaraz

Fort Raguse

Pontoon Bridge

Albalat Bridge

Fort Napoleon

Romangordo

Casas de Miravete

Fort Colbert

Fort Miravete

Fort Senarmont

Fortified Venta

0   Miles   2

N

To Jaraicejo

across the border into Portugal. If the bridge at Almaraz was destroyed any French troops moving north or south would have to march by a longer route, giving Wellington the time to bring together his own forces or, if necessary, withdraw.

Hill sent Lieutenant George Hillier into French territory to gather the intelligence that Wellington required. In the meantime, Ciudad Rodrigo was successfully stormed on 19 January after being besieged for only 11 days. Wellington immediately began to make plans to take Badajoz next, and the operation to destroy the bridge remained a priority. On 28 January he wrote to Hill with very detailed instructions:

When we shall attack Badajoz, we must expect that the Army of Portugal, consisting of eight divisions of Infantry, the whole of which are now in Castille, & the Army of the South, will co-operate to oblige us to raise the siege. The Army of Portugal would naturally cross the Tagus by their bridge at Almaraz; and they would be obliged at the season of the year in which I propose to undertake this operation, to go round even by Toledo, if we could destroy their bridge and other establishments at that place.

This is what I wish you to attempt.

You probably went to look at the bridge of Almaraz when the army were at Jaraicejo in the Month of August, 1809. As well as I recollect, the Puerto de Mirabete commands the whole ground to the River, the descent from the Puerto being about a league. The French have there three Works defended by 15 pieces of cannon eight pounders and a howitzer; that is to say, one, I believe, at the Puerto: & two others below, to defend the Bridge, one being at each side of the River. I am not quite certain however of the locality of the Works; & some accounts have given me reason to believe that the Works besides the one at the Puerto de Mirabete, are Redoubts thrown up for the defence of a small village called Lugar Nuevo, on one side of the River & of another called Casas del Puerto, at the left side; & about a mile and a half below the Puerto de Mirabete. If this be true, it would be possible to destroy the bridge with out taking the Works; and at all events if it is not true, & that the Works are near the River & properly têtes de pont, they must be very bad ones, as I recollect perfectly that the ground falls on the left side to the banks of the River, from the Puerto de Mirabete, & almost an equal distance on the right side.

Under these circumstances it appears to me that you will have no difficulty in destroying the enemy's bridge at Almaraz; and I hope that you may have it in your power to destroy their stores and establishments there.

The Garrison of the three Works consists of 450 Men, including Artillery Men, sappers, &c.; and as long as the Enemy remain in Castille, they cannot be assisted or reinforced. If I should find that the enemy move from Castille again into Estremadura, I could easily apprise you of their movement in time to stop you, if it should be necessary.

The equipment which you should take with you for the purposes of this operation, should be eight or ten ladders, from eighteen to twenty feet in length; about twenty felling Axes, and 3 or 4 Crow Bars; a coil of good rope might be of use to enable you to tow the Boats to a situation in which you could burn them. Besides I would recommend you to take 4 or 5 of the 24 pdr Carronades which are going into the Alentejo for the purposes of the Siege of Badajoz. These Carronades are mounted upon Travelling Carriages; with Axle Tees of the same span as the Portuguese Artillery & the carts of the country. They can therefore travel anywhere. They weigh the same in travelling as our Nine and heavy 6 pdrs; and are drawn by eight horses. They are now travelling with bullocks; but I will tomorrow send you the route by which they are to march; and I recommend to you to send horses belonging to your Heavy Brigade, or to your Horse Artillery, to meet & bring them up to you quicker than the bullocks can bring them. Each of them has on its Carriage every thing for its use, excepting Shot, Powder, and

The 16th Century Albalat Bridge, which was partially destroyed by the Spanish in 1809. (Author's Photo)

Cartridges; and it is desirable that you should without delay adopt the following measures to procure these Articles.

You should send to Elvas to have selected from the stores there, 100 English 24 pdr shot for each Carronade that you will take. I say English 24 pdr shot, because any thing larger will not fit them. You should likewise draw from the stores of the army, either at Elvas or Abrantes 50, 5½ inch shells for each; and about twenty 5½ inch Spherical Case for each; if there are so many. The stores at Elvas will supply the quantity of Powder sufficient for these shot and shells.

The Commissary must get mule carts if possible to carry these stores upon your Expedition if not bullock carts. 30 or 40 Shot or Shells will go in a cart easily. That part of the equipment taken from Elvas might be given out to be for the use of Campo Mayor, Ouguela, & Albuquerque.

I should hope that all the preparations would be made by the time that the Carronades would arrive at Portalegre.

I would then recommend the following disposition to you. That General Hamilton & the Portuguese Division, & Portuguese Cavalry should observe the Garrison of Badajoz. That Generals Morillo & the Conde de Penne Villemur should observe the Bridge of Merida, and the movements of the 5th corps in Lower Estremadura, while you should move with the 2d division, the British Cavalry, & such part of the 6 pdr Brigade, and of the Horse Artillery, as should be equipped after equipping the Howitzers as above desired, by Caceres direct upon Jaraicejo, & thence upon the Puerto de Mirabete.[4]

---

4   Wellington to Hill 28 January 1812, BL Add. MS, 35059, pp.520-4.

Hillier had reached Almaraz, drawn a plan of the French positions and written a report for Hill by 16 January. The French fortifications were formidable and included forts on either side of the bridge, which was itself protected by smaller works. Additionally, the main pass through the hills at Miravete was protected by a hilltop position and fortified houses on the road. Hillier also noted that most of the bridge had been dismantled and that only two of the pontoons were on the river and that the rest were on carriages on the northern bank. This meant that any attempt to destroy the bridge would also have to involve a force crossing the river elsewhere and attacking on both banks, greatly complicating the operation. Hill included Hillier's report in his reply to Wellington on 30 January:

> I have the honour to acknowledge the receipt of your Lordship's letter of the 28th, marked secret and confidential, and will use my best endeavours to fulfil the instructions which it contains. Your Lordship will perceive, by Mr. Hillier's report on Almaraz, dated the 16th instant, that I have not been inattentive to your wishes on the subject of the destruction of the enemy's works at that place. You will likewise observe, that on the 16th the enemy had only two boats on the river, and the others, nine in number, were on the north bank of the river, mounted on carriages, and two spare carriages.[5]

Hillier's information forced Wellington to reassess his plan for the operation, but not to abandon it. On 1 February he wrote again to Hill:

> I did not see Lieut. Hillier's very clear report to you of the 16th January till this day, when I received your letter of the 30th. It is very obvious to me that unless you can send a detachment to the right of the Tagus to cut off the retreat of the Boats the principal object of your expedition which is to destroy these boats, must fail.
>
> I can supply you with the means of sending a detachment across the Tagus; but the first point to be ascertained is whether wheel carriages can go to the Tagus by any road excepting by that of Mirabete, or so near Mirabete that they must be perceived. As well as I can recollect of the country, it is impossible to get down to the Tagus with wheel carriages, anywhere between the junction of the Tietar and the junction of the Ibor, excepting by the Puerto de Mirabete. I beg that you will have enquiry made by Lieut. Hillier upon this point. It would also be well if he were to enquire whether the enemy have any means of moving off the 9 Boats which are under their Work, marked B in his Sketch.
>
> If you cannot get down to the Tagus with wheel carriages, excepting by the Puerto, it is not worth while to attempt the operation, for as well as I can recollect, the Enemy have in that part of the country a large quantity of oxen. If, however, you can get down to the Tagus, it would be desirable to send over a sufficient detachment to endeavor to surprise and get possession of the work C; while the Castle of Mirabete or the work A should be attacked on the left bank, & to cut off and destroy the Boats.

---

5   Hill to Wellington, 30 January 1812, BL Add. MS, 35062, p.122.

The view downstream from the Albalat Bridge towards the site of the French pontoon bridge. The Tagus is wider than it was in 1811, due to a series of dams further down the river. (Author's Photo)

The view upstream from the Albalat Bridge, illustrating how mountainous the terrain is and why crossing points were so infrequent along the Tagus. (Author's Photo)

We have at Villa Velha six tin pontoons, with all their equipments, carriages, &c. They are very light, and, as well as I recollect; are drawn each by four pairs of bullocks, but Major Squire can tell exactly. You must desire Mr. Routh to provide bullocks to draw them; and with these you can form a flying bridge fully equal to take over the Tagus any detachment which you might think proper to send to the Right Bank. They would even carry over some of the Carronades if you should think proper to send them; but from Lieut. Hillier's description of the Enemy's works at the bridge, I should scarcely think it necessary to take these carronades. I should think that under the fire of your heavy six pounders and howitzers, and by keeping a heavy fire of musketry upon the parapet, while the storming party should advance, your troops would escalade any of these works. All the preparations, however, for the carronades, as detailed in my letter of the 28th January, might still go on, and Mr. Routh might get the bullocks for the pontoons, & the pontoons might be moved up to Portalegre, as they will be of use in our ulterior operations. But you will proceed upon your expedition, or not, according to the information which you will receive from Lieut. Hillier, whether or not you can get your pontoons down to the Tagus; not passing by Mirabete.

I do not believe the Work C is commanded by the road on which A stands; but I am quite certain that the Work B is completely commanded both by the ground A and C. I was at the old castle of Mirabete; the ascent to it is very rugged indeed; but I should think that no garrison could remain in it against your Howitzers.[6]

Unfortunately Hillier's diagram has not survived, so it is not clear which fortifications are referred to by which letters.

On the 4th Wellington wrote again to Hill to inform him that the carronades had been delayed by bad weather and poor roads. On the 7th he asked Hill to send 200 men to help speed their progress, but told Hill to make sure they did not beat the bullocks or mistreat the drivers. On the 9th he informed Hill that a French division was at Talavera with detachments at Navalmoral and Oropesa, but that he still thought the operation should go ahead.[7]

On 6 February Hill wrote to Wellington:

I beg to inclose a copy of a letter just in from Mr Hillier and also the examination of four deserters, one of them appears to be an intelligent fellow. It gives some interesting information regarding the works at Almaraz they all correlate Mr Hillier's report with respect to there being no Bridge at present on the River, except the two boats in two small flying bridges.[8]

The new information revealed that the pontoons on carriages had been sent away from Almaraz. The deserters also confirmed that the fortifications at Almaraz were of sufficient strength to make bombardment with the carronades a desirable element in any assault. On the 10th Hill wrote again to Wellington, after receiving Hillier's information that there were no other

---

6   Wellington to Hill 1 February 1812, BL Add. MS, 35059, pp.528-30.
7   Wellington to Hill 4, 7, & 9 February 1812, BL Add. MS, 35059, pp.531-8.
8   Hill to Wellington 1 February 1812, BL Add. MS, 35062, p.123.

routes for carriages to the Tagus. Given that it would be impossible to destroy the pontoons on the northern bank Hill wrote: 'taking every circumstance into consideration I do not think I aught to undertake the Expedition against Almaraz'.[9]

Wellington concurred with Hill's assessment:

I have received your letter of the 10th, and I agree with you in thinking that you would not succeed in obtaining possession of the Enemy's Boats on the Tagus near Almaraz, although you might destroy their Works. This last is not so important an object, and at all events, this is not the moment at which it ought to be attempted. But it is desirable that we should keep this object in view; that we should have as far as possible all the preparations made for the operation; and that we should endeavor to acquire all the information to be procured on these Works.[10]

Wellington, the siege train, and a large portion of his army, made their way from Cuidad Rodrigo to Badajoz during February and early March. Wellington took the opportunity to invest both Graham and Hill into the Order of the Bath on 12 March. Graham had been granted the honour for his victory at Barossa, and Hill for Arroyomolinos. Sir Rowland was initially reluctant to be addressed by his new title. One of his staff commented 'When he was knighted there was not one of us dared for nearly six months to call him *Sir Rowland*: he was quite distressed at being called any thing but *General*; and it was only very gradually that he could be driven to bear his honour'.[11]

As the siege of Badajoz began on 16 March Hill's command, along with Graham's of three divisions, covered the approaches to the town. Hill occupied Almendralejo, again, and then advanced east to Medellín. When he heard that Soult was gathering his forces at Seville Hill retired back to Merida and came under pressure from advanced elements of the French. Hill destroyed the central arches of the bridge over the Guadiana at Merida, and then joined Graham at Albuera on 6 April as Soult approached to raise the siege with 28,000 men, slightly less than the combined allies. On the same day Badajoz was successfully stormed, but with very heavy casualties. The allied soldiers sacked the town and it was almost three days before order was restored. Soult's mission became pointless and he withdrew.[12]

On 10 April Wellington learned that Marmont had crossed into Portugal in the north and was threatening Ciudad Rodrigo. He marched quickly northwards with the bulk of the army, leaving Hill to cover Badajoz while the fortifications were repaired. The 2nd Division and Hamilton's Portuguese were asked to contribute masons, bricklayers, carpenters, sawyers, wheelwrights, miners, smiths, and an entire brigade to assist in the repairs.[13] Marmont, who had advanced somewhat reluctantly, opted not to give battle and soon

---

9   Hill to Wellington 10 February 1812, BL Add. MS, 35062, p.125.
10   Wellington to Hill 12 February 1812, BL Add. MS, 35059, pp.542-3.
11   Sidney, *Life of Hill*, p.186.
12   Teffeteller, *Surpriser*, pp.121-3.
13   Wellington to Hill 11 April 1812, in Gurwood, *Dispatches*, Vol.IX, pp.51-3.

withdrew as the allies approached. Wellington had made significant gains early in the campaigning season, but his ability to hold on to Badajoz and Ciudad Rodrigo rested on the French armies not uniting against him. To this end he made plans for the Royal Navy to conduct raids on the north coast of Spain and work with the guerrillas there, he asked for an expedition to be made by the British forces in Sicily to the east coast of Spain, and he requested various diversionary operations from the Spanish. He also returned to the idea of destroying the bridge at Almaraz, on 24 April he wrote to Hill:

> Marmont has retired, and I shall immediately get provisions into Ciudad Rodrigo. I propose, while this operation shall be going on, to send some of the troops back across the Tagus, and to distribute the whole in such a manner as that they can be easily subsisted.
>
> I think that you might avail yourself of this opportunity to strike your blow at Almaraz. I think that one of your British brigades, and two Portuguese brigades, or one and a half British, and one strong Portuguese brigade, would do your business as to the French in that neighbourhood.
>
> All the iron howitzers are now in Elvas, and you might employ, to draw six of them, the mules attached to one of General Hamilton's brigades of Portuguese artillery. If Dickson has not got the ammunition carriages prepared for the brigade of howitzers, which I proposed should be in the reserve of the artillery, you might then get mule carts, to carry the quantity of shot, and of howitzers and spherical shells, which you might think it expedient to take. See Dickson in regard to this equipment, and settle the whole with him. You had better take him on the expedition with you. The equipment might be prepared at Elvas, and might join you at Truxillo or Jaraicejo by Caceres. Besides the gun equipment, you should take with you six of our small pontoons, to enable you to make a flying bridge if you should require it. The pontoons and bullocks are at S. Vicente, near Elvas; Lieut. Piper, of the Engineers, is in charge of them, and will do whatever you order him; each of them should march with a double proportion of bullocks.
>
> Make all your preparations in secret for this expedition. I shall watch from hence the course of the enemy's retreat, and will let you know if it should appear to me that you have anything to fear from any of the divisions of the army of Portugal going near Almaraz. Of course you will not march till you shall hear further from me.[14]

The operation was back on and Hill and his men would again have the chance to do more than march, counter-march, and skirmish.

---

14   Wellington to Hill 24 April 1812, in Gurwwod, *Dispatches*, Vol.IX, p.80.

10

The Allies at Alamaraz

On 14 April 1812 Lieutenant General Christopher Tilson Chowne was appointed to the command of the 2nd Division 'under the orders of Lieutenant General Sir Rowland Hill K.B'.[1] This was a recognition of Hill's broader responsibilities; he kept the nominal command to retain the use of the staff while Chowne took care of the day-to-day running of the division. Chowne had been called Tilson until the start of 1812 when he had to change his name as part of the conditions of an inheritance. As Tilson he had commanded a brigade from 1809 but was forced to go home on leave in 1810 to recover from a fever. He had been appointed a local Lieutenant General in November 1811.[2] The only other significant changes to Hill's staff were that his brother, Clement, and Edward Currie had both secured their promotions to major, and Hill's own local rank of lieutenant general had been made army wide, and not just local.[3] There was also at least one other addition to the numbers at headquarters; Mrs Currie had given birth to a son early in the year.

The troops that Hill selected for the raid on the bridge at Almaraz were largely a subset of those that had fought at Arroyomolinos; Howard's and Wilson's Brigades from the 2nd Division, Ashworth's Portuguese Brigade, and the 13th Light Dragoons from Long's Brigade.

Howard's Brigade

Major General Kenneth Howard's brigade contained all the units that it had the previous autumn; the first battalions of the 50th, 71st and 92nd Foot, plus Captain Peter Blassiere's No.8 Company of the 5/60th. Howard carried out the half-yearly inspections of his brigade during May, and the field returns and confidential reports give a very good insight into the state of the brigade. The field returns contain tables of the men's nationalities (English, Scotch,

---

1   General Order 14 April 1812, Anon., *General Orders Spain & Portugal*, Vol.IV, p.64.
2   Anon., *The Royal Military Calendar*, Vol.II, pp.302-3 & *General Orders Spain & Portugal*, Vol.III, p.254.
3   Army List 1812, TNA, WO 65/62.

Irish or Foreign – the Welsh were included under English), their ages, length of service, and height. There are also returns of the numbers and states of arms, accoutrements and clothing. The 1/50th had 590 Englishmen, 26 Scots, 307 Irish and 10 foreigners. The average height was around 5 foot 6 inches, the average age was between 25 and 30 years old and the average length of service was six years. The confidential report was very complimentary of both the battalion and its commander, Lieutenant Colonel Charles Stewart, finding that the battalion was 'in a perfect state of discipline'. However, the fact that 300 men were under 5 foot 6 was commented upon.[4] The minimum height for recruits was supposed to be 5 foot 5 inches, but this was often flouted and was reduced in 1812 to 5 foot 4 inches.[5]

The heights, ages and service of the 1/71st were similar to the 1/50th. Their field return, unsurprisingly, showed Scots as being in the majority with 642, but also 42 English, 320 Irish and five foreigners. The report praised their commander, Lieutenant Colonel Henry Cadogan, noting the level of care and attention that he gave the regiment and again the perfect state of discipline. One officer, Lieutenant James Stewart, was however singled out for lacking zeal and being 'not qualified for light infantry'. The duties of light infantry did often require higher levels of fitness, and a greater level of responsibility for junior officers. In a letter attached to the report Cadogan writes that Stewart 'from ill health no less than want of zeal is unequal to perform his duty' and requests that he be removed from the regiment. Stewart was transferred to the 3rd Garrison Battalion in 1813. The report also notes that the privates were clean but not 'very robust', and comments that as many of the men came from the city of Glasgow they were not as strong as men from the country.[6]

The 1/92nd had a higher proportion of Scots with 1,013 and only 49 English, 68 Irish and no foreigners. The 150 men under 5 foot 5 inches was commented upon in Howard's report, which stated that the battalion 'was not a tall body of men' but were strong and fit for service. They were generally well behaved but he did note that for two or three days after receiving their pay there were frequent cases of drunkenness, despite the officers' best efforts. The report found that commanding officer Lieutenant Colonel John Cameron was 'a zealous officer who has the honour of the regiment at heart', but also noted that some of the officers 'appear at present from age, infirmity or other cause to be unfit for the service'.[7]

The report on Blassiere's rifle company also says that it was also 'in a perfect state of discipline', and Howard praised the NCOs, and stated that the men were 'sober and orderly', but did note that some were 'old soldiers'. The report concludes with: 'In short it is a very efficient company which conducts itself in an orderly fashion on a march and in quarters'.[8] As of 25 April Howards Brigade had a total strength of 2,090 effective rank and file,

---

4   Field return and confidential report 1/50th, May 1812, TNA, WO 27/107.
5   K. Linch, *Britain and Wellington's Army* (Basingstoke: Palgrave, 2011) p.87.
6   Field return and confidential report 1/71st May 1812, TNA, WO 27/107, and Army List 1813, WO 65/63.
7   Field return and confidential report 1/92nd May 1812, TNA, WO 27/107.
8   Confidential report Captain Blassiere's Company 5/60th May 1812, TNA, WO 27/107.

Uniforms of the 92nd Foot 1808-10, by Harry Payne, from Gardyne, *The Life of a Regiment.*

with the 1/50th mustering 593, the 1/71st 695, the 1/92nd 758 and the rifle company 44.[9] The brigade still had over 500 men sick,[10] including Lieutenant John Macdonald of the 50th who had suffered 'a fit of insanity', escaped the care of a sergeant and two privates escorting him to the rear, and was then found in Lisbon. He was sent home to recover his health.[11]

---

9   Army in Spain and Portugal by Brigades and Divisions April 1812, TNA, WO 17/2469.
10   General Monthly Return 25 April 1812, TNA, WO 17/2469.
11   Regimental Return 1/50th 25 April 1812, TNA, WO 17/164.

Wilson's Brigade

Brevet Colonel George Wilson was still in command of his brigade, but he had seen one significant change in its composition in that the 2nd battalion of the 39th Foot had been replaced by the 1st battalion of the same regiment. The 1st battalion had left Sicily in August 1811 and had landed in Lisbon in mid-October. They marched from there a month later to join Wilson's Brigade and replace the 2nd battalion, but a medical inspection found that many of the men were suffering from ophthalmia; an eye condition that had plagued them in the Mediterranean. The 50 worst cases were hospitalised and the battalion was quartered in Crato, near Portalegre, until just after Christmas when most of the men and some of the officers of the 2nd battalion joined the 1st, and the remaining cadre of the 2nd returned to Britain to recruit.[12] The battalion's introduction into campaigning in the Peninsula was an arduous one with Lieutenant Exham Vincent writing in his diary in February:

> During the last six weeks the troops have been exposed to the most severe fatigue. The marches were generally long, and the weather extremely wet. The country at one time was so deluged with rain, that in the course of one day's march we had seven rivers to ford, some of them so deep and rapid that many accidents occurred. A good deal of baggage and ammunition was lost and several mules carried away in the current. It frequently happened that after a long days [sic] march, under incessant rain, the troops were halted in the open field where they slept in the same clothes, and without any covering than a wet blanket.[13]

The 1/39th was commanded by Brevet Colonel Robert William O'Callaghan, who had been with the regiment since 1803 and had last seen action commanding a battalion of grenadier companies at the Battle of Maida.[14]

Wilson also inspected his brigade in May. The height, age and service of the men of the 1/28th were similar to those of Howard's brigade. The field return also listed 35 women, three children aged over 10, and 12 under that age. The confidential report praised the commanding officer, Lieutenant Colonel Alexander Abercromby, and the comments on the officers and NCOs are peppered with terms such as 'zealous', 'attentive' and 'intelligent'. The privates were noted as being 'a good body of men with a general appearance of health and cleanliness,' and 'generally speaking sober and well behaved.' The battalion was fairly evenly split between the English and Irish with 499 of the former and 511of the latter, plus 12 Scots and single foreigner.[15]

The 1/39th, overstrength because of the merging of the battalions, was more predominantly English with 1,080, and then 10 Scots, 175 Irish and 12 foreigners. The report was also uniformly complimentary and referred to the

---

12　Diary of Captain Exham Vincent 54th and 39th Regiments 1800-1813, NAM, 2006-05-69, pp.49-51.

13　Diary of Captain Vincent, NAM, 2006-05-69, pp.55.

14　*The Naval & Military Magazine*, Vol.I, March 1827, p.101; Anon., *The Royal Military Calendar*, Vol.III, p.375.

15　Field return and confidential report 1/28th May 1812, TNA, WO 27/106.

men as 'not tall but of a serviceable size' and noted the continued many cases of 'weak eyes.'[16] The returns and reports for the 2/34th and Captain John McMahon's No.4 Company of the 5/60th are absent from the archives. On 25 April the brigade had a strength of 2,307 effective rank and file. The 1/28th mustered 776, the 2/34th 537, the 1/39th 967, and the rifle company just 27. There were around 450 on the sick list.[17]

Ashworth's Brigade

Coronel Charles Ashworth's Brigade still consisted of Regimento de Infantaria n.º 6 and n.º 18, plus Batalhão de Caçadores n.º 6. *Capitão* Richard Brunton of the caçadores characterised the early part of 1812, saying: 'we were constantly on the alert, moving in different directions on the frontier of Spain, and formed part of the covering Army under Ld. Hill during the siege of Badajos.'[18] N.º 6 had 1,459 effectives across its two battalions, n.º 18 had 1,511, and the caçadores fielded 616.[19]

Long's Cavalry

Major General Robert Ballard Long's cavalry command this time consisted only of the 13th Light Dragoons. Long's letters of the spring of 1812 reveal not only his usual criticism of the progress of the war and his superiors, but also a deepening dissatisfaction with the life of a soldier. In March he had written to his brother:

> I dislike butchery in all its forms and shapes, and of all kinds of butchery that of the human species is to me the most odious. No ambition, no love of reputation can conquer this feeling. A profession that is at constant war with one's feelings cannot be an agreeable one; Lord W. talks of *expending* such and such Battalions in such and such affairs, as you would talk of expending so much shot and powder on the 1st Sept. To him, War must have every charm that can fascinate a man's heart. He is a *thorough-bred* soldier. I make the distinction between the duty that summons every man to the field to defend his own country and rights; but Armies which are formed for other purposes (and all of them are) should be made up of Volunteers, those who adopt the profession from preference and predilection, who love War as a trade, in all its forms and features, and follow what they like. I say honestly that *I* have no business among *this* class of men, for I dislike the thing, and always have.[20]

---

16 Field return and confidential report 1/39th May 1812, TNA, WO 27/107.
17 Army in Spain and Portugal by Brigades and Divisions, & General Monthly Return 25 April 1812, TNA, WO 17/2469.
18 Narrative of the Service of Lt. Col. Richard Brunton, NAM, 1968-07-461.
19 Return of Portuguese infantry 18 April 1812, TNA, WO17/2466.
20 Long to C.B. Long 14 March 1812, in McGuffie, *Cavalry General*, p.172.

The 13th, which had an effective strength of 303,[21] were now commanded by Lieutenant Colonel Patrick Doherty, who had joined them in April. The regiment had been very actively employed on outpost duties during the winter and spring. The men and horses were fit and healthy and the regiment had done all it could to put equipment in order for the coming campaign. The 13th moved to Merida in early May, and on 10 May captured a gang of 15 bandits who had been operating in the area.[22]

Engineers & Artillery

John Squire was still the senior officer of the Royal Engineers attached to the 2nd Division and had been promoted to major in December 1811.[23] He was assisted by Lieutenant Peter Wright and their first task would be to repair the bridge at Merida so the troops could cross on their way north. In charge of the artillery for the expedition was Lieutenant Colonel Alexander Dickson. Hill wrote to Dickson on 29 April:

> I received a letter last night from Lord Wellington by which I am truly happy to find that I am to have your assistance in an expedition to Almaraz.
>
> In order to make you master of Lord Wellington's sentiments & wishes on the occasion I send you a copy of his letter to me.
>
> I also send an extract of a letter from his Lordship to me, dated 28th January last, at which time you know it was in contemplation to make a march upon Almaraz.
>
> I also enclose a letter from Squire on the same subject.
>
> In order to accomplish, as far as possible, the required arrangements for the service [in] question, I feel I need only beg of you to do what you may find necessary on the occasion. I think you had better not come over here at present. You will be more useful where you are.
>
> In the meantime while Squire will get the bridge at Merida put to rights, and I will have the troops cantoned in readiness to move. All our preparations I trust will be made with secrecy.[24]

The enclosed letter from Squire included:

> With this you will receive the copy of a letter written by Lord Wellington to Sir Rowland Hill, relative to an attack on Almaraz. That letter I have also seen & I am desired to Sir Rowland to request you will order the following entrenching tools to be prepared for immediate conveyance, viz.,
>
> 12 ladders (I think those that were used at the castle of Badajoz are the longest and best)

---

21   General Monthly Return 25 April 1812, TNA, WO 17/2469.
22   Barret, *XIII Hussars*, p.171.
23   Army List 1812, TNA, WO 65/62.
24   Leslie, *The Dickson Manuscripts*, Series C, Vol. VI, p.635-6.

20 Felling axes (well sharpened).

6 crow bars & a coil of rope.

Lord Wellington also directs 6 English pontoons be sent to Sir R. Hill's Corps from there under charge of Lieut. Piper of the Engineers, now at S. Vincente. Will you be good enough to mention this circumstance to him & say that it is intended to make three flying bridges with them & to desire that he will send everything necessary for that purpose with the proper proportion of men, & if he himself comes, it will much forward the service. The whole should be immediately got ready to move at a moment's notice, & wait for further orders, or perhaps they may be brought to Elvas, so as to be ready to move with the other stores, which you will have prepared there.[25]

Mr Packenham, master pontonier, had with him with 28 soldiers and four sailors.[26] The gunners and artillery drivers to serve the six 24-pdr carronades that would be going with the expedition came from 185 men from *Capitão* Sebastião José de Arriaga's brigade of Portuguese artillery and 80 men from Captain Glubb's company of the Royal Artillery, commanded by Captain William Power. Dickson listed the equipment that marched to join Hill on 7 May:

6 24pdr Howitzers with 6 wagons, forge, spare carriage &c.

32 mule carts, Spanish

2 Portuguese block carriages, each conveying 6 long ladders, 30 feet long each

6 tin pontoons.

The ladder wagons were drawn by four pair Spanish hired mules each, the pontoons by three pair of do. [ditto] each, and the howitzers by the mules of the Portuguese brigade, viz:–

6 howitzers	48 mules
6 waggons	36 mules
1 forge	6 mules
1 spare carriage	8 mules
3 store carts	6 mules
mounted	10 mules
Total	118

The ammunition conveyed in the limber wagons and Spanish mule carts is as follows:–

24 Pr. Round	600
5½ inch common shells	300
5½ inch spherical	240
5½ inch common case	60
1200 with powder compleat[27]	

---

25 Leslie, *Dickson Manuscripts*, Series C, Vol.VI, p.636.

26 Leslie, *Dickson Manuscripts*, Series C, Vol.VI, p.642.

27 Leslie, *Dickson Manuscripts*, Series C, Vol.VI, p.642-3.

Dickson's column marched on the northern side of the Guadiana river via Montijo to Merida. On 8 May an extra 10 mule carts had to be added as the carts carrying the ammunition were overloaded. The artillery and engineering train reached Merida the next day and waited for the bridge to be repaired so that Hill's infantry and cavalry could join them from the south.[28]

Hill reviewed the 2nd Division on a plain near Almendralejo on the 11th and 'expressed himself highly pleased with the appearance of every regiment of which it is composed'.[29] The troops marched just before daylight on 12 March and that afternoon camped in an olive grove a mile from Merida. The 1/39th however, stayed at Almendralejo for three more days and then followed on.

On 12 May Hill's assistant adjutant-general Lieutenant Colonel John Rooke wrote to his brother:

> We march from here this day on an Expedition against Almaraz, which has been long talked of in the English papers, as one for which Sir R Hill's Corps was destined. The object is to destroy the works which the Enemy have thrown up at that point, and if possible to get possession of the Bridge of Pontoons which they have there under the protection of the said works. The Enemy are said to be moving more troops to same point, but I trust we shall be beforehand with them, should we however find that they have anticipated us and are too numerous for us, you must not be much disappointed. The object so desirable to attain but it is not of that importance which the newspapers seem to imagine and I should think that nothing will be attempted, unless it can be done without serious risk. Sir Rowland only takes about 4,000 men with him. The remainder of his Corps continues here as before.
>
> In about ten or twelve days we shall have returned to our present positions whether the expedition succeeds or not.[30]

---

28 J.T. Jones, *Journals of Sieges Carried on by the Army under the Duke of Wellington* (London: Egerton, 1827), Vol. I, p.248.

29 Hope, *Letters*, p.71.

30 J.C. Rooke to W. Rooke, 12 May 1812, Gloucestershire Archives, D1833/F14, p.65.

11

The French at Almaraz

The bridge at Almaraz came under the responsibility of *Maréchal* Auguste Marmont, commander of the Armée de Portugal. It is worth noting that while most British accounts always refer to the bridge being at Almaraz, the French often referred to the crossing being at Lugar Nuevo, which was the small settlement nearest the bridge. The village of Almaraz was over two miles from the bridge. The bridge itself was made up of small boats with planks laid across them, all securely lashed together with ropes.

Writing in his memoir about the period following the fall of Ciudad Rodrigo Marmont stated:

> Subsequently I caused the passage of the Tagus at Almaraz to be fortified with the greatest care in order to keep open the communications of the army of Portugal with that of the South of Spain. Works, revetted with masonry and provided with redoubts, covered the left bank; advanced forts defended the only passage by which the enemy's artillery could pass. This post of Almaraz was of great importance; I had placed garrisons there of sufficient strength. But the troops were of mixed character, and the bad ones were in a majority, especially a German battalion called Prussian. The good troops occupied the advanced posts which defended the Col of Mirabete.[1]

The good troops to which Marmont was referring were probably a detachment of the 6e Légère, which had been ordered to reinforce the garrison after *Général de Division* Maximilien Foy had been informed that Hill had advanced to Trujillo.[2] The 6e Légère was designated as light infantry but there was less difference in role between line and light regiments in the French army, with both being expected to be able to fight in line and as skirmishers. However, the light regiments were seen as senior to those of the line and had a reputation for possessing greater ésprit de corps. The 6e had been in Spain since 1809 and had fought in many of Napoleon's major

---

1 A.F. Lendy (translator), *On Modern Armies by Marshal Marmont* (London: Mitchell, 1865), pp.29-30.
2 Foy to Drouet 31 May 1812, in M. Girod de l'Ain, *Vie militaire du général Foy* (Paris: Plon, 1900), pp.374-6.

battles before that.[3] Also at Almaraz was a battalion of the 39e Ligne, led by *Chef de Batallion* Piere Teppe. The regiment had a similarly solid record and long experience in the Peninsula, marred only by losing an eagle during a panicked river crossing at Foz de Arouce in 1811.[4]

The bad troops Marmont referred to were the 4e Régiment Étranger. Until August 1811 the regiment had been the Régiment de Prusse, and they had been in Spain from the outset of the campaign. The regiment had been formed in 1806 in Leipzig. The officers were to be selected from prisoners of war from the Prussian army after Jena and Auerstadt, and the rank and file were to come from deserters from the Prussian army. However, a generous bounty and enthusiastic recruiters filled the ranks with a range of nationalities and men of sometimes dubious character. Hundreds deserted as the regiment marched to France. In 1808 the 1er battailon was part of the French army in Spain, whilst the 2e and 3e battailons garrisoned Flushing on the island of Walcheren, and were subsequently taken prisoner by the British when they briefly occupied the island. Many of the men then volunteered for British service.

The 2e battailon was rebuilt from recruits and marched to Spain in 1810. On the way there were many instances of ill-discipline and Napoleon was prompted to write: 'In general, it seems that such troops will make things worse rather than better in Spain.'[5] The 2e battailon soon gained a reputation for a high level of desertion. The 1er battailon seems to have had a better character and in August 1810 the two battalions were merged into one. The new battalion took part in the invasion of Portugal in 1810. The harsh conditions of that campaign, the winter, and then the retreat that followed, severely reduced the strength of the battalion and it was relegated to garrison duty.[6]

There was also a company of artillery and another of sappers at the crossing. The whole garrison was around 1,000 strong, including those in the works on and above the Miravete pass. The commander of the garrison was *Major* Aubert, of the 24e Légère. Aubert, whose first name is not included in any of the accounts, came from Piedmont.[7]

The French troops were housed in the various fortifications at the bridge and at the pass. On the northern bank of the river there was Fort Raguse, named for Marmont who was the Duc de Raguse (often anglicised to Ragusa). The fort was a strong redoubt with a stone tower 25 feet high in the centre, and occupied high ground overlooking the river bank. The northern end of the bridge was protected by a triangular earthwork, open to the rear, known as a flèche. On the southern bank was a larger Tête de Pont, with stone-faced ramparts and guns, enclosing a *venta*, or inn, and several houses that had been converted to storehouses and barracks. On high ground nearby stood

---

3   D. Smith, *Napoleon's Regiments* (London: Greenhill, 2000), pp.186-7.
4   Smith, *Napoleon's Regiments*, p.95.
5   Quoted in G. Dempsey, *Napoleon's Mercenaries* (London: Greenhill, 2002), p.239.
6   Dempsey, *Mercenaries*, pp.236-40.
7   A. Marmont, *Mémoires du Marechal Marmont, Duc de Raguse de 1792 a 1841* (Paris: Perrotin, 1857), Vol.4, pp.210.

Fort Napoleon, which had a raised retrenchment across its northern section, with a loopholed tower in its centre seven metres high. Both forts were at least partially surrounded by ditches and had room for garrisons of over 400 men. At Fort Napoleon the ditch probably did not extend along the eastern and western sides where the ground sloped steeply away.

The road from the south to the bridge passed though the Miravete pass high in the hills. On the summit of the mountain overlooking the pass the French had strengthened an old Moorish watchtower, adding outer works 3.5 metres high and mounting several guns there. On the road they had fortified an inn, and built two smaller works between there and the castle, connecting them with a covered trench.[8] The two smaller, but still substantial, works were Forts Senarmont and Colbert, both named for French generals who had fallen in Spain. Senarmont was the larger at around 40 metres by 10 metres and sat between the peak and the road. Colbert, on the northern side of the hills, was nearly square and approximately 13 metres on each side.[9]

The disposition of the garrison is unclear, with sources such as Napier and Oman differing.[10] Most accounts agree that the 4e Étranger held Fort Raguse and the crossing. *Capitaine* Nicolas Marcel of the 69e, who was with the first troops to reach Almaraz after the battle, places 350 men from two companies of the 6e Légère and two of the 39e in Fort Napoleon, with another 150 men of the 6e Légère occupying the positions on the Miravete pass.[11]

Fort Napoleon mounted four 12-pounder cannon, one 6-pounder, one 4-pounder and three 6-inch howitzers. The Tête de Pont had two 6-pounders and one 10-inch howitzer. Fort Raguse had three 12-pounder cannon, two 6-pounders and a 6-inch howitzer.[12] It was a formidable array of artillery that had the potential to inflict heavy casualties on any attacking force. Marmont thought that the positions were fortified well enough to require a siege to be taken, and he felt that the works at Miravete would have to be tackled first by any attackers so they could bring their artillery down to the river.[13] However, in June 1811 he had written to Napoleon saying:

> I will put in good defence the passage of the Tagus at Lugar-Nuevo, near Almaraz. This post will be one of my main stores of food and ammunition. The general instructions given to the troops, in case of attack by the enemy, will be, for those of the left bank, to cross the Tagus, and for those of the right bank to cross the Tietar, on which I am going to build a good tête de pont. I will establish my headquarters in the neighbourhood of Navalmoral, and so I will find myself able to carry either to Ciudad-Rodrigo or Badajoz.[14]

---

8   Jones, *Sieges*, Vol. I, pp.231-3; N. Marcel, *Campagnes du Capitaine Marcel, du 69e de ligne, en Espagne* (Paris: Plon, 1913), pp.154.

9   Historia de Romangordo, <http://www.romangordo.info/historia/miravete/mirav_1.htm> (accessed October 2019).

10   Oman, *Peninsular War*, Vol.V, p.324; W. Napier, *History of the War in the Peninsula & in the South of France* (London: Warne, 1886), Vol.IV, p.162.

11   Marcel, *Campagnes du Capitaine Marcel*, pp.156-7.

12   Return of Ordnance and Stores Captured at the Bridge of Almaraz, TNA, WO 1/254.

13   Marmont, *Mémoires*, Vol.4, pp.209-10.

14   Marmont to Napoleon 21 June 1811, in Marmont, *Mémoires*, Vol.4 pp.105.

This implies that, in the event of the attack, the troops on the southern bank were to cross the river, presumably taking up the bridge behind them, whilst those on the northern bank were to retreat to the Tietar river further to the north. This seems at odds with his later statements and it may be that the instructions changed after the works were completed.

Looking towards the Albalat Bridge from Fort Napoleon. (Author's photo)

The pontoon bridge spanned the Tagus, narrower and faster flowing at the time, on the line from the trees on the left to the right bank. The steam rising in the centre is from the cooling towers of the Almaraz nuclear power station. (Author's photo)

The hill above the site of the bridge with the remaining walls of Fort Napoleon just visible in the centre of the picture. (Author's photo)

View across the river to where the northern end of the pontoon bridge was anchored. The ruins of Fort Raguse, now fenced off, are just visible in the trees on the high ground to the right of centre. (Author's photo)

The site of the pontoon bridge, showing the ruins of the *venta* on the right. There would have been several other small buildings here at the time as well, probably enclosed by the tête-de-pont. The building on the left was part of a now derelict small hotel complex. The original line of the road to the Albalat Bridge can be seen crossing from left to right. A new road was constructed higher up when the river rose after dams were built downstream. (Author's photo)

The Puerto de Miravete, taken from the peak. (Author's photo)

Looking from the peak towards the village Romangordo (at the end of the hills in the middle ground) and over the remains of Fort Senarmont (on the flatter area in the centre). The fortified *venta* was on the other side of the road, roughly where the track leading up to the peak branches off the road. The site of the bridge is on the left of the frame, as indicated by the arrow. (Author's photo)

The communication towers and fire-watch station that now occupy the top of the peak, where the old watchtower stood and which was fortified by the French. (Author's photo)

Looking northwards at the peak and the pass of Miravete from the road to Jaraicejo. The flatter area in the centre was the site of Fort Senarmont. The road is in the trees on the right. (Author's photo)

The remains of Fort Napoleon, taken from the south. It is unclear whether the remains of the low wall in the middle ground is associated with the defences or is later. This face of the fort was probably the sector protected by a ditch. (Author's photo)

12

Hill's Advance

The march of Hill's troops on 12 May had been delayed by more than a week by difficulties with the repair of the bridge over the Guadiana river at Merida. It had been built by the Romans with 60 arches spanning just over 700 metres, and had been perfectly sound before Hill had destroyed two of the arches. On 1 May Hill had written to Wellington that the timber sent for the repair was too short and that he was attempting to find an alternative supply, and then on 3rd he wrote again to say that it was being sent from Badajoz.[1] On 10 May he had to write again to say that it was still not repaired but that he had been assured by the engineers that it would be by the 12th.[2] As well as the lack of timber, the repair had been delayed by a shortage of tools and other materials, some of which had to be taken from nearby ruined buildings.[3] Major Squire was still with Hill's headquarters and was urging Lieutenant Wright, who was supervising the repairs, to make every exertion to get the repairs completed whilst also trying to secure him the tools that he needed.[4] The gap that had to be bridged was just over 66 feet wide and Major Squire had designed a simple temporary wooden structure supported from beneath on what remained of the two arches, and with a central support standing on the pier in the river.[5] On 8 May Colonel Offeney, Hill's assistant quartermaster general, had written to Lieutenant Colonel Dickson:

> Unfortunately the delay in repairing the bridge at Merida is greater than what Sir Rowland Hill was first led to suppose. It will certainly not be ready before the 11th & perhaps not till the 12th inst.
>
> The whole of the heavy equipment being drawn by mules, Sir Rowland considers it best that you should move with us on the high road by S.Pedro, Miajadas, &c., as in case the present rainy weather continues, you might meet with difficulties on the other roads without having sufficient assistance at hand, and they would also

---

1   Hill to Wellington 1 & 3 May 1812, BL Add. MS 35062, pp.149-50.
2   Hill to Wellington 10 May 1812, BL Add. MS 35062, pp.152-3.
3   Jones, *Sieges*, pp.248-9.
4   Hill to Churchill 8 May 1812, BL Add. MS 35060, p.50.
5   Squire to Burgoyne 27 April 1812, Royal Engineers Museum, 4601-74.

Watercolour of the Roman bridge at Merida, by John Varley. (Yale Center for British Art, Paul Mellon Collection)

take you a good deal out of your way. If however you should see any objections to this plan, the General begs you will communicate them to him.

Tomorrow, the 9th, the General wishes you to march to Merida, there to express your anxiety to have the bridge ready for you to cross, and to make enquiries about the best roads leading to the castle of Belalcázar, so as to mislead the people in their conjectures. In this part of the country they talk of nothing but a movement to the south. You may also speak of Sir Thomas Graham's corps as being expected to cross at Merida.

Mr Wright of the R. Engineers is employed in repairing the bridge and will I dare say be glad to receive your advice upon it. He is not in the secret about our move.[6]

Hill was evidently cognisant of the risks of any delays and the chance of the French learning the true destination of his force. He was attempting to convince any observers that the repair to the bridge was necessary for Dickson's column to cross to the southern bank rather than to enable his own force to cross to the northern side. On 9 May he wrote to Wellington:

Dickson's march towards Merida I think can not excite any great suspicion as to our real intentions. He will give out that the Pontoons are intended for the Guadiana at Medelin, but upon reflection it strikes me that the objections of making the movement so near the Enemy might be greater than two days delay. In the mean while I hope the weather will improve.[7]

Hill left Sir William Erskine in command of his remaining forces in front of Badajoz, which included Byng's Brigade, most of the cavalry, and Hamilton's Portuguese Division. On 10 May he wrote to Wellington again, stating that he was certain the true destination of the expedition remained a secret and that the prevailing opinion in the area was that the troops would be attempting to capture Belalcázar over 80 miles to the south-east of Merida.[8] Hill's friend Sir Thomas Graham was given orders to move to Portalegre with

---

6   Offeney to Dickson 8 May 1812, in Leslie, *Dickson Manuscripts*, Series C, Vol. VI, p.644.
7   Hill to Wellington 9 May 1812, BL Add. MS 35062, pp.151-2.
8   Hill to Wellington 10 May 1812, BL Add. MS 35062, pp.152-3.

his 1st Division and Wellington also placed the 6th Division and cavalry at Graham's disposal in case any attempt was made on Badajoz while Hill was absent.[9] As long as the destination remained secret there was little chance of the French intercepting Hill, but there was a risk that they could move to cut off his retreat back to Merida. The nearest French troops that might come to the aid of the garrison at Almaraz were *Général de Division* Maximilien Foy's division at Talavera de la Reina, who would take two or three days to get to the crossing. Intercepted dispatches had kept Wellington well informed about both the dispositions of the French forces and also the animosities and lack of coordination between Marmont and Soult. For their part the French were aware that Hill was on the move, but at first believed that his destination was Andalusia. When it did become clear Hill was moving north the information reaching Foy greatly overestimated the size of Hill's forces and did not reveal his destination.[10]

The bridge repairs were finally completed on 12 May and early on the morning of the 13th the infantry began to march carefully across the narrow repaired section. The men went over in files of two and only one mule was allowed to cross at a time. Even so the heavily laden mule carrying Major General Long's baggage jumped, or fell, into the river but was retrieved uninjured, with its load intact.[11] The column marched 10 miles to San Pedro de Merida and then halted for the night. When the 1/39th arrived at Merida the following day the battalion remained there to secure the crossing.

The expedition marched nearly 30 miles on the 14th to Villamesías and then 16 miles the day after. As the column moved north, they marched through a landscape ravaged by the war. Houses, convents and other buildings had been looted and wrecked. Most of the local population had long since fled. When they reached Trujillo on the 15th, they found the town practically in ruins. Part of the 1/71st was quartered in the once grand residence of the conquistador Francisco Pizarro, which had been reduced to not much more than a shell.

While at Trujillo the men of the 2/34th made preparations to mark the anniversary of the Battle of Albuera the following day:

> A celebrated sutler, one Tamet, a Turk, always followed our division with a supply of good things; such as English hams, tea, sugar, pickles, and a variety of other luxuries, all at famine prices; but Senor Tamet was a goodnatured fellow, and gave some people tick until the next issue of pay, and continued to give credit to those who paid according to agreement. He now furnished our regiment with what we required for our banquet. We selected a pretty spot outside the town, under some cork-trees, marked out the size of our table on the green sod, and cut a trench all round. Our legs in the trench, we sat on the ground, with the *table* in front, but without a table-cloth. This was our arrangement.

---

9   Wellington to Graham 7 May 1812, Gurwood, *Dispatches*, Vol.IX, pp.128-9.
10   Napier, *History of the War*, Vol.IV p.162; Oman, *Peninsular War*, Vol.V, p.322.
11   Bell, *Rough Notes*, p.34 & Barret, *XIII Hussars*, pp.171-2.

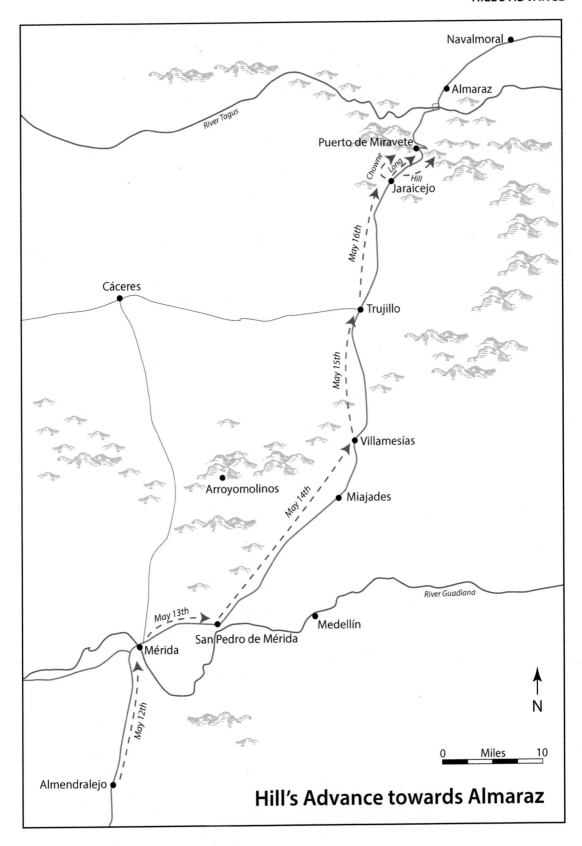

Hill's Advance towards Almaraz

We were like school-boys about Christmas, looking out for a jollification dinner; but all was rough, and nothing at all smooth in these days.[12]

Unfortunately, the troops received orders to cook three days' rations and march that night, so the dinner was postponed. One man who would march no further was Major John Squire of the engineers. He became severely ill, suffering from a paralytic stroke, and died on the 17th.[13]

The women and baggage were left at Trujillo, with a small party from each regiment. Lieutenant Colonel Rooke's memoranda regarding the march to be made on 16 May to Lieutenant Colonel Dickson of the artillery stated:

I have the honour to communicate to you by order of Lieut. General Sir Rowland Hill, the following memoranda which you will be pleased to cause to be carried into effect as far as relates to your Park.

The troops to be formed in close column of half companies tomorrow morning on the road leading to Jaraicejo, so as to be ready to move off at two o'clock right in front & in the following order:

Captain P. Blassiere's company 60th regiment
71st regiment Light Infantry
13th Light Dragoons
Major General K.A. Howard's Brigade
Colonel G. Wilson's brigade
Colonel C. Ashworth's brigade
Captain S. Maxwell's artillery
Lieut. Colonel A. Dickson's Park
The baggage & commissariat stores
A rear guard of two companies from the rear regiment.

The baggage to be left in Trujillo with the exception of one mule for each Field Officer, one per company, & the Camp Kettles.

One Field Officer from the 2nd division of Infantry, one subaltern per brigade from the 13th Light Dragoons, and 1 serjeant per regiment with as small a proportion of batmen as possible, the latter to form the guard. The Officers & serjeants to meet the Field Officer in the Square at daylight.

The men to carry three day's bread or as much as the Commissaries can supply.

Bullocks to be taken for four day's consumption.

Rum & forage corn for the same number of days. No other description of Commissariat stores to be taken.

Major General Long has been directed to leave a subaltern & twenty men of the 13th Light Dragoons in Trujillo.[14]

Blassiere's rifle company would have formed the advance guard, as the companies of the 5/60th often did. The light infantry manual specified that a

---

12   Bell, *Rough Notes*, p.38.
13   M.S. Thompson, *Wellington's Engineers* (Barnsley: Pen & Sword, 2015), p.144.
14   Leslie, *Dickson Manuscripts*, Series C, Vol.IV, p.647.

company forming an advance guard should be split into four parts. The first part would be 500 paces ahead of the main column, with another 200 paces further forward and then a sergeant and six men 100 paces beyond that. The two other parts would be placed 300 paces on either flank of the first part, with small parties 100 paces ahead and further to flanks. The company would form an arrowhead that would scour the area surrounding the line of march, investigating every building, climbing every high point, questioning anyone they came across, and looking for any sign of the enemy.[15]

After covering around 15 miles during the night the column stopped in a wood just short of Jaraicejo at daybreak on 16 May, to cook their breakfast and also to practice climbing the scaling ladders, as Ensign James Hope of the 92nd wrote:

Here we cooked; and those friends who were to lead the storming party, had their limbs pretty well exercised, by running one hundred and one times up ladders placed against the front of an old stone bridge. On hearing one of the party, a jolly ensign, afterwards complain of stiffness of the joints, a friend of his, who overheard him, turned round and said, 'Be thankful, my good-fellow, if your limbs are not stiffer to-morrow; what you have received to-day, is only in part payment of what you, as a member of the forlorn club, may expect to receive at day-light to-morrow morning.' Being a married man, the joke was not at all well received.[16]

The column remained concealed in the wood during the day and that evening marched again, passing through Jaraicejo at around midnight. Bell of the 34th recalled:

We marched away by moonlight; the men slung their arms, to prevent the enemy seeing our line of march and calculating our numbers, for the barrels were bright in those days and might be seen glistening a long way off by moonlight. The daily polishing of the old flint firelock gave the men an infinity of bother and trouble; rainy days and night dews gave them a rust which was never permitted on parade, as we were more particular about clean arms and powder dry than anything else. We moved on all quiet, the muleteer alone singing a serenade to beguile the passing hour. We marched through rugged mountain passes nearly all the night, halting about every quarter of an hour, in consequence of the many obstacles in front; and at every halt I was fast asleep on the sod, and everybody else also perhaps;– but let every one write a book for himself, and tell his own story. I can't undertake it, but may say in truth that twenty men of any perception or interest in their *trade* might write a history of a campaign or a battle, each one clear in his story, yet all differing in narrative.[17]

---

15 F. de Rottenburg, *Regulations for the Exercise of Riflemen and Light Infantry and Instructions for their Conduct in the Field* (London: Egerton, 1803), pp.26-7.

16 Hope, *Memoirs*, p.145.

17 Bell, *Rough Notes*, p.39.

At Jaraicejo, 12 miles from the crossing, the column was split into three. Lieutenant General Chowne would take the 28th and 34th of Wilson's Brigade, plus the caçadores, through the hills on the left to attack Fort Miravete from the rear. Major General Long would carry on down the main road with the rest of Ashworth's Brigade, the artillery and his dragoons to make a diversionary attack on the Miravete pass. Hill would take Howard's Brigade to the right, down to the river via Romangordo and assault Fort Napoleon and the bridge. The left and right columns would carry the scaling ladders and Hill hoped that either or both of the objectives could be taken, if circumstances proved to be favourable. If Fort Miravete fell and the pass was forced then the artillery could move down to the river and support the attack there, if it had not already succeeded.

As Chowne's column approached Fort Miravete it was led by the forlorn hope; the party of volunteers that would be the first to assault the works. Lieutenant James Sullivan, of the 34th, was in command with the men coming from his regiment and the 28th. The grenadier and the light companies of the 28th followed in support, with Major Edward Mullens in command of the whole assault party. Lieutenant John Coen, of the 28th, commanded the small group carrying the scaling-ladders and explosive petards. Lastly, the pioneers carried axes and crowbars to create openings in palisades or gates. The rest of Chowne's force were drawn up in column behind.[18] Second Lieutenant Henry Thiele of the KGL artillery accompanied the attackers, with a sergeant and 20 artillerymen drawn from the British and Portuguese gunners. They carried the petards; boxes containing 50lbs of gunpowder designed for blowing gaps in the defences, plus the port fires and linstocks needed to set them off, and hammers and spikes to disable the French guns.[19]

George Bell of the 34th recalled the attack:

> About four o'clock in the morning my regiment was ordered to halt, the rest of the division pushing on, and now Colonel F[enwick] explained our plan of attack in a few words. On the top of a mountain, just above, stood the castle of 'Mirabete,' garrisoned by 1,000 French soldiers and eight guns with a rampart twelve feet high; to storm this place by coup-de-main, by an escalade in the old style, and as quickly as possible, was our part of the night's amusement. Volunteers were called for the forlorn hope, and they jumped to the front in a minute, with an officer, Lieutenant Sullivan, at their head. Being myself orderly officer for the day, I was detailed to go in front with the scaling-ladders to place against the walls, a position I considered at the time equal to a wooden leg; but it never can be too often repeated that war, however adorned by splendid strokes of skill, is commonly a series of errors and accidents. We crawled up this steep ascent with great caution and silence; but just as we approached the tower, a solitary shot was fired at the foot of the hill, and the next moment the castle was in a blaze. Luckily for us it was not yet daylight, and that a cloud of mist hung over the castle top we could not be seen, but the garrison kept up a random fire, all their shot passing over our heads as we lay on the heather. It was now too late to surprise our

---

18   Cadell, *Narrative*, p.131.
19   Jones, *Sieges*, Vol.I, p254.

Appearance of the Pass of Miravete from the Front or South (TNA, WO 1/254). Included with Hill's dispatch, this sketch shows (from left to right) Fort Miravete, Fort Senarmont and the fortified *venta*.

Looking eastwards from the Miravete peak at the ground over which Chowne would have approached, probably coming around the end of the ridge left of centre. (Author's photo)

friends, as they rather surprised us with their *feu d'enfer* [French: hellfire], and so we retired a little way down and got under cover before dawn; there we lay all the day waiting for fresh orders.[20]

Bell blamed the shot that alerted the French garrison on his servant, who was following the column with Chowne's groom. They missed a turn and were seen by a French picquet, which opened fire. The groom was killed and Bell's servant fled.[21] Both Cadell of the 28th, who would have been with Chowne's main body, and Brunton with the caçadores, placed their arrival at the base of the Miravete hill after dawn due to the poor paths and

---

20   Bell, *Rough Notes*, pp.39-40.
21   Bell, *Rough Notes*, pp.40-1.

The long line of hills to the right of the Miravete pass, through which Hill attempted to approach the Tagus on the night of 16 May 1812. (Author's photo)

circuitous route, and stated that they were then spotted by the French who proceeded to open fire.[22]

With the French putting down a considerable weight of fire Chowne quickly judged that the fort could not be taken without artillery support. He halted the attack and withdrew the forlorn hope. The light companies were left in position until nightfall. Long's column also discovered that the pass was too well defended to be forced, and Hill was having even less luck. The tortuous path of the Puerta de Cueva to Romangordo slowed the descent of Howard's Brigade to the extent that as dawn broke they were not half-way down the mountainside. It had taken the column five hours to travel one and half miles of the path.[23]

With the cover of darkness gone and the element of surprise lost, Hill retraced his steps and withdrew the columns back behind a nearby ridge and out of sight of the French positions. Lieutenant John Patterson of the 1/50th wrote a typically vivid description of the trials of the night in his memoir:

> By daybreak, on the morning of the 17th, we found ourselves on the declivity of a range of steep and craggy mountains, the broken and precipitous sides of which we had been ascending for some hours before, by a narrow pathway among the rocks, all trace of its windings being almost lost amidst the wilderness of heath and broom.
>
> The night was bleak and chilling, while we were thus endeavouring to explore the passage, that lay in the direction of the river, upon the banks of which the forts were situated. In consequence of the main road being commanded by the castle of Miravete, our further progress in that line was arrested, and we proceeded, by a similar path to that which we had already travelled, into a still more wild and desolate region. With much toil and labour, we pursued our dark and lonesome way, in some parts hardly better than a sheepwalk, which did not seem to have ever been trodden by human footsteps.
>
> The Sierra upon which we had the felicity of being perched had somewhat of an Alpine character – huge grey rocks and broken and desert hills forming throughout a dreary and inhospitable prospect. The silence of the barren waste was interrupted only by the foot steps of our troops, and the moaning sound of

---

22   Cadell, *Narrative*, p.131; Narrative of the Service of Lt. Col. Richard Brunton, NAM, 1968-07-461.

23   Rooke to W. Rooke 26 May 1812, Gloucestershire Archives, D1833/F14, p.62.

the wind, mingled with the screaming of sundry birds of prey, which seemed to reproach their intruders for breaking in upon their haunts, where for ages their race had lived secure from the ruthless violence of man. On this mountain ridge we remained during the 17th, getting all in readiness for the delicate piece of work which was cut out for us. Pickets and guards were thrown out upon the most commanding points, secured by whose vigilance we made all the requisite arrangements for the intended assault.[24]

---

24   Patterson, *Adventures*, pp.194-5.

13

The Assault

Hill now had two options. He could make a concerted attempt to force the pass and take the forts, using more troops than last time and having them supported by the artillery. Alternatively, he could attempt to bypass the Miravete positions and find another way down to the bridge, probably without his artillery. Neither option was ideal, both risked heavy casualties, and time was now of the essence as he knew that the French may well have sent for reinforcements.

As his troops rested from the ordeals of the night, Hill sent officers and scouts out during the day on 17 May, to gather more information both on the defences at the pass and alternative routes. A patrol of the 13th Light Dragoons was spotted from Fort Napoleon and this, along with word of the British strength and positions brought by a Spanish woman from Romangordo, caused *Major* Aubert to reinforce the fort's garrison.[1] On the morning of the 18th Lieutenant Wright of the engineers was sent forward to make another assessment of the French defences, and the artillery officers renewed their search for an alternative route down to the bridge for the guns. No other way was found and the strength of the enemy's works was confirmed. Hill decided to attempt to escalade the forts at the bridge without any artillery support. He reinforced Howard's Brigade with the Regimento de Infantaria n.º 6 from Ashworth's Brigade, the rifle company from Wilson's Brigade, and 20 artillerymen. He also ordered Chowne to make a diversionary attack at the pass, to distract the French at the bridge.

At 9 o'clock on the evening of the 18th, the men of Hill's column, assisted by local guides, began to make their way up over the sierras and down the narrow goat tracks towards Romangordo, taking a winding pass known as the Puerta de Cueva, through the ridge several miles to the right of the road at Miravete. The long ladders had to be cut in half to enable them to carried through the tight twists and turns. Approximately 3,500 men were soon strung out, stumbling in the dark, in a long single-file line down the mountainside. Hill had hoped to arrive at the fort while it was still dark but by dawn on 19 May his troops had only reached the village of Romangordo,

---

1   Napier, *War in the Peninsula*, Vol.IV, pp.163-4.

still nearly three miles from the Tagus. The men had a brief rest and then continued on. The long march over rough country had spread the column out, as one soldier of the 71st later wrote 'we were scattered all over the foot of the hill like strayed sheep, not more in one place than were held together by a ladder'.[2] Fortunately the rolling hills allowed Hill to gather his men together and to continue to approach, unseen by the French in Fort Napoleon. Patterson of the 50th wrote of the march:

> We moved off the alarm-post about night fall on the 18th, and continued our way across the mountain ridge in a direction unmarked by any distinguishable track. It was at first intended to surprise the forts before daylight. The difficult nature of the road rendered it, however, impossible to effect this object, and we had, in consequence, no alternative but to march boldly on. Having gained the open country, we were halted under cover of some rising ground, sloping downwards to the fort. Here we waited for the rear of the column to move up, as well as for the signal to advance; and having had some breathing time, we were soon in readiness for the word. The morning was clear and pleasant, and it continued fine throughout the day.[3]

The troops lay down and waited. An attack in full daylight was inherently more risky, and likely to result in heavy casualties, but Hill resolved to continue. High on the hills to the left the diversionary attack on the Miravete positions had already started. *Capitão* Richard Brunton of Batalhão de Caçadores n.º 6. was with the troops preparing to attack Fort Miravete:

Looking towards the Tagus from the road from Romangordo. (Author's photo)

2   Anon., *Journal of a Soldier of the 71st*, p.153.
3   Patterson, *Adventures*, pp.195-6.

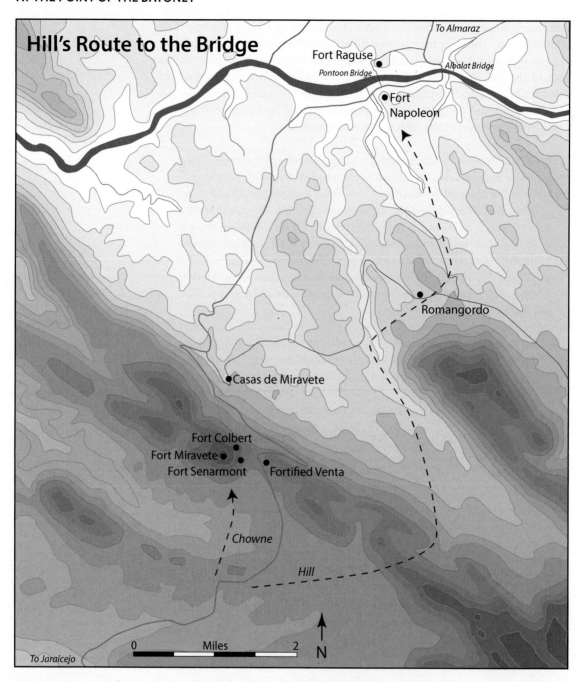

Hill's Route to the Bridge

The Light Companies of the 28th and 34th were selected for this duty, and 100 picked men of the Caçadores were called for, of which I volunteered to take the Command, – the whole under the orders of Capt. Baker of the 34th – Accordingly at dusk we moved with scaling ladders, as far as was thought necessary, up the mountain, and lay down until the proper time arrived for our advancing. In the middle of the night however we got orders that ours was only to be a feint, but to be conducted with such vigour as to deceive the Enemy into a supposition that a real attack was intended. This was entirely confided to me, and accordingly at the proper time before daybreak

I commenced climbing the Height. I had with me a section of the 34th or 28th (I am not sure which) and my Caçadores, the others remained in reserve, we had the greatest difficulties to encounter in getting up in the dark, but arrived silently and tolerably well closed up, exactly at the proper moment on the French Picquet who challenged, and immediately after fired a volley on us and retired – We rushed after them and our road was made clear to us by the Tower &c. becoming a blaze of light. We took up our stations as well as we could amongst the rocks and stones close around it, too close as I afterwards proved, for some of my men had actually got under cover of their outward defences. – We kept up as heavy a fire as we could, which was retuned, and all the effects produced on lookers on at a distance of a real attack, and it appears that it distracted the attention of the Enemy at the Forts, exactly as was intended. – Sometime after daylight I received orders to retire; and the question now became, how was it to be done, without the loss of many lives, as, when leaving their hiding places close to the wall the men must fall a prey to the murderous fire of those within, who were of course anxiously watching their opportunity. – I therefore determined to remain, and wait for a favourable moment, and not very long afterwards it occurred, for as if by an interposition of Providence, the whole Peak became enveloped in a dense cloud. – I immediately sounded the Retreat, and got my men off, with the loss only of one Officer and two men wounded.[4]

Whilst the diversion drew the attention of the French at the bridge and hopefully convinced them that the allies were going to force the pass before tackling the forts, Hill organised Howard's Brigade into three columns for the attack. The attack on Fort Napoleon would be made by the 1/50th, with one wing of the 1/71st. Lieutenant Colonel Charles Stewart would lead one wing of the 1/50th and Major John Bacon Harrison the other. Major Charles Cother commanded the men of the 1/71st detailed to attack the fort. Each column would attack a different face of the fort. The remainder of the 1/71st and the 1/92nd were positioned to either support the attack on the fort if necessary, or to take the tête de pont. The two rifle companies of the 5/60th and the Regimento de Infantaria n.º 6 were to be held in reserve under *Coronel* Ashworth. Lieutenant William John Hemsworth of the 50th led the forlorn hope, which consisted of one sergeant and 21 privates.[5]

The site of Fort Napoleon viewed from the road from Romangordo, showing the rise behind which Hill gathered his troops. (Author's photo)

4 Narrative of the Service of Lt. Col. Richard Brunton, NAM, 1968-07-461.
5 Fyler, *History of the 50th*, p.140; Patterson, *Adventures*, pp.196-7; Hope, *Military Memoirs*, p.148. Patterson names Hemsworth as John W. The army list names him as Thomas, see also Hall, *Biographical Index*, p.272.

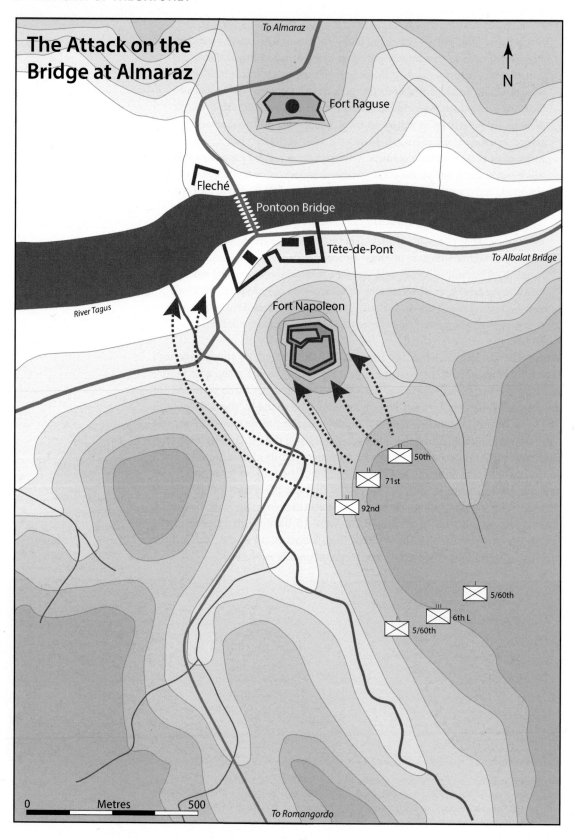

The Attack on the Bridge at Almaraz

To Almaraz

N

Fort Raguse

Fleché

Pontoon Bridge

Tête-de-Pont

To Albalat Bridge

River Tagus

Fort Napoleon

50th

71st

92nd

5/60th

6th L

5/60th

0   Metres   500

To Romangordo

Fort Napoleon lies at the end of a low ridge. Behind it the land falls away to the river. On either side there are steep slopes down into a small valley on the right, when facing the river, and on the left down to the track from Romangordo and a stream. The front of the fort, facing Romangordo along the ridge, was the easiest approach. A shallow slope of around 150 metres from the face of the fort falls to a saddle, and then the ridge rises again, becoming covered with small trees. It was behind this wooded rise that Hill waited while the rest of Howard's Brigade and the Portuguese came up. The Portuguese were in the rear and with time passing and the sun rising higher Hill gave the order to attack as soon as Howard's Brigade was ready:

> The word to advance was instantly hailed by the troops, while at the same time they made a rapid and steady movement to the front, and pressed onward towards the summit of the hill. The moment our caps appeared we were saluted with a volley of round shot, canister and small arms; by way of sample, or as an earnest of the reception we might expect. Nothing daunted, however, by this very rough treatment, our little columns still rushed on, though under such a galling shower, and the whole of the glacis was speedily covered by our men.[6]

Stewart had ordered the 1/50th not to load their muskets until they got to the walls so that they would not pause to fire and he urged them to close quickly and use their bayonets.[7] The canister rounds, tins of musket balls like a giant shot-gun cartridges, cut down many as they ran to the foot of the ramparts. Major General Howard charged with his men and received a ball through his hat. Those carrying the ladders planted them in position as soon as they could but after having been cut in half to facilitate their transport down the mountain paths the ladders were not now long enough to reach across the ditch surrounding part of the wall and up to the parapet. The troops at the ditch, under constant fire, had to either lash the ladders together, or cross the ditch to the berm and then bring up the ladders. In the meantime, the French threw everything they had into the defence:

> By this mischance considerable havoc was occasioned; for while we were endeavouring to raise the ladders, the French grenadiers, whose great bearskin caps and whiskered faces ornamented the breastwork overhead, hurled down upon us with ruthless vengeance an infinite variety of missiles. Anxious to dislodge such ugly customers, they were in nowise particular as to what they made use of for the purpose; rolling down fragments of rock, stones of huge dimensions, round shot, glass bottles, and many other articles in the small way, so that had our pates been composed of adamantine stuff they could scarcely have resisted an avalanche so direful.[8]

---

6   Patterson, *Adventures*, p.196.
7   J. MacCarthy, *Recollections of the Storming of the Castle of Badajos* (Staplehurst: Spellmount, 2001), p.74.
8   Patterson, *Adventures*, p.198.

The view along the ridge from Fort Napoleon towards Romangordo, showing the area across which the assaulting columns had to travel. The tree-line would have almost certainly been further back at the time. (Author's photo)

View from the walls of Fort Napoleon showing how steeply the land falls away on the left, facing towards Romangordo. The slope would have made it difficult and unnecessary to add a defensive ditch. (Author's photo)

The tallest section of the walls on the north-east side was assaulted by No.4 Company of the 1/50th led by Captain Robert Candler, 34 years old and from Colchester in Essex. Candler was first up one of the ladders. He waived his sword, urging his men to push forward and then jumped down onto the parapet, where he was quickly hit by several shots and fell dead inside the fort.[9] Patterson wrote of Candler:

> From the coolness with which Captain Candler of the 50th, who fell upon the parapet, settled his affairs, on the evening previous to the to the assault, it was evident that he felt as though the business would end fatally for him. There was something so peculiar about his manner, that if ever an individual going upon a dangerous service had forebodings of his near approach to death, I should affirm that Candler was the man. We buried him on the spot he fell, where an honourable grave received the remains of as spirited a soldier as ever breathed.[10]

Hemsworth, leading the forlorn hope, was severely wounded in the head and Lieutenant Patrick Plunket took command of the party. Plunket saw a longer ladder to the rear and with Lieutenant Roger North ran back to get it, succeeded in placing it against the wall, and then climbed it, followed by a handful of men. The grenadiers of the 1/50th also gained entry into the fort and the French began to withdraw back to the entrenchment around the tower. North captured two French officers who were attempting to rally their men.[11]

View showing the steepness of the slope on the right, looking towards Romangordo. The site of Fort Miravete can be seen on the peak on the right. (Author's photo)

9   Patterson, *Adventures*, p.199; Hall, *Biographical Dictionary*, p.111; MacCarthy, *Recollections*, p.75.
10   J. Patterson, *Camps and Quarters, or Scenes and Impressions, of Military Life* (London: Saunders & Otley, 1840), Vol.II, pp.146-7.
11   Fyler, *History of the 50th*, pp.140-2.

The remains of part of the raised retrenchment at the northern end of Fort Napoleon. (Author's photo)

The north-eastern section of wall where Captain Candler was killed. (Author's photo)

Major Crother, leading the five companies of the 1/71st, ordered two to extend and provide covering fire whilst the other three advanced towards the fort:

We had a hollow to pass through to get at the battery. The French had cut a part of the brae-face away, and had a gun that swept right through into the hollow. We made a rush past it, to get under the brae [Scots: bank] on the other side. The French were busy cooking, and preparing to support the other fort, thinking we would attack it first, as we had lain next it. On our approach the French sentinel fired and, retired. We halted, fixed bayonets, and moved on in double quick time: we did not receive above four shot from the battery until we were under the works, and had the ladders placed to the walls. Their entrenchment proved deeper than we expected, which caused us to splice our ladders under the wall, during which time they annoyed us much by throwing grenades, stones, and logs over it; but not a Frenchman durst be seen on the top, for we stood with our pieces cocked and presented. As soon as the ladders were spliced, we forced them from the works, and out of the town, at the point of the bayonet, down the hill and over the bridge.[12]

It is possible that the 'other fort' that the soldier refers to was the tête de pont. The description of the hollow they had to pass through does not tally with the ground as it is today, unless he is referring to slopes to the side of the fort. Another of the highlanders watched the attack on the castle from the other wing of the 1/71st:

Our comrades were now to be seen mounting the ladders, regardless of the heavy fire which the enemy poured down upon them; the fire was returned from some at the foot of the walls, yet a number of the men were shot or thrust off the ladders with bayonets before an entrance was effected, which was done at length, every opposition being borne down, a 71st man entering the place first of all, – a thing very gratifying to us, of course.[13]

Doubtless the men of the 1/50th would have argued about who got in first, but almost as soon as the British troops gained a foothold within the defences French resistance began to crumble. *Capitaine* Gabriel Seve of the 6e Légere accused the grenadiers of the 39e Ligne of being the first to break, and this

The south-west corner of Fort Napoleon. (Author's photo)

12   Anon., *Journal of a Soldier of the 71st*, pp.153-4.
13   Anon., *Vicissitudes*, pp.206-7.

was confirmed by their commander *Chef de Batallion* Pierre Teppe, who said that many of them abandoned the walls and hid in the bakehouses.[14] Another French account, which being third-hand and perhaps prone to hyperbole needs to be treated with caution, comes from *Capitaine* Marcel of the 69e Ligne:

> A captain of the 6e Léger obtained authorisation to go and take money to one of his comrades who had been taken prisoner in one of the forts in Lugar-Nuevo. When the officer got back he gave us the details on the manner in which the attack took place. The garrison of the fort, which was on the left bank of the Tagus, was made up of two companies of the 6e Léger and two companies of the 39e, in total 350 men, and was sufficient in order to guard the fort. In the evening, the enemy appeared on the surrounding hills everyone took up arms and chased away those coming too close. At one in the morning, two English regiments came in mass at the edge of the moat of the first fort. The soldiers of the 6e Léger fought like lions. The officers fired and used bayonets like simple soldiers of the line, as soon as the English were pushed off at one point they were running to another place, always encouraging their men with cold blooded calm so typical of a French officer. Such a reception caused the English to falter, but when a panic broke out in the grenadiers of the 39eme who cowardly left their positions, cut the ropes of the draw-bridge, and threw themselves at a boat moored on the shore of the Tagus, and in the rush the boat overturned and nearly all of them perished, the enemy came back with a charge and finding the fort open entered easily. The brave officers of the 6eme Léger were all wounded. Major Aubert of the 24eme Léger, who was Commander in charge, received four bayonet wounds and three musket ball wounds, he stood on the draw bridge by the cowardly 39eme and ran through with his sword every Englishman that came his way. Two old sergeants of the 6eme Léger, after having fought as valiantly as the officers blew out their brains rather than surrender. These brave companies of the 6eme Léger who for a decade have been brigaded with us, called at the moment of the assault for the officers and soldiers of the 69eme.

According to Patterson, the 'governor' of the fort, who he names as Clarimont rather than Aubert, fought with his back to the wall of the tower and refused to surrender before being stabbed by Sergeant Checker of the 1/50th's light company. Aubert was buried with military honours by his captors when he later succumbed to his wound at Merida.[15] Patterson also did not escape the storming of the fort unscathed, writing wryly in his memoir: 'I myself was wounded by another of those 'crooked' random shots, which, for some time at least, completely spoiled my dancing'.[16]

With the garrison of Fort Napoleon surrendering, or escaping from a sally-port at the rear of the fort, it was time for the 1/92nd and the other half of the 1/71st to attack the tête de pont and cut them off. As the troops headed towards the river around the left flank of the fort, trying to keep to dead

---

14   Oman, *Peninsular War*, Vol.V, p.327.
15   Patterson, *Adventures*, p.200.
16   Patterson, *Adventures*, p.146.

ground, they came under fire from the guns of Fort Raguse. The French on northern bank also began to fire on Fort Napoleon once it was obvious that it had fallen. However, Second Lieutenant James Love of the Royal Artillery got his men to turn the guns of Fort Napoleon onto Fort Raguse, and after just a few rounds the commandant, the commander of the 4e Étranger's carabinier company, quickly marched his men off towards Navalmoral.[17]

The French fleeing from Fort Napoleon saw the men of the 1/92nd and 1/71st moving to block their escape. Sergeant David Robertson of the 92nd was with a party that were to seize the *venta* being used as a barracks near the bridge, but, when they entered, they found all the able-bodied men had left, leaving only some wounded.[18] Ensign James Hope of the 92nd was with the men advancing to the bridge:

> Perceiving that our object was to cut off their retreat, the enemy, on retiring from Napoleon, rushed towards the bridge in order to escape. But some of their own people having previously cut the bridge, and drawn two or three of the pontoons to the right bank, a great many of them to preserve their liberty, threw themselves into the dark rolling current, where, instead of that inestimable blessing, not a few of them found a watery grave. All the others surrendered at discretion.[19]

Patterson commented on the alacrity with which the tête de pont was taken:

> The Tete du pont, in like manner, fell before the bayonets of the 71st and 92nd. The Gordon Highlanders, being rather fond of introducing the cold steel upon all occasions, made free to give their opponents a specimen of their abilities in that line, and so completely did they settle the business, that we were scarcely lodged in Fort Napoleon, when they were at the water side in full possession of their defences.[20]

Estimates for the length of the action vary between less than 15 minutes to around 40 with the shorter estimates perhaps referring only to the taking of Fort Napoleon.[21] However, it was a quick victory won at a high cost and the butcher's bill was a long one, especially for the 1/50th.

17　Jones, *Sieges*, Vol.I, pp.260-1.
18　Glover, *Journal of Sergeant David Robertson*, p.118.
19　Hope, *Memoirs*, p.150.
20　Patterson, *Adventures*, pp.201-2.
21　Hope, *Memoirs*, p.150; Anon., *Vicissitudes*, p.207; Patterson, *Adventures*, p.205.

14

Aftermath

The brunt of the British casualties were sustained by the 1/50th. As well as Captain Candler a further 27 rank and file were listed as killed in action on the post-battle casualty return. Seven officers, six sergeants and 87 rank and file were wounded.[1] Candler's death left a wife, Mary Ann, and large family without a means of support and Hill later successfully lobbied for Parliament to grant his widow a pension of £40 per year.[2] The regimental casualty return lists only 22 as killed in action, but has a further 11 who died of wounds soon afterwards. The monthly regimental return for 25 May mentions that 26 were killed on the 19th and six subsequently died of their wounds.[3]

Rank	Forename	Surname	From	Trade	Death
Private	Samuel	Basket	Suffolk	Labourer	KIA 19/5
Private	Benjamin	Berry	Idle, Yorkshire	Shoemaker	KIA 19/5
Private	Partick	Casey	Connaught, Westmeath	Labourer	KIA 19/5
Private	Bartholomew	Cuff	Mullingar, Westmeath	Labourer	KIA 19/5
Private	William	Deacon	Nottingham	Labourer	KIA 19/5
Corporal	Stephen	Egan	Loughrea, Galway	Cooper	KIA 19/5
Private	Arthur	French	Galway	Labourer	DOW 25/5
Corporal	Francis	Gilchrist	Loth, Sutherlandshire	Labourer	KIA 19/5
Private	Joseph	Glenholmes	Killenny, Down	Labourer	DOW 21/5
Private	William	Griffin	Stowe, Wiltshire	Labourer	DOW 25/5
Private	James	Hawes	Norwich	Shoemaker	KIA 19/5
Corporal	Joseph	Hill	Coventry, Warwickshire	Silkweaver	KIA 19/5
Private	William	Hinton	Warminster, Wiltshire	Labourer	KIA 19/5
Private	William	Hudson	Idle, Yorkshire	Clothmaker	DOW 24/5
Private	William	Jew	Gloucester	Tailor	KIA 19/5

---

1   Return of Killed and Wounded 19 May 1812, TNA, WO 1/254, p.423
2   Journals of the House of Commons, Vol. 71, p.587.
3   Regimental Return 1/50th May 1812, TNA, WO 17/164.

Rank	Forename	Surname	From	Trade	Death
Private	Michael	Lally	Loughrea, Galway	Labourer	KIA 19/5
Sergeant Major	John	Lewes	St. Mary's, Glamorganshire	Land Surveyor	DOW 1/6
Private	Robert	Lockhart	Stowmarket, Suffolk	Labourer	KIA 19/5
Private	John	Mullen	Ballygally, Antrim	Labourer	KIA 19/5
Private	John	Murdaugh	Mayo	Labourer	KIA 19/5
Private	George	Nash	Painswick, Gloucestershire	Labourer	DOW 21/5
Private	John	Nugent	Dublin	Brassfounder	KIA 19/5
Private	James	Oilleally	Castle Bar, Galway	Labourer	DOW 24/5
Private	Edward	Page	Cheltenham	Labourer	DOW 21/5
Private	Michael	Reynolds	Tynagh, Galway	Labourer	KIA 19/5
Private	William	Robinson	Loughrea, Galway	Labourer	DOW 22/5
Private	John	Rollinson	Coventry, Warwickshire	Weaver	DOW 24/5
Private	Michael	Ryan	Galway	Weaver	KIA 19/5
Private	Joseph	Sinclair	Tantenden, Wiltshire	Shearman	DOW 24/5
Private	John	Varnell	Horsham, Sussex	Labourer	KIA 19/5
Private	Patrick	Whelan	Spancill Hill, Clare	Labourer	KIA 19/5
Private	John	Williams	Worcester	Labourer	KIA 19/5
Corporal	William	Williamson	Staffordhsire	Stockingweaver	KIA 19/5

Source: Casualty Return, 1st Battalion 50th Foot, 25 March - 25 June 1812, TNA, WO 25/1837.

Varnell, Casey, and Glenholmes all had wives with the battalion to whom their outstanding pay and prize money was paid. Ryan and Egan both had brothers serving with the battalion, and Gilchrist had a cousin. John Patterson remembered the Egan brothers in his memoir, although he refers to Stephen as Patrick:

> An affecting interview took place after the surrender of the fort, between two brothers, Laurence and Patrick Egan, who were so strongly attached that they were never content on separate duties – The eldest, Laurence, or Larry as his comrades called him, being a batman, was consequently ordered to remain in charge of the baggage of his company, on the march of the Regiment. Prompted by a noble feeling, as well as an ardent desire to be near his brother, this spirited young soldier begged so earnestly for leave to join and meet the enemy with his own companions, that he was at length permitted to do so.
>
> The brothers behaved gallantly on the occasion, and maintained the character of Irishmen. Patrick was mortally wounded during the escalade, being one of the first to mount the ladder. Lying on the rampart in a most painful state, he lingered out for some hours. Poor Larry, in the joy of his heart on our success, ran to find out his brother, whom he soon discovered extended in the agonies of death! A more touching or affecting scene could not be witnessed, and, though it was in humble life, it was moving to the hearts of all around. Many who had long been callous to the horrors of a battle-field, and familiarized to the work of slaughter, could have wept over the deep sorrows of those truly brave and affectionate brothers. The mournful Larry never regained his spirits, and fell in one of the

subsequent engagements. They were both excellent soldiers, having a good claim to this feeble record of their worth.[4]

Lawrence received £1 19s 9d of his brother's pay, but probably did not live long enough to receive the Walcheren prize money. James Hope of the 92nd may have also observed Lawrence, or possibly the brother of Michael Ryan:

> About an hour after the capture of Fort Napoleon, I observed a private soldier of the 50th regiment, bending over the lifeless trunk of one of his comrades, and apparently wiping away the tear from his eye. Anxious to ascertain the cause of his grief, I stepped forward, and diverted his attention from the melancholy scene before him, by inquiring the name of the deceased. Till I spoke, the poor man imagined he was pouring out his grief in secret, for on lifting his head he blushed, and instantly dried up the fountain of tears. In answer to my query, I was informed that the deceased was my informant's brother, and the third of the family who had given their lives for their country. Perceiving that previous to my arrival he had been endeavouring to dig a grave for his brother on the counterscarp, with nothing but his fingers and his bayonet, I, on moving away, kept my eyes upon him for some time, and was not less astonished than delighted to see him succeed in forming a grave sufficiently capacious to contain the mangled remains of his beloved brother.[5]

Captain Robert Fitzgerald Sandys, from County Kerry, was severely injured and died of wounds at Ciudad Rodrigo in November. His obituary mentions 'a fever, occasioned by excessive fatigue' so it is not clear if the fatal wounds were those he received at Almaraz but Patterson did attribute his eventual death to them.[6] Lieutenant William John Hemsworth, who sustained a head injury leading the forlorn hope, did receive a promotion to captain in the 31st as his reward, but he was still suffering from his wound two years later when he claimed a pension of £70 per year and went on half-pay, unable to serve any longer.[7] Lieutenant Edward Richardson and Ensign George Anthony Goddard were also severely wounded. Lieutenant John Patterson, and Ensigns William Crofton and George Anthony Goddard were slightly wounded.[8] The casualties sustained by the 1/50th equate to approximately a third of the officers and a fifth of the rank and file present.[9] Officers were often more likely than the rank and file to be casualties in battle because they generally led from the front and were easily distinguishable.

The 1/71st lost one sergeant and three rank and file killed. Four sergeants, one bugler and 23 rank were file wounded.[10] The sergeant killed in action was Peter Sally, from Fain in Scotland. His £9 2s ¼d pay, along with his

4   Patterson, *Adventures*, pp.204-5.
5   Hope, *Memoirs*, p.154.
6   Hall, *Biographical Dictionary*, pp.506-7; Patterson, *Adventures*, p.203. Sandys is listed as a lieutenant in the Army List for 1812 but referred to as captain in the casualty return and by Patterson.
7   Hall, *Biographical Dictionary*, p.272.
8   Return of Officers Killed or Wounded 19 May 1812, TNA, WO 1/254, p.422.
9   Based on the Regimental Returns 1/50th for April and May 1812, TNA, WO 17/164.
10   Return of Killed and Wounded 19 May 1812, TNA, WO 1/254, p.423.

prize money for the Cape of Good Hope, Buenos Aires, the *La Volontaire* frigate that sailed into Table Bay at the Cape, and the Battle of Oporto, was paid to his wife in 1815. The three privates were: Thomas Reid, a weaver from Kiltimagh, County Mayo; Alexander Short, a tailor from Glasgow; and William Fidley, a labourer from County Tyrone. Sergeant Barnaby Doude, a weaver from Portadown, and Private Lachlin MacDonald from Perth both died of wounds within a few days of the battle, as did a further corporal and three privates in June.[11] Captain Lewis Grant died of his wounds on the day of the battle. He was unmarried and his possessions were auctioned, as was the custom, raising £102 9s. Lieutenant William Lockwood was severely wounded, and Lieutenant Donald Ross and Ensign Colin Mackenzie were slightly wounded. Mackenzie was killed in action a year later at Vittoria.[12]

The 1/92nd only had two rank and file wounded. Three of the Royal Artillery and two of the Portuguese gunners were wounded in the attack, and so was Lieutenant Peter Wright of the Engineers. One *caçadore* and *Alferes* Luiz Pereira Cotinho de Vilhena were wounded during the diversionary action at Miravete.[13]

The only French officer recorded as killed was *Lieutenant* Braun of the 4e Battalion Sapeurs. Amongst the wounded were: *Major* Aubert; *Chef de Batallion* Teppe and *Sous Lieutenant* Coutamy of the 39e Ligne; *Capitaine* D'Owidzki and *Lieutenants* Raynardi de Sainte-Margueritte and Tabor of the 4e Étranger: Capitaine Lebel of the 4e Battalion Sapeurs;[14] and *Capitaine* Sèves of the 6e Légere.[15]

A total of 259 French prisoners were taken, including ten officers. The 4e Étranger made up the bulk of the prisoners with 102 soldiers taken, with 64 coming from the 39e Ligne and 42 from the 6e Léger, with the remainder coming from the engineers, artillery and commissariat.[16] Lieutenant Colonel Rooke estimated the total French losses at over 400 men[17], so it is possible that the French lost at least another 150 dead at the fort and in the river. Aubert died at Merida, and on 1 June Major General Long wrote to his brother:

> We have this morning buried with military honors the French Governor of the Forts on the Tagus, who died of his wounds. He was most highly spoken of for his skill and bravery, and his body showed ample marks of determined resistance. It is reported that the Governor of Fort Ragusa, with nine men, have been condemned to be shot for misbehaviour, and they deserve it for their conduct was most dastardly.[18]

11 Casualty returns 1/71st May & June 1812, TNA, WO 25/1994.
12 Return of Officers Killed or Wounded 19 May 1812, TNA, WO 1/254, p.422; Hall, *Biographical Dictionary*, pp.245-6, p.372.
13 Return of Officers Killed or Wounded 19 May 1812, TNA, WO 1/254, p.422; Return of Killed and Wounded p.423.
14 Martinien, *Tableaux*, p.209, p.500 & p.668. Aubert does not appear in Martinien's lists.
15 A. Martinien, *Tableaux, par Corps et par Batailles, des Officiers Tués et Blessés Pendant les Guerres de l'Empire (1805-1815) Supplement* (Paris: Fournier, 1909) p.67.
16 Return of Prisoners of War, TNA, WO 1/254, p.417.
17 Rooke to W. Rooke 26 May 1812, Gloucestershire Archives, D1833/F14, p.62.
18 Long to C.B. Long, 1 June 1812, in McGuffie, *Cavalry General*, p.191.

The battle had been brief but hard-fought, and the men were eager for their traditional reward of booty. One of the 71st, who had not been part of the storming party, recalled:

> Liberty was now given to pile arms; and we spectators set off full speed towards the fort, for the purpose of coming in for a share of whatever booty was going: some stingy officers attempted to throw obstructions in the way, but General Hill commanded them to desist, saying, that 'we had wrought hard enough for any thing which might be obtained.' Reaching the desired haven, we found that an interesting scene of noise and confusion was taking place since the din of war had ended: numbers of tame goats were running about on all sides, flying from the men, who were eagerly pursuing them with no friendly intent. It seems that almost every one of the French garrison had been possessed of a goat or two, either for pets or for their milk, or perhaps for both purposes. Immense magazines of provisions and spirits were also laid open to our attacks,– they consisted of rice, biscuits, hams, brandy, &c.: the filling of haversacks and canteens gave employment for some time, in consequence of this God-send. But a 50th man was the most successful of any, he coming out of some secret place or other with his cap filled with gold doubloons: each of these coins is equivalent to £3 17s sterling; it may be judged, therefore, that a capful of them would constitute a pretty round sum. A 71st man had the good fortune to find a colour belonging to the corps étranger; for, to be candid, I must say, that he had not an opportunity of taking it by force of arms, but the difference of the honour is merely ideal; for what, in reality, is the honour of a stained rag?[19]

The colour, possibly found on the banks of the river, was sent to Wellington and was later displayed in London. Also in the fort was a French artillery officer's wife, dressed in the military style with a travelling cap, pelisse and trousers, She was quickly placed under the protection of British officers, but while her honour remained intact her baggage did not.[20]

Many of the men made immediate use of the plentiful rations:

> Collected together in knots and parties, with the green sward for our table-cloth, forgetful of the past, and careless about the future, we feasted most sumptuously, drinking to our foes in their own generous wine, and wishing that, in future campaigns, our adventures might be terminated in an equally agreeable and fortunate manner.[21]

Once the troops had filled their haversacks and helped themselves to whatever they could they were ordered to bivouac half a mile back from the river. Later that day Howard issued a brigade order thanking his men:

> Major-General Howard cannot delay expressing his warmest acknowledgements to Lieut.-Colonel Stewart and Major Harrison of the Fiftieth Regiment, and

---

19 Anon., *Vicissitudes*, pp.207-9.
20 MacCarthy, *Recollections*, pp.77-8.
21 Patterson, *Adventures*, pp.207-8.

Major Cother of the Seventy-first Regiment who commanded the three columns of attack this morning on Fort Napoleon, and the works on the Tagus, for the gallant and distinguished manner in which they led the columns intrusted to them, as well as to all the other officers, non-commissioned officers, and privates, for their bravery and good conduct, which produced the brilliant result of the capture of the works in question.[22]

The venta and the site of the store houses and crossing. The tête-de-pont would have been in the foreground. Later development has removed all trace of it. (Author's Photo)

Parties of each regiment were detailed to deal with the dead and injured, and a more systematic destruction of the forts, bridge, stores and batteries began. Two grenadiers of the 1/92nd, Privates James Gauld and Walter Sommerville, swam the river to bring back the boats that had been drawn across so the bridge could be re-established. Hill ordered each to be given two doubloons reward. Gauld was also later granted a pension for the feat.[23]

The return of stores captured in the forts and the houses near the river was impressive and proves what an important position Almaraz was for the French. The amounts are in number of soldier's rations rather than by weight or volume:

---

22 A. Mckenzie, 'Lieutenant-Colonel Charles Cother (1777-1855), 71st (Highland) Regiment (Light Infantry), and later of the 83rd Regiment', *Journal of the Society for Army Historical Research*, Vol.49, No.197(Spring, 1971), p.11

23 Gardyne, *Life of a Regiment*, p.239.

Bread – 33
Biscuit – 29,961
Rice – 65,961
Vegetables – 2,554
Salt -23,926
Oil – 4,428
Wine – 1,718
Brandy – 27,814
Live Cattle – 16,848
Salt Meat – 18,086[24]

Exactly how many rations a live cow contained would of course vary but nearly 17,000 portions presumably equated to a significant number of cows. As well as the 18 guns of various calibres and types captured in the forts and other works, the French magazines were found to contain 120,000 musket cartridges, 300 6-inch shells, 380 case shot rounds, and 413 muskets with bayonets. In addition, 20 pontoon boats with their associated carriages, timber, ropes and anchors were also taken.[25] These pontoons were Marmont's only means of creating another crossing. With the Miravete pass still in French hands Hill did not have the means to carry off much of the stores and ordnance, and so most of it was destroyed.

The guns were loaded, fired at each other, and then thrown into the river. The wooden palisades taken up and piled with the pontoon carriages and other timber and burnt, as were the store houses. Second Lieutenant Henry Thiele of the KGL artillery was charged with the destruction of Fort Raguse. He had disabled the guns and placed around 1,000lbs of gunpowder in the tower. He had a French port-fire to use as a fuse but worried that it would not be good enough and so asked Lieutenant Colonel Dickson for an English one. After receiving one, Thiele then returned to the fort. Dickson later wrote:

He went into the tower, staid some time, came out again, left the fort with his men, soon returned, went into the tower again, and scarcely entered the door when the explosion took place, and he was blown to atoms. I find that – instead of going into the tower with a slow match, he took a lighted port-fire up with him, the sparks of which must have communicated with the powder in some manner.[26]

Howard's brigade order thanking his troops went on to say:

He must also notice the promptitude with which Lieut. Love of the Royal Artillery furnished his personal assistance in turning the guns of Fort Napoleon on the enemy as soon as it was in our possession. The melancholy accident which has

---

24   State of Provisions in the Forts at the Bridge of Almaraz on the Morning of the 19th May 1812. Taken from a Return signed by the French Commissary dated 11th of May 1812, TNA WO1/254 p.418.
25   Return of Ordnance and Stores Captured, TNA, WO 1/254, p.419.
26   Dickson to Franningham, 23 May 1812, in Beamish, *History of the KGL*, Vol.II, p.415.

since befel [sic] Lieut. Thiel, of the same corps, now makes my thanks to him nugatory.[27]

Once everything on the northern bank was destroyed, disabled or burning, the boats, ropes and planks of the bridge were pulled over to the southern bank and set alight.[28] Fort Napoleon was blown up and as night fell Hill withdrew most of his men back to the Puerta de Cueva, leaving only a small detachment to watch the flames and cover the men still working to destroy everything that they could. On the morning of 20 May the positions were inspected to ensure that nothing of use remained and one magazine near the now ruined tower of Fort Napoleon that had escaped notice was detonated. Hill then marched his entire force to back to Jaraicejo.

Captain William Webber, Royal Artillery, was at Almaraz in September 1812 and wrote in his journal: 'I was able to walk up to Fort Napoleon and never saw works more completely dismantled. Several good brass 12-pounders were lying in the ditch, all spiked, together with shot and shells innumerable, besides a great many human skulls and bones'.[29]

---

27   Quoted in Leslie, *Dickson Manuscripts*, Series C, vol.VI, p.651.
28   Jones, *Sieges*, Vol.I, pp.240-1.
29   R.H. Wollocombe, *With the Guns in the Peninsula* (Barnsley: Frontline, 2017), p.64.

15

This Brilliant Exploit

Hill's withdrawal on 20 May was precipitated by news he had received the day before from Major General Sir William Erskine that *Maréchal* Soult was on the move into Estremadura. Ideally Hill would have liked to have taken and destroyed the works at Miravete before marching south, but that could have taken several days of bombardment and then an escalade with potentially heavy casualties. It was four day's march back to Merida. He could not afford to take the risk of being cut off from his line of retreat.[1]

Général de Division Maximilien Foy, at Talavera, had been aware of Hill arriving at Trujillo on 16 May. On the 17th companies of the 6e Légere were moved towards the bridge in response, but Foy was uncertain of Hill's intentions at that point and the report had inflated the size of Hill's force so that Foy reacted cautiously. The nearest French troops, at Navalmoral, only a day's march from the bridge, were the Frankfurt Battalion of the army of the Confederation of the Rhine. This battalion had also been ordered forward to reinforce the bridge but were slow to move and on 19 May, when they met the troops fleeing from Hill's attack, the commander of the battalion opted to withdraw rather than advance further. Foy was gathering his troops at Talavera and preparing to march himself, but not until he had gone ahead with a planned ball which lasted until 6:00 a.m. on the morning the division was meant to leave. Foy eventually reached the bridge three days after Hill had left, by which time the allied expedition was back at Trujillo.[2]

The movement that Erskine interpreted as Soult preparing to enter Extremadura was in fact only his subordinate Drouet, who had received intelligence of Hill's march north, moving his advance guard to Medellín on the 17th. French cavalry patrols crossed the Guadiana a day later and came into contact with Erskine's outposts. Erskine's information severely overestimated the size of the French force and he sent off messages to Wellington, Hill and Graham. The latter advanced with his divisions to help cover Hill's withdrawal. Erskine's reaction was precisely what Soult had hoped for. The marshal wrote to King Joseph in June:

---

1   Hill to Wellington 26 May 1812, BL Add. MS 35060, p.65.
2   Foy to Drouet 31 May 1812, in M. Girod de l'Ain, *Vie Militaire du Général Foy* (Paris: Plon, 1900), pp.374-6; Oman, *Peninsular War*, Vol.V, p.329; Marcel, *Campagnes*, p154.

Your Majesty will see, through my correspondence, that I have continued to hold General Hill's corps in check, and that, when he turned to Almaraz, I forced him to return to the Guadiana, a diversion which made General Graham to go with his divisions to the aid of General Hill.[3]

On 21 May Wellington wrote to Graham, not having heard yet from Hill and, it seems, not fully convinced of Erskine's interpretation of the enemy's movements:

The enemy are evidently moving upon Hill's rear, probably in larger force than that which has hitherto been under the command of Drouet. The last I heard of Soult was, that he had left Seville for the Puertos on the 10th and 11th; and on the same day there were about 2500 men near Ayamonte, it was said, under Gazan. It is not probable, therefore, that the whole army of the South are in motion.

I apprised Hill of the probability of this movement; and it is most likely that he heard of the enemy being at Don Benito on the 17th as soon as Sir William Erskine.

If this is the case, he will have arrived at Aldea del Obispo, so as to open the road to Caceres on the 19th; and he will be at Caceres this day, whether successful or other wise in the enterprise which was the object of the expedition.

If he should be a day later, I think he will still be in time, as it is probable that the troops which were at La Granja on the 18th are intended to pass the Guadiana at Medellin, which they cannot do before the 20th. I have therefore but little anxiety respecting Hill's retreat.

I was apprehensive that the enemy would make this movement in consequence of the delays which took place; and the movement of the equipment upon Merida instead of upon Caceres. However, I hope that the evil will be confined to the disappointment of my views upon Almaraz for this time.

The 1st division cannot move in a better direction than towards Caceres; but if Hill's retreat should have been effected, it would be best to get the troops back to their stations, as matters are getting very forward here.[4]

However, Hill was retreating to Merida rather than towards Cáceres and a day later Wellington wrote again to Graham saying that he had heard that Soult had arrived near Cadiz and that he thought Erskine had been misinformed. As he felt Hill's retreat was now secure, he asked Graham to return his divisions back to their previous positions.[5]

Hill's column reached Jaraicejo on the evening of the 20th and then Trujillo on the 21st. When the 2/34th arrived back at Trujillo, hoping to at last have their much delayed Albuera dinner, they found that a foraging party of French dragoons had raided the town and carried all the food away. The wine had escaped but, fearing another raid, the regiment's surgeon and a few other of the officers who had also been left behind had drunk it all before it

---

3   Soult to Joseph 8 June 1812, in Du Casse, *Mémoires et Correspondance Politique et Militaire du Roi Joseph*, Vol.9, p.25

4   Wellington to Graham 21 May 1812, in Gurwood, *Dispatches*, Vol.IX, pp.158-9.

5   Wellington to Graham 22 May 1812, in Gurwood, *Dispatches*, Vol.IX, p.160.

fell into the hands of the enemy.[6] The populace of Trujillo put on a bull fight in the main square to celebrate the success of the operation. Hill had the time to write his dispatch to Wellington, having already sent Major Currie with a verbal report immediately after the action on the 19th. The dispatch is reproduced in the appendix to this work, and in it Hill outlined the course of the operation, the failure of the columns to reach their targets on the night of 16 May, his subsequent judgement that taking Miravete would involve too great a loss, and that instead he would attempt the attack without his artillery via Romangordo. He praised Major General Howard, the 1/71st and 1/50th in particular for their assault on Fort Napoleon, but also acknowledged all the units and their commanders for the parts that they played in the victory. Currie, having already arrived at Wellington's headquarters on the 22nd, officially delivered the dispatch, when it arrived, to Wellington, along with the captured colour of the 4e Étranger. He subsequently took both on to London. Currie had written to Hill on 23 May:

> I arrived here at five o'clock yesterday afternoon, after very great fatigue and exertion. Lord Wellington expressed the great joy and satisfaction at what had been done: in a word, he seems fully to appreciate the merits of the troops and every body connected with the expedition. Foy, he says, has been prettily humbugged, and must now go round by Toledo. When I mentioned our small loss, and the extent of the enemy's establishments at Almaraz, he said, 'Yes, Hill has done it well and ably: and I will send you to England; it will give you a step.' From letters which he received last night from Sir W. Erskine, and which he did not seem altogether pleased with, he said, 'he was afraid you would be hurried back to stop Drouet before you had completed the destruction, of every thing at Almaraz.'

Currie continued:

> Half-past nine o'clock. Lord W. has just repeated before his staff that he will send me to England, and that I had better stop here until the arrival of your despatch. The Marshal and every body offer a thousand congratulations; and they are known to attach a great deal of consequence to your late services, and particularly to the manner in which, according to Lord W.'s own words, things have been uniformly managed.
>
> I have no time to say a word more, as the post is just going off, and I waited till the last moment for his Lordship's commands. Ten thousand thanks for the very kind and considerate manner in which you have put me in a fair way of promotion. I can never forget your brother's kindness neither.[7]

In his letter to Lord Liverpool that accompanied Hill's dispatch Wellington wrote:

---

6   Bell, *Rough Notes*, p.41.
7   Currie to Hill 23 May 1812, in Sidney, *Life of Hill*, pp.197-8.

I have the honour to enclose Lieut. General Sir Rowland Hill's report of this brilliant exploit; and I beg to draw your Lordship's attention to the difficulties, with which he had to contend, as well from the nature of the country, as from the works which the Enemy had constructed; and to the Ability and Characteristic qualities displayed by Lieut. General Sir Rowland Hill, in persevering in the line, and confining himself to the objects chalked out by his Instructions, notwithstanding the various obstacles opposed to his progress.

I have nothing to add to Lieut. General Sir Rowland Hill's report of the Conduct of the Officers and Troops under his Command, excepting to express my concurrence in all he says in their praise. Too much cannot be said of the Brave Officers and Troops who took by storm, without the assistance of Cannon, such works as the Enemy's Forts on both banks of the Tagus, fully garrisoned, and in good Order, and defended by 18 pieces of Artillery.[8]

In the meantime Hill had marched his men back to Merida, whilst Foy stayed in Trujillo. On 28 May Hill wrote to Wellington:

I am inclined to think Foy will not remain long where he is. The enclosed Spanish paper, written by an intelligent man in observation, confirms my opinion respecting Foy's intention to return to the other side of the Tagus by Arzobispo. I am also inclined to think the enemy will abandon Mirabete. I could easily oblige Foy to go off from Truxillo, but under present circumstances I do not think it would be advisable for me to go so far to my left; and on the other hand, adverting to Foy's situation, I do not like to take all my force so far to the right as Almandralejo. Therefore, for a day or two, I will halt here, which will give my troops a little rest, and time to mend their shoes, &c.; and in the mean while, probably, I shall hear from your Lordship.[9]

Hill's Assistant Adjutant General, Lieutenant Colonel John Rooke, took the time to write to his brother from Merida, giving him a good summary of the expedition, the difficulties the troops had faced, and the strength of the French positions at Miravete:

Our expedition to Almaraz has succeeded far beyond my warmest expectations. The Enemy not only marched from us, but we have been inabled sufficiently to destroy their establishments at that place, and those establishments were of a far more valuable and extensive description than I had imagined. We reached Jaraicejo on the morning of the 16th and that night proceeded with the view of effecting our work we were met however with delays and it was not carried into execution until the morning of the 19th. The Gazette will give you all the particulars as detailed as I could pretend to give them. I will not therefore trouble you with a repetition of them. The Coup has we flatter ourselves some sparkling of brilliancy about it, and will do credit to the troops; tho' not of that magnitude to attract much notice after the greater events which have in recently occurred. The very large Depot and the strength of the works which the Enemy had formed

---

8   Wellington to Liverpool 28 May 1812, TNA, WO 1/254, pp.377-87.
9   Hill to Wellington 28 May 1812, BL Add. MS 35062, p.154.

at Almaraz means that they must have considered it as an interesting point, and Lord Wellington considered it in the same light. When I last wrote to you I was of a different opinion, but am now satisfied I was wrong. The principal difficulty we met with were the roads, tho' even that tended in great measure to our success, for roads the Enemy conceived impracticable for us to get at them, as we did, they would have probably taken greater precautions and we would not have gained the bridge, which was the main object of the Expedition. It will give you some idea of the nature of the road we had to pass when I tell you that with every exertion of Officers and Men, we were five hours passing one mile and half of it, altho' the Column did not exceed 2500 Men. Nothing could exceed the conduct of the troops – Cool and steady but with an invincible determination to overcome all obstacles, they soon made themselves masters of Fort Napoleon, a work calculated in every way to stand a regular siege – and it adds not a little to their merit that it was done in broad daylight, the enemy in a full sate of preparation. Our ladders were rather short for the state of the roads had rendered it absolutely necessary to cut them. The coolness and intelligences however of the Officers and Men soon found remedies for this. The Enemy fought bravely at first, but when our own men got a footing within the work, they stuck so close to them with the Bayonet that they had not time to make a stand at their interior entrenchments before our fellows were amongst them. I should estimate their loss at upwards of 400. Men however were not our object. The destruction of the Bridge and Depot were the great pursuits, and these could not have been more satisfyingly accomplished. That Miravete also could not have been taken is to be regretted, but it was impossible, without greater sacrifices that it was worth. Had our Troops been able to reach it the first night that they advanced, to have attacked it before day, it might have been gained, but when the Enemy were on their guard it became too severe an undertaking. Thus entrenched at the summit of an almost impossible peak, and with works within works which would enable it with a good garrison (which it had) to make a desperate defence. What our next operation is to be I know not but I rather think something else is preparing for us. During the time we were away the French force in this quarter made some partial movements against the Troops which Sir R Hill left behind, but they have now fallen back and we shall for a few days at least resume our former quarters. Lord Wellington sends home one of Sir R Hill's Aides de Camp with the dispatch, which shows that he attaches some importance to the Expedition, indeed he has expressed himself highly satisfied with the manner in which the whole business has been executed.[10]

However, Wellington may have been highly satisfied but he was not entirely satisfied. In his postscript to Hill on the 23rd Currie had written, 'Lord W. asked me how I thought the garrison of Mirabete would get away. Could it not be starved out? and would it not have been well to have left something to blockade it? I mentioned the Guerilla force in the neighbourhood'.[11] On the 25th, before he received Hill's dispatch, Wellington wrote to his subordinate: 'I wish you would take measures to know exactly what passes at Mirabete, if you have not got that garrison as Prisoners. It is my opinion that they will

10   Rooke to W. Rooke 26 May 1812, Gloucestershire Archives, D1833/F14, p.62.
11   Currie to Hill 23 May 1812, in Sidney, *Life of Hill*, pp.197-8.

abandon the place as soon as they can; and I shall be glad to hear from you when they will abandon it'.[12]

In a letter written on the 26th, before he had received the above enquiry, Hill had written to Wellington outlining the measures he had taken to destroy the bridge and its defences, and then added:

> With respect to Mirabete, I certainly shall have been very glad to have got hold of the Place, but it appeared impossible to get guns up to bear on it in any reasonable time, and to have attempted to have assaulted it would in all probability have cost us very dear indeed. I at one time had an idea of Blockading Mirabete, but ascertaining they had provisions in the place for six weeks I did not think it was right for me to delay my return, particularly as Foy and Drouet both appeared to be in motion.[13]

On 28 May Wellington wrote to Liverpool:

> You will be as well pleased as I am with General Hill's success, which certainly would have been still more satisfactory if he had taken the garrison of Mirabete, which he would have done if General Chowne had got on a little better in the night of the 16th, and if Sir W. Erskine had not alarmed him, by informing him that Soult's whole army were in movement, and in Estremadura. Sir Rowland, therefore, according to his instructions came back on the 21st, whereas, if he had stayed a day or two he would have brought his heavy howitzers to bear on the castle, and he could either have stormed it under their fire, or the garrison would have surrendered.
>
> Your Lordship will observe that I have marked some paragraphs in Hill's report not to be published. My opinion is that the enemy must evacuate the tower of Mirabete; and indeed it is useless to keep that post, unless they have another bridge, which I doubt. But if they see that we entertain a formidable opinion of the strength of Mirabete, they will keep their garrison there, which might be inconvenient to us hereafter, if we should wish to establish there our own bridge.[14]

Chowne has been criticised for his failure to escalade Fort Miravete on the night of the 16th, with William Napier in his *History of the War in the Peninsula* commenting, 'if Chowne had not been negligent he might have carried the castle of Mirabete before daylight.'[15] However, George Bell's account does suggest that Chowne's column had reached their position at the base of the Miravete hill prior to daylight, albeit not by much, and that it was the weight of fire from an alerted garrison that stalled the attack. Hill, characteristically perhaps, seems to have placed no blame on Chowne and his subsequent assessment of the position confirmed Chowne's judgement that any attempt to press the assault would have resulted in very heavy casualties. The goat tracks on which Chowne's column had to march on the

---

12   Wellington to Hill 25 May 1812, BL Add. MS 35060, p.60.
13   Hill to Wellington 26 May 1812, BL Add. MS 35060, p.65.
14   Wellington to Liverpool 28 May 1812, in Gurwood, *Dispatches*, Vol.IX, pp.189-90.
15   Napier, *War in the Peninsula*, Vol.IV, p.162.

night of the 16th, with the moon only one-third full, wound through brush-filled steep slopes and wooded valleys, and it is hardly surprising that they did not make the time that the plan had called for. Neither, of course, did Hill's own column.

The French withdrew the garrison from Miravete in July and by September Lieutenant Robert Piper, Royal Engineers, had overseen the construction of a pontoon bridge to replace the French one. In October Captain Alexander Todd, Royal Staff Corps, began work on repairing the old stone bridge.[16] In December Lieutenant Peter Wright was ordered to destroy Fort Miravete, and also to destroy what remained of Fort Napoleon. Wright was assisted and escorted by a battalion of the Spanish Regimiento de la Unión, from Morillo's command.[17]

Concerns about Miravete did little to lessen the praise that Hill and his men received for the operation. The 50th, 71st and 92nd were all later granted permission to add the battle honour 'Almaraz' to their colours.[18] Lord Bathurst, who took over as Secretary of State for War from Liverpool in June, wrote to Wellington:

> Your Lordship will have the goodness to take the earliest opportunity of conveying to Sir Rowland Hill his Royal Highness's approbation of the distinguished skill, decision and vigour displayed by Sir Rowland Hill on this occasion, and of the firmness and intrepidity so eminently manifested in the reduction of the redoubt of Fort Napoleon by Major General Howard, and the officers and troops under his command. I am commanded by his Royal Highness to mark his satisfaction of the loss of officers and men being, comparatively speaking, so small, more especially as it appears that it is in a great measure owing to the judicious arrangements made by Sir Rowland Hill previous to his making the attack.[19]

As far as the French soldiers who had been at Almaraz were concerned, *Major* Aubert was singled out for his brave attempt to rally his men, but for the officers and soldiers who had fled from Almaraz rather than stand and fight Foy outlined a series of punishments. Those from the elite grenadier or voltigeur companies who fled without arms would be placed back in centre companies; they would lose seniority; would be denied advancement; and their shame could only be removed by future bravery in combat. The garrison of Fort Raguse was exempted as they had followed the orders of their commander, who was put under arrest at Talavera and then court martialled.[20] He was convicted of cowardice and shot.[21]

The strategic consequences of the destruction of the bridge for the French were as severe as the personal consequences for those who abandoned it. On 25 May Wellington wrote to Hill and commented that Hill's success

---

16   Thompson, *Wellington's Engineers*, pp.156-7.
17   J.A.P. Rubio, *Revista de Estudios Extremeños*, 2013, Tomo LXIX, Número I, p.331.
18   *The United Services Journal*, 1830, Part I, pp.516-7.
19   Quoted in Sidney, *Life of Hill*, pp.199-200.
20   Order of the day 1 June 1812, in Girod de l'Ain, *Vie Militaire du Général Foy*, pp.376-7.
21   Dempsey, *Mercenaries*, p.240.

A not very accurate engraving of the storming of Fort Napoleon and the capture of the bridge published in July 1812, soon after the news arrived in Britain. (Anne S.K. Brown Military Collection)

had forestalled the plans of both Soult and Marmont, and also that Hill should now feel himself secure to act against Drouet and keep him out of Extremadura.[22] The destruction of the bridge gave Wellington much more freedom of movement. On 28 May, in his letter to Liverpool, he wrote:

> Your Lordship is aware that the Road of Almaraz affords the only good military communication across the Tagus, and from the Tagus to the Guadiana below Toledo. All the permanent bridges below the Bridge of Arzobispo have been destroyed, during the war by one or other of the Belligerents, and the Enemy have found it impossible to repair them. Their bridge, which Lieut. General Sir Rowland Hill has destroyed, was one of Boats; and I doubt their having the means of replacing it, or that they will again form such an Establishment at that point, however important it is to their objects, as that of which he has deprived them.
>
> The communications from the bridges of Arzobispo and Talavera to the Guadiana are very difficult, and cannot be deemed military communications for a large army. The result then of Lieut. General Hill's expedition has been to cut off the shortest and best communication between the armies of the South

22   Wellington to Hill 25 May 1812, BL Add. MS 35060, p.60.

and of Portugal, which, under existing circumstances, it will be difficult, if not impossible, to reestablish.[23]

Wellington could now advance into Castille, north of the Tagus, with his right flank secure from French troops in the south moving north; if he needed to withdraw to the Portuguese frontier again, he could safely use the Tagus valley as his route. He ordered the repair of the bridge at Alacantra, to the west of Almaraz, in order to improve the communication between himself and Hill. In a letter to Lord Burghersh, a friend and the husband of Wellington's niece, he claimed that the victory at Almaraz assured the success of his plans for the rest of the campaign:

> I think we are now in a great situation. The blow which I made Hill strike a few days ago upon the enemy's establishment at Almaraz has given me the choice of lines of operation for the remainder of the campaign, and do what we will we shall be safe. If I have luck we may do great things; at all events, the campaign is ours, I believe.[24]

Lieutenant Colonel Colin Campbell, commandant of Wellington's headquarters, wrote to a friend on 30 May that Wellington had been informed by his spies that Marmont expected an attack on Madrid after the Almaraz operation and moved towards Talàvera, leaving Salamanca vulnerable. Campbell continued to say that a lack of money and transport stopped Wellington making an immediate move on Salamanca. Wellington also hoped that when he did advance on Marmont the destruction of the bridge meant it was possible that, in order to support, him Soult would be obliged to abandon southern Spain.[25] Wellington did subsequently advance towards Madrid, defeating Marmont at Salamanca on 22 July. In the same month Hill prepared to fight Drouet at Albuera but the French, outnumbered, withdrew. Wellington ordered Hill to drive the French from Extremadura and to threaten Andalusia, but Drouet carried on moving southwards. The allies occupied the Spanish capital on 12 August. Soult, his position now untenable, was ordered to withdraw from southern Spain and this in turn freed Hill to also march to Madrid, ending his troops' role of a corps of observation in the south. Wellington moved further north and attempted to take the castle at Burgos in a badly handled siege before being forced, by the concentration of the French armies against him, to withdraw back to the Portuguese frontier in a costly retreat. Hill, who had been left at Madrid with four divisions under his command, had to abandon the Spanish capital and join Wellington. However, with the French having left southern Spain the stage was set for the next year's campaign, which would see the allied army defeat the French again at Vittoria and then advance to the Pyrenees and across the borders of France itself.

---

23   Wellington to Liverpool 28 May 1812, TNA, WO 1/254, pp.377-87.

24   R. Weigall, *The Correspondence of Lord Burghersh* (London: Murray, 1912), p.51.

25   Abstract of Lieutenant Colonel Colin Campbell's letters in Wellington, *Supplementary Despatches*, Vol. VII, pp.361-2.

The destruction of the bridge at Almaraz and the subsequent events of the campaign brought peace to war-weary Extremadura. The province would not have to suffer the constant advance and retreat of the allied and French armies across it, and the depredations upon the population that involved. *Brigadeiro* Benjamin D'Urban, *Marechal* Beresford's chief of staff, wrote in his journal of Almaraz:

> The French had collected here very considerable Magazines of Provisions and Ammunition, a Dock Yard for Boat Building, and an Arsenal of Cable, Timber, and River Stores; and had in fact formed an extensive Permanent Establishment. This therefore had become an Entrepôt for the Supply of anything moving upon, or acting in Estremadura with which it was the point of Communication, and to which it was the Key. Its Capture and Destruction is of infinite importance both real and moral, and is indeed the most advantageous Coup of the Second Class during the War.[26]

---

26   B. D'Urban, *The Peninsular Journal Of Major-General Sir Benjamin D'Urban: 1808-1817.* Kindle Edition. (Kindle Locations 4686-4694).

16

Afterwards

The victories at Arroyomolinos and Almaraz were the making of Hill's reputation. The reports of each reached Britain just when good news was needed; Arroyomolinos came at the end of a frustrating year of victories but little progress, and Almaraz soon after the murder of Prime Minister Spencer Perceval. Such positive news helped those arguing for a continuation of the war in the Peninsula and for giving Wellington the resources that he needed.

Hill had already proved himself a capable commander in battle and a reliable subordinate to Wellington prior to 1811, but the two actions covered in this book display a level of measured aggression and risk taking that goes beyond his reputation as 'Daddy Hill' and a safe pair of hands. He had, and would continue to have, the welfare of his men at the forefront of his mind but that did not mean he would not drive them hard and sacrifice their lives to gain his objectives. After Girard had left Cáceres, Hill could have just let the French march away unmolested, perhaps following a day or so behind to keep up the pressure. Instead he led his men, already weary from several days marching in bad weather, in further forced marches to close with the enemy. It is true that Hill outnumbered Girard, and that the French commander's negligence contributed greatly to his defeat, but Hill's meticulous operational planning secured a tactical victory which was never in doubt once the battle was joined. Had the weather been slightly better and the attack able to start earlier, the allies would have quite likely defeated Girard's whole division rather than slightly more than half of it.

The strategic effects of the victory at Arroyomolinos were limited mainly to morale to and enabling Castaños' troops access to greater resources. However, the strategic value of the crossing at Almaraz made its destruction a clear priority for Wellington in his planning for the campaign of 1812. He was typically detailed in his instructions to Hill but it was Hill's reaction to the difficulty of the ground and the strength of the positions blocking the Miravete pass, and the bravery of his troops, that delivered the victory. Hill adjusted his plans from an attack heavily supported by artillery, to using just a portion of his force and undertaking a very risky daylight escalade on a strong position. Major General Long wrote to his brother: 'A great deal of luck, as usual, has attended this enterprise. Had the works been better manned or more vigorously defended, our loss would have been enormous and success problematical'.[1] He went on to say that the French could have spiked the guns and withdrawn across the bridge, taking the boats to the other bank. Hill though had already planned for that possibility and sent the 1/92nd and the rest of the 1/71st around the flank to hinder any withdrawal across the river. He also had substantial forces in reserve. The rapid collapse of the defence of Fort Napoleon reduced allied casualties but it is difficult to see how the action would have ended any differently had they held out longer. Given how quickly the 1/50th and 1/71st gained access, it would seem that Marmont's confidence that the forts would hold out long enough for him to arrive with reinforcements was severely misplaced and the positions, with the exception of Fort Miravete, were not as strong as he thought.

Of course, the victories at Arroyomolinos and Almaraz were not Hill's alone. He had an able staff, solid brigade commanders, and good troops who were well led. The Spanish army is often much maligned in British memoirs from the Peninsula, but at Arroyomolinos Gíron, Penne Villemur, Morillo, and the men under them, supported Hill admirably and were integral to the success of the operation. It was undoubtedly Hill's famed affability that enabled him to work well with his allies, his subordinates, and with Wellington. It is also clear that it was his evident and genuine concern for his men that helped him to get the best from them. Their pleasure and satisfaction in delivering him both the victories is evident in their memoirs. Charles Oman, near the end of *A History of the Peninsular War*, wrote 'I have never seen a hard word of 'Daddy Hill' in any of the hundred Peninsular diaries that I have read'.[2]

Hill's semi-independent role came to an end in 1812, after almost three years, but he continued to play a key role by commanding the right wing of Wellington's army through the campaigns of 1813 and into the final battles of 1814. The core of his command continued to be the 2nd Division, plus the Portuguese and Spanish troops he had under his command in the south, but he was also often given additional divisions when needed. At Vittoria, the key victory of 1813 that sealed the fate of the French in Spain, Hill opened the battle with an attack, led by Morillo, on high ground on the French left flank. The fighting was fierce but the repeated French counterattacks weakened their line and aided Wellington in the centre, while Graham attacked on the opposite flank.

As the army advanced into the Pyrenees and up to the borders of France itself Hill obtained perhaps his hardest won victory at St Pierre. Soult massed his divisions for an attack on Hill's isolated British and Portuguese troops. The French columns advanced on a narrow front and Hill's men first fought them to a standstill, despite two battalion commanders losing their nerve, and then successfully counter-attacked. Wellington rode up with reinforcements late in the battle, after the victory was more or less won, and said 'Hill, the day's your own'.[3]

Following the French surrender and Napoleon's abdication in the spring of 1814 Hill returned to Shropshire. He was raised to the peerage, as 1st

---

1   Long to C.B. Long 23 May 1812, in McGuffie, *Cavalry General*, p.186.
2   Oman, *Peninsular War*, Vol.VII, p.525.
3   Bell, *Rough Notes*, p.140.

Baron Hill of Almaraz and of Hawkstone, for his services to the country. As early as December 1813 the editor of *The Shrewsbury Chronicle* had proposed the erection of a column to honour Hill:

> It is suggested therefore, that by erecting a COLUMN, or some other Building, DEVOTED to General Sir Rowland HILL we may... by a SUITABLE INSCRIPTION enumerate some of the GREAT TRANSACTIONS OF THE PRESENT DAY – the expulsion of invaders – the restoration of millions of inhabitants to national independence – and the March into France of triumphant British Soldiers, conducted by a SALOPIAN CHIEFTAN.[4]

Construction started in December 1814 and was completed on 18 June 1816, the first anniversary of Waterloo. The five-metre-high statue of Hill on a 40-metre-high column still stands, and is a taller column than Nelson's in Trafalgar Square, if one ignores the pedestal that the latter stands upon.

Lord Hill's column, Shrewsbury.

Hill was recalled to duty when Napoleon escaped from Elba and at Waterloo he commanded the allied II Corps. Sergeant David Robertson recalled that when the 92nd saw Hill:

> We all stood up and gave him three hearty cheers, as we had long been under his command in the Peninsula, and loved him dearly, on account of his kind and fatherly conduct towards us. When he came among us he spoke in a very kindly manner and enquired concerning our welfare.[5]

Hill survived the battle, despite having a horse shot from under him, but many of his Peninsular veterans did not.

After Napoleon's second abdication Hill commanded part of the army of occupation, but then in 1818 he retired to Shropshire and the life of a country gentleman. He refused several positions and commands, including the post of Master General of Ordnance, but in 1828 when Wellington, then the Prime Minister, offered him the post of commander-in-chief of the Army he accepted. Due to his lack of seniority he had to be termed 'the senior general on the staff, performing the duties of commander-in-chief', but his role was the same as Wellignton's had been before him.[6] His tenure saw the

---

4   Quoted in *Follies Magazine*, Spring 2020, p.12.
5   Glover, *Robertson*, p.191.
6   Teffeteller, *Surpriser*, p.199.

British Army through some turbulent times when it was frequently used to quell social unrest. He also oversaw reform of the system of military discipline. Unsurprisingly, he was noted as being extremely fair and impartial when it came to dispensing the considerable powers of patronage that his position entailed. He finally retired in 1842, and was made a viscount in recognition of his long service. Unfortunately, his health was already failing and he died a few months later.

HER MAJESTY VICTORIA 1ST
ATTENDED BY THE DUKE OF WELLINGTON, THE KING OF THE BELGIANS, LORD HILL &c. &c. DEPARTING FROM WINDSOR CASTLE. TO REVIEW THE TROOPS.

Queen Victoria attended by the Duke of Wellington (right) and Lord Hill (left) departing from Windsor Castle to review the troops in 1838, during his tenure as commander-in-chief. (Anne S.K. Brown Military Collection)

On his death Wellington wrote to Sir Rowland Hill, Viscount Hill's nephew:

> Your letter of the 10th, giving me the melancholy account of the death on that morning of your uncle, my old companion and friend, Lord Hill, reached me yesterday.
>
> You may conceive better than I can express how much I have felt his loss. More than thirty five years have elapsed since I had the satisfaction of being first connected with and assisted by him in the public service; and I must say that, from that moment up to the latest period of his valuable and honourable life, nothing ever occurred to interrupt for one moment the friendly and intimate relations which subsisted between us.
>
> During many years, when both were employed in the service of our Sovereign, he invariably did every thing in his power to promote my views. The habits then established continued up to the latest period of his holding the Command in Chief of the army. He knew that he could rely upon my support and assistance upon every occasion of difficulty or annoyance to him. I performed no more than my duty in affording both; but I have the satisfaction of feeling that he knew that it was performed willingly and heartily.[7]

The letter very much places Hill's service in the context of Wellington's own career, and this is perhaps the most common way that Hill is still seen; as an able subordinate of Wellington, who once said of him 'The best of Hill is that I always know where to find him'.[8] Despite Hill's evident ability and potential he was doomed to be always in Wellington's shadow, and Wellington seems to have thought that in his shadow was where Hill served best. When Bathurst was seeking his opinion on generals to take over the command in North America in the autumn of 1814 Wellington wrote:

> Hill is an excellent fellow; but I should say that he wants a commander. He likes his troops in order, but he is too good natured to exert himself about it, and he would require some assistance in that way. He has talents and God knows experience enough for any situation, and he might command in chief as well as anybody else; but I should be inclined to doubt it; and to have him fail as well as our troops would be terrible.[9]

Part of the issue is, possibly, their very different styles of command and their personalities. Wellington had a dominant and domineering character, and micro-managed his subordinates. Hill was far more affable and delegated to those he commanded effectively and efficiently. It is often the case that alpha males, such as Wellington, do not see that there are different, and equally effective, ways to achieve success and manage or command others.

---

7   Wellington to R. Hill 12 December 1842, in Sidney, *Life of Hill*, p.389.

8   G.C. Moore Smith, *The Life of John Colborne, Field Marshal Lord Seaton* (London: Murray, 1903), p.140.

9   Wellington to Bathurst 30 October 1814, in F. Bickley, *Report on the Manuscripts of Earl Bathurst, preserved a Cirencester Park* (London: HM Stationary Office, 1923), p.303.

Hill's performances at Arroyomolinos, Almaraz, and later at St Pierre, make it clear that had he was much more than a general who was good at following Wellington's often exhaustive instructions.

Many of the staff and subordinates who supported Hill so ably sadly did not survive the wars. Edward Currie was killed towards the end of the Battle of Waterloo. Clement Hill and Chatham Churchill did survive and both rose to be major generals, only to subsequently die in India; the former of natural causes in 1845 and the latter of wounds sustained at the Battle of Maharajpoor in 1843. John Rooke was wounded at the Battle of the Nivelle in October 1813 and died in December. Wilhelm Offeney, who fell ill on the march to Almaraz, eventually died at Belem hospital in August 1812.

Sir William Erskine, having long suffered from mental illness, threw himself to his death from a Lisbon window in February 1813. Kenneth Howard survived until 1845, becoming the 1st Earl of Effingham. George Wilson died of a fever in January 1813. None of the unit commanders of Howard's Brigade, which played such a prominent part at both Arroyomolinos and Almaraz, survived to enjoy a well-earned retirement. Charles Stewart died following the long hard retreat in December 1812. Henry Cadogan was mortally wounded at Vittoria, as was John Cameron at Quatre Bras. Peter Blassiere led his rifle company all the way into France, but died of his wounds following a small skirmish near the Joyeuse river in February 1814.

Charles Ashworth did survive the war and died in 1832. Pedro Agustín Girón died in 1842 after having served two brief terms as the Spanish Minister of War, a post also held by Louis de Penne Villemur before his death in 1836. Pablo Morillo was made Captain General of Venezuela after the end of the Peninsular War and tried in vain to quell revolts in the Spanish colonies. He went on to fight the French again in 1823 and fought in the First Carlist War before he died in 1837.

Captain James Gubbins, 13th Light Dragoons. Killed at Waterloo. From C.R.B Barret, *History of the XIII Hussars*, Vol.I. (Reproduced with the permission of The Light Dragoons Regimental Association).

Those who later published memoirs, such as Patterson, Blakeney, and Hope, obviously survived the war, as did those who left behind diaries and journals, with the exception of James Gubbins who fell at Waterloo. The fate of the rank and file that Hill led across Spain and into France is harder to summarise. It is likely that only a small proportion survived the war unscathed. The anonymous soldier of the 71st and author of *Vicissitudes in the Life of a Scottish Soldier* wrote of the end of the Peninsular Campaign:

> In making a calculation of our numbers, it was found, that out of the 600 picked men who went to Portugal in 1810 only 75 remained. I do not mean to say that every individual out of this mighty deficiency was actually dead; some were in existence, but in a disabled state, although perhaps not just 'at the town's end for life'.[10]

---

10   Anon., *Vicissitudes*, p.343.

Even for those who did survive life carried on being hard, and in the long depression that followed the victory over Napoleon there was often little work for former soldiers. The other anonymous writer from the 71st penned a final letter, dated May 1818, to the friend to whom he gave the manuscript that became *Journal of a Soldier of the 71st.* He wrote:

> These three months, I can find nothing to do. I am a burden on Jeanie and her husband. I wish I was a soldier again. I cannot even get labouring work. God will bless those, I hope, who have been good to me. I have seen my folly. I would be useful, but can get nothing to do. My mother is at her rest, — God receive her soul! I will go to South America...
>
> ...Farewell! John, this is all I have to leave you. It is yours: do with it as you think proper. If I succeed in the South, I will return and lay my bones beside my parents: if not, I will never come back.[11]

---

11   Anon., *Journal*, pp.231-2.

Appendix

Reports & Dispatches

Hill's Arroyomolinos Dispatch

Merida October 30 1811

My Lord,

In pursuance of the instructions which I received from your Lordship to drive the Enemy out of that part of Estremadura which lies between the Tagus and the Guadiana, and to replace the Corps under the Command of Brig. General the Count de Penne Villemur, in Caceres, from which town it had been obliged to retire by the superior force of the Enemy I put a portion of the Troops under my Orders in motion on the 22d Inst. from their Cantonments in the neighbourhood of Portalegre, and advanced with them towards the Spanish Frontier.

On the 23d the Head of the column reached Alburquerque, where I learnt that the Enemy, who had advanced to Aliseda, had fallen back to Arroyo del Puerco, and that the Spaniards were again in possession of Aliseda.

On the 24th I had a brigade of British Infantry, half a Brigade of Portuguese artillery (six pounders), and some of my Cavalry at Aliseda, and the remainder of my Cavalry, another brigade of British Infantry, and half a Brigade of Portuguese six pounders at Casa de Castillana, about a league distant.

On the 25th the Count de Penne Villemur made a reconnaissance with his cavalry, and drove the enemy from Arroyo del Puerco. The Enemy retired to Malpartida, which place he occupied as an Advanced Post with about 300 Cavalry and some Infantry, his main body being still at Caceres.

On the 26th at day break, the Troops arrived at Malpartida, and found that the enemy had left that place, retiring towards Caceres, followed by a small party of the 2d Hussars, who skirmished with his rearguard. I was shortly afterwards informed that the whole of the Enemy's force had left Caceres, but the want of certainty as to the direction he had taken, and the extreme badness of the weather, induced me to halt the Portuguese and British Troops at Malpartida for that night. The Spaniards moved on to Caceres.

Having received certain information that the Enemy had marched on Torremocha, I put the Troops at Malpartida in motion on the morning of the 27th and advanced by the road leading to Merida through Aldea del Cano and Casa de Don Antonio, being a shorter route than that followed by the Enemy, and which afforded a hope of being able to intercept and bring him to action, and I was here joined by the Spaniards from Caceres. On the march I received information that the Enemy had only left Torremocha that morning, and that he had again halted his main body at Arroyo del Molino, leaving a rear guard at Albala, which was a satisfactory proof that he was ignorant of the movements of the Troops under my command.

I therefore made a forced march to Alcuesca that Evening, where the Troops were so placed as to be out of sight of the Enemy, and no fires were allowed to be made. On my arrival at Alcuesca, which is within a league of Arroyo del Molino, everything tended to confirm me in the opinion that the Enemy was not only in total ignorance of my near approach, but extremely off his guard; and I determined upon attempting to surprize, or at least to bring him to action before he should march in the morning, and the necessary dispositions were made for that purpose.

The town of Arroyo del Molino is situated at the foot of one extremity of the Sierra of Montanches, the mountain running from it to the Rear in the form of a Crescent, almost every where inaccessible, the two points being about two miles asunder. The Truxillo Road runs round that to the Eastward.

The Road leading from the town to Merida runs at right angles with that from Alcuesca, and the Road to Medellin passes between those to Truxillo and Merida, the ground over which the Troops had to manoeuvre being a plain thinly scattered with Oak and Cork Trees. My object of course was to place a body of Troops so as to cut off the retreat of the enemy by any of these Roads.

The Troops moved from their Bivouack near Alcuesca about two o'clock in the morning of the 28th, in one column, right in front, direct on Arroyo del Molino, and in the following order: Major General Howard's Brigade of Infantry (1st battn. 50th, 71st, and 92d regiments, and one Company of the 60th) Colonel Wilson's Brigade (1st batt. 28th, 2d battn. 34th and 2d battn. 39th, and one Company of the 60th) 6th Portuguese Regt. of the Line, and 6th Cacadores, under Colonel Ashworth, the Spanish Infantry under Brig. General Morillo; M. General Long's Brigade of Cavalry (2d Hussars, 9th and 13th Lt. Dragoons); and the Spanish cavalry, under the Conde de Penne Villemur. They moved in this order until within half a mile of the Town of Arroyo del Molino, where under Cover of a low ridge the Column closed, and divided into three columns. M. General Howard's Brigade, and three Six Pounders under Lt. Colonel Stewart, supported by Brig. General Morillo's Infantry, the left; Colonel Wilson's Brigade, the Portuguese Infantry under Colonel Ashworth, two Six Pounders and a Howitzer, the right, under Major General Howard; and the cavalry the centre.

As the day dawned a violent storm of Rain and thick mist came on, under cover of which the Columns advanced in the direction and in the Order which had been pointed out to them. The left column, under Lt.Colonel Stewart, marched direct upon the town. The 71st, one company of the 60th, and 92d regiments, at Quarter distance, and the 50th in close column, somewhat in the rear with the guns as a reserve.

The right column, under M. General Howard, having the 39th Regiment as a Reserve, broke off to the right so as to turn the Enemy's left, and having gained about the distance of a Cannon Shot to that flank, it marched in a circular direction upon the further point of the Crescent, on the mountain above mentioned.

The cavalry under Lt. General Sir Wm. Erskine moved between the two Columns of Infantry, ready to act in front, or move round either of them as occasion might require.

The advance of our Columns was unperceived by the Enemy until they approached very near, at which moment he was filing out of the Town upon the Merida Road; the rear of his Column, some of his cavalry, and part of his baggage being still in it. One Brigade of his Infantry had marched for Medellin an hour before daylight.

The 71st and 92d Regiments charged into the Town with cheers, and drove the Enemy every where at the point of the Bayonet, having a few of their men cut down by the Enemy's Cavalry.

The Enemy's Infantry, which had got out of the Town, had, by the time these Regiments arrived at the extremity of it, formed into two Squares, with the Cavalry on their left: the whole were posted between the Merida and Medellin Roads, fronting Alcuesca; the Right Square being formed within half musket shot of the Town, the Garden Walls of which were promptly lined by the 71st Lt. Infantry, while the 92d Regt. filed out and formed line on their right, perpendicular to the Enemy's right Flank, which was much annoyed by the well directed fire of the 71st. In the mean time one wing of the 50th Regiment occupied the town, and secured the Prisoners, and the other wing along with the three 6 Pounders skirted the outside of it, the Artillery as soon as within range firing with great effect upon the Squares.

Whilst the Enemy was thus occupied on his right, M. General Howard's column continued moving round his left, and our Cavalry advancing and crossing the head of their Column, cut off the Enemy's Cavalry from his Infantry, charging it repeatedly, and putting it to the Rout. The 13th Lt. Dragoons, at the same time, took possession of the Enemy's Artillery. One of the charges made by two Squadrons of the 2d Hussars and one of the 9th Lt. Dragoons was particularly gallant, the latter commanded by Captain Gore, and the whole under Major Busche of the Hussars. I ought previously to have mentioned that the British cavalry having, through the darkness of the night and the badness of the roads, been somewhat delayed, the Spanish Cavalry under the Count de Penne Villemur was on this occasion the first to form upon the plain and engage the Enemy, until the British were enabled to come up.

The Enemy was now in full retreat, but M. General Howard's Column having gained the point to which it was directed, and the left column gaining fast upon him, he had no resource but to surrender, or to disperse and ascend the mountain. He preferred the latter, and ascending near the eastern extremity of the crescent, and which might have been deemed inaccessible, was followed closely by the 28th and 34th Regiments, whilst the 39th Regiment and Col. Ashworth's brigade of Portuguese Infantry, followed round the foot of the mountain by the Truxillo Road, to take him again in flank. At the same time Brig. Genl. Morillo's Infantry ascended at some distance to the left with the same view.

As may be imagined the Enemy's troops were by this time in the utmost panick, his Cavalry was flying in every direction. The infantry threw away their Arms, and the only effort of either was to escape. The Troops under M. Genl. Howard's immediate Command, as well as those he had sent round the point of the mountain, pursued them over the Rocks, making prisoners at every step, until his own men became so exhausted and few in number, that it was necessary for him to halt, and secure the Prisoners, and leave the further pursuit to the Spanish Infantry under General Morillo, who from the direction in which they had ascended had now become the most advanced. The Force General Girard had with him at the Commencement, which consisted of 2500 Infantry and 600 Cavalry, being at this time totally dispersed. In the course of these operations Brig. General Campbell's Brigade of Portuguese infantry (the 4th and 10th Regts.), and the 18th Portuguese Infantry, joined from Casas de Don Antonio, where they had halted for the preceding night; and as soon as I judged they could no longer be required at the scene of Action, I detached them with the Brigade consisting of the 50th, 71st, and 92d Regiments, and Major General Long's Brigade of Cavalry, towards Merida; they reached St. Pedro that night, and entered Merida this morning; the Enemy having in the Course of the night retreated from hence in great alarm to Almendralejo. The Count de Penne Villemur formed the Advanced Guard with his Cavalry, and had entered the Town, previous to the arrival of the British.

The ultimate consequences of these operations I need not point out to your Lordship; their immediate result is the Capture of one General of Cavalry (Bron), one Colonel of Cavalry the Prince d'Aremberg, one Lt. Colonel Chief of the Etat Major, one Aide de Camp of General Girard, two Lt. Colonels, one Commissaire de Guerre, 30 Captains and Inferior Officers, and upwards of 1000 Non Commissioned Officers and Soldiers already sent off under an Escort to Portalegre. The whole of the Enemy's Artillery, Baggage, and Commissariat, some Magazines of Corn, which he had collected at Caceres and Merida and the contribution of money which he had levied on the former Town, besides the total dispersion of General Girard's Corps. The loss of the Enemy in killed must also have been severe, while that on our side was comparatively trifling, as appears by the accompanying return, in which your Lordship will lament to see the name of Lieut. Strenuwitz, Aide de Camp to Lieut. General Sir Wm. Erskine, whose extreme gallantry led him into the midst of the Enemy's Cavalry, and occasioned his being taken prisoner.

Thus has ended an Expedition which, although not bringing into play to the full extent the gallantry and spirit of those engaged, will, I trust, give them a claim to your Lordship's approbation. No praise of mine can do justice to their admirable conduct, the patience and good will shewn by all Ranks during forced marches in the Worst of Weather, their strict attention to the orders they received, the precision with which they moved to the Attack, and their obedience to command during the action, in short, the manner in which every one has performed his duty from the first commencement of the operations, merits my warmest thanks, and will not I am sure pass unobserved by your Lordship.

To Lt. General Sir William Erskine I must express my obligations for his assistance and advice upon all occasions; To Major Genl. Howard, who dismounted and headed his Troops up the difficult ascent of the Sierra, and throughout most ably conducted his Column; and to Major General Long, for his exertions at the head of his Brigade, I feel myself particularly indebted. I must also express my obligations to Colonel Wilson, Colonel Ashworth, and Lt. Colonel Stewart, commanding Brigades for the able manner in which they led them.

Lt. Colonel Cameron, the Hon. Lt. Colonel Cadogan, the Hon. Lt. Colonel Abercromby, and Lt. Col. Fenwick, Muter, and Lindesay, Majors Harrison and Busche, Major Parke Commanding the Light Companies and Captain Gore Commanding the 9th Lt. Dragoons, Major Hartmann Commanding the Artillery, Lt. Colonel Grant and Major Birmingham of the Portuguese Service, Captain Arresaga of the Portuguese Artillery, whose guns did so much execution, severally merit my warmest approbation by their conduct; and I must not omit to mention the exertions made by Brig. Genl. Campbell and his Troops to arrive in time to give their Assistance. General Giron the Chief of General Castaños' Staff, and second in command of the 5th Spanish Army, has done me the honour to accompany me during these operations; and I feel much indebted to him for his assistance and valuable advice. Brig. General the Count de Penne Villemur, Brig. Genl. Morillo, Colonel Downie, and the Spanish Officers and Soldiers in general have conducted themselves in a manner to excite my warmest approbation.

Having now, I hope, accomplished the object of your Lordship's wishes with the Troops under my Command, I shall give them one day's rest at this place, and then return towards the Portuguese Frontier for the purpose of replacing them in cantonments.

To Lt. Colonel Rooke Assist. Adjt. General and Lt. Col. Offeney, Assist. Quarter Master General, for the able manner in which they have conducted their departments, and also for the valuable Assistance and Advice which I have at all times received from them, to the Officers of the Adjutant and Quarter Master General's Departments; To Capt. Squire of the Royal Engineers for his intelligence and indefatigable exertions during the whole operations, and to Captain Currie and my personal staff, my warmest thanks are due.

This dispatch will be delivered to your Lordship by Capt. Hill, my first Aid de Camp, to whom I beg to refer your Lordship for all further particulars.

I have the honour to be, &c.

R. Hill, Lt. General.

P.S. Since writing the above report a good many more prisoners have been made, and I doubt not but the whole will amount to 13 or 1400.

Brig. Genl. Morillo has just returned from the pursuit of the dispersed, whom he followed for eight leagues. He reports that, besides those killed in the plains, upwards of Six Hundred dead were found in the Woods and Mountains.

General Girard escaped in the direction of Serena with two or three Hundred men mostly without Arms, and is stated by his own Aid de Camp to be wounded.[1]

Giron's Dispatch to Castaños

Excellent Sir – In consequence of your Excellency's orders, I marched from this place on 23rd instant, to take the command of the troops of this army, destined to co-operate with his Excellency General Hill, Commander in Chief of the Allied Army of the Alentejo, and on the 24th accomplished this object in the town of Aliseda, where General Hill had just arrived, and which place the Conde de Penne Villemur reached the preceding day, with the vanguard of his troops. The enemy were in Caceres, and occupied Arroyo del Puerco with 300 horse.

On the 25th, at day-break, Gen. Conde de Penne marched with his cavalry to make a reconnaissance upon Arroyo del Puerco, at whose approach the enemy evacuated that place, and retired to Malpartida. The Conde Penne remained in Arroyo. General Hill then determined to march the following morning with two brigades of his infantry, all ours and the cavalry of both nations.

On the 26th, at two in the morning, we put ourselves in motion in the midst of a heavy storm, but not withstanding that, and the darkness of the night, we marched so well, that at day-break our troops were ready to attack Malpartida, the column of the Conde de Penne, which marched from Arroyo, being ready to act with us; but the enemy evacuated the place a little after midnight, and retired upon Caceres.

The Conde de Penne, with his horse, and 200 English hussars, followed to that place, supported by the Spanish infantry, under the second Commandant of the van guard, Brigadier P. Morillo. The remainder of the English horse, and allied infantry and artillery, remained in Malpartida.

Gen. Girard, who was in Caceres with the division under his command, commenced his retreat as soon as he discovered, by his advance cavalry, this movement; and although the Spaniards and Allies under Conde de Penne, endeavoured to overtake them, a few shots only were exchanged between our advance parties and the sharp-shooters of the enemy's rear. Girard that day marched to Torremocha, and Conde de Penne remained in Caceres, with the main body of the vanguard.

On the 27th, before light, the English cavalry marched from Malpartida, towards Alcuescar, and General Conde de Penne took the same direction with the vanguard. At eight the following morning, the Allied infantry and artillery followed the route of the horse, and all troops united at night-fall in the village of Alcuescar. Upon arriving at it, we found, to our great astonishment, that the division of General Girard was in Arroyo del Molino, a village situated at a short league's distance from Alcuescar, which when

---

1   TNA, WO 1/251, pp.107-129.

General Hill had ascertained, he made proper dispositions for attacking them the following day.

At two in the morning of the 28th, the troops moved for this purpose. The weather was horrible, but the heavy rain and strong wind, which was on our backs, was greatly favourable to us. The troops marched with the utmost precision, notwithstanding the difficulties which night and the tempest presented, and before day General Hill was directing the columns of attack, in a valley at a short distance from Arroyo del Molino. A column of allied infantry, with which proceeded the artillery, marched upon the place, another formed of Spanish infantry, directed by Brigadier Morillo, took a direction to flank the place upon the left, and a third column of allied infantry proceeded by the right to cut off the enemy from the roads of Merida and Medellin, and attack them from that point.

Our cavalry, conducted by Conde de Penne, marched upon the right of this last column, and the British horse on the left of the same. Thus disposed, and in the finest order imaginable, our troops marched upon the place, and in a few moments saw the enemy, who had scarcely got out of it, by the road of Merida. To see, attack, defeat and completely disperse them, without firing a shot, was but the work of an instant; nothing could equal the boldness and valour of the Spanish allied troops employed on this occasion, and to this is owing that the enemy was so completely surprised, though formed, and in march, that they could make no disposition, nor do any thing else than fly, surrender, or die.

Gen. Girard, with some part of his infantry, succeeded in gaining a mountain very close to the road; but, pursued thither by my infantry, and part of the allied, almost all his were killed or made prisoners in the course of the day, and he himself being wounded, fled through the mountain with a handful of men; it is still possible he may fall into our power.

The Spanish and allied horse first charged, and afterwards pursued the enemy in all directions, with the greatest ardour, not giving them time to turn, nor think of rallying.

The result of this glorious action has been 1,400 prisoners, among them the Duke D'Aremberg, the General of Brigade Brune, Jose, Chief of Staff; two Commandants, thirty Officers and four hundred men, were left dead upon the field of battle, among who were, the General of Brigade Dubrocoukie, and twenty officers. – We took all their artillery.

One stand of colours were taken by the British troops, and by those under my command, the flag of the 40th Regt. of the Infantry of the Line, which I have the honour of transmitting your Excellency, and an immense number of muskets, swords, knapsacks, and horses, together with the whole of the baggage and equipage of the division. The enemy likewise lost an Eagle, but we have not yet been able to find it.

Such has been, Excellent Sir, the result of the fortunate day of Arroyo de Molino, in which was totally destroyed, or rather annihilated, the most flourishing division of the enemy's army in the middle of Spain.

The simple narration of this action, and movements superior to it, will be sufficient to enable all military men to do due justice to the profound knowledge displayed by General Hill during this operation, to which is entirely owing the glory of so complete and signal an advantage; but it is requisite to have been in it, to properly appreciate the valour, bravery, and ardour of the British troops, Generals, Chiefs, and Officers; their conduct was above all eulogium.

[General Giron twice praises the conduct of different officers; and among others Colonel Don Juan Dounie, who, he observes, takes every opportunity of evincing his brilliant courage.]

Our loss in all does not exceed 20 killed and 100 wounded; such has been, and such ever must be the result of decided attacks prepared by a wise combination. I cannot omit informing your Excellency of the repeated proofs of consideration and respect which I have constantly received from Gen. Hill, nor be silent upon the interest which this worthy General and all his army take in the sacred cause in which we are engaged. God preserve your Excellency, &c.

P.A. Giron[2]

Girard's Reports on Arroyomolinos

Letter from Girard to Soult, 4 November 1811
Marshal – The Count D'Erlon directed my Aide-de-Camp to deliver to your Excellency the report of the battle of Arroyo Molinos. Your Excellency will see that I was in march, that I could have retired and avoided fighting with my rear guard, but the cavalry had compromised themselves, and it would have been requisite to have abandoned them.

The enemy was numerous; I considered but the honour of his Majesty – the duty of a devoted soldier. I marched upon the English, and by drawing upon myself all the forces of the enemy, disengaged the light cavalry.

We have suffered sensible losses, but disengaged ourselves with honour from a difficult situation. Three times surrounded, three times we opened ourselves a passage with the bayonet.

Marshal – I shall be in despair if the results of the unfortunate affair should make me forfeit the confidence of his Majesty. I merit it by the sentiments which directed me – by those which animate me.

Girard's Report to Drouet, 2 November 1811
My General – I send my Aid-de-Camp to you, with the details of the battle of Arroyo Molinos.

On my departure from Caceres, some reports, but without foundation, announced a movement of the English. I quitted that position, to come and pass the night at Turee Moyha, and on the 27th at Arroyo Molinos. During these two days, no demonstration gave reason to believe in the march of an enemy's corps.

I was to proceed on the 28th to Merida. Gen Remond had orders to repair to Medellin. The troops assembled at six o'clock and immediately began their

---

2   *The Globe*, Tuesday 3 December 1811.

march. The rear-guard put itself in motion at half past seven, when shouts and discharges of muskets announced that the troops of the enemy had entered the town, which was only occupied by patroles of the rear guard. I hastened thither. General Dombrowski was forming in column the troops of the rear guard, and ordered the second battalion of the 34th, commanded by M. Mouellard, to check the English tirailleurs, who began to debouche from, and to disengage the light cavalry, which was in front of the village, and which I supposed had already engaged. – I knew the force of the enemy, but I would not abandon the cavalry. I made a movement forward. The English columns then wavered, and advanced upon me. I had not more that 1500 men under my command; they resisted their first shock, and repulsed the charges of the cavalry; but the enemy made at the same time, a great movement on my left, and manoeuvred to surround me. The road of Merida was already intersected and my equipages taken. – Our cavalry did not shew itself. I gave orders for a retreat. The English then threw themselves by their right in my rear. I was surrounded. The enemy's General summoned me to surrender. I pierced through with the bayonet, and we slowly made our retrograde movement. By an unheard of fatality, our artillery did not follow me! The rain had extinguished the matches, while the artillery of the enemy played on our battalions, and I lost a great number of men. I then saw that it was impossible for me longer to keep the plain, not being supported by the cavalry; I resolved to retreat by the mountains, but I was obliged to abandon my three pieces of artillery.

I ordered a movement to the right, and there myself on the heights which range towards Montaches. The enemy pursued me briskly, and I every moment stopped to repulse his attack; my flanks were in like manner assailed, my march being retarded by these attacks. I had been anticipated on the passage of Montaches on my left, I followed the mountains which range upon Sarza.– The enemy already occupied this defile; General Dombrowski rallied the troops; I threw myself into the plain, and charged with the bayonet the enemy who attempted to stop me.

A second flag of truce came to General Dombrowski and myself, but was sent back with contempt as before. I continued my retreat in the plain, without ceasing to engage the enemy, till I reached the height of Ibahernando, where I took up a position, and the enemy ceased his attacks. I stopped some hours at Ibahernando. I afterwards proceeded to Zoveta, then to Naval Villar and Orelland, where I passed the Guada.

I lost a number of men in the long combats in which I was engaged during the great part of the day, with a superior force. The enemy had more than 7000 infantry. I set at liberty, in one charge, a great number of prisoners taken in the mountains. General Dombrowski displayed great firmness of character. He conducted the troops with equal bravery and coolness. His behaviour merits a grateful reward.

The officers Guillot, Veiten, Morvilland, and Voiral, gave proofs of valour. My Chief of the Staff H. Audry, has been made prisoner: this is a loss which will be sensibly felt.

M. M. Veiten and Voiral are wounded, and in power of the enemy.

General Dombrowksi has lost every thing. – His noble conduct and bravery merit a recompense. I solicit for him advancement in the Legion of Honour.[3]

Hill's Almaraz Dispatch

Sections in italics were marked for omission from publication by Wellington.

Truxillo May 21st 1812

My Lord,

I have the satisfaction to acquaint your Lordship, that your instructions relative to the capture and destruction of the Enemy's works at Almaraz have been most fully carried into effect by a Detachment of troops under my Orders, which marched from Almendralejo on the 12th instant.

The bridge was, as your Lordship knows protected by strong works, thrown up by the French on both sides of the River, and further covered on the Southern side by the Castle and Redoubts of Mirabete, about a league off, commanding the pass of that name, through which runs the Road to Madrid, being the only one passable for Carriages of any description, by which the Bridge can be approached.

The works on the left bank of the River were a tête de pont, built of Masonry, and strongly intrenched, and on the high ground above it, a large and well constructed Fort, called Napoleon, with an interior intrenchment and loopholed Tower in its centre. This Fort contained nine pieces of Cannon, with a garrison of between 4 and 500 Men, there being also on the opposite side of the River, on a height immediately above the Bridge, a very complete Fort, recently constructed, which flanked and added much to its defence.

On the morning of the 16th, the Troops reached Jaraicejo and the same Evening marched in three Columns; the left Column, commanded by Lieut. General Chowne, (28th and 34th regiments under Colonel Wilson and the 6th Portuguese Caçadores), towards the Castle of Mirabete; the right Column, under M General Howard (50th, 71st, and 92nd regiments) which I accompanied myself to a pass in the Mountains, through which a most difficult and circuitous footpath leads by the village of Romangordo to the bridge; the centre column under M General Long, (6th and 18th Portuguese infantry under Colonel Ashworth, and 13th Lt. Dragoons, with the Artillery,) advanced upon the high road to the pass of Mirabete.

The two flank columns were provided with Ladders, and it was intended that either of them should proceed to escalade the Forts against which they were directed, had circumstances proved favorable; the difficulties, however, which each had to encounter on its march, were such, that it was impossible for them to reach their respective points before day break; I judged it best, therefore, as there was no longer a possibility of surprize, to defer the attack,

---

3   Du Casse, *Voluntaire, pp.357-66,* & English translation taken from *The Caledonian Mercury,* Thursday 9 January 1812.

until we should be better acquainted with the nature, and position of the works; and the troops bivouacked on the Sierra.

On further examination *of the Mirabete works, I was satisfied that any attempt to force that pass however successful, must be attended by so serious a loss, that* I determined on endeavouring to penetrate to the Bridge by the Mountain Paths leading through the village of Romangordo, although, by that means, I should be deprived of the use of my artillery.

On the evening of the 18th, I moved with M General Howard's Brigade and the 6th Portuguese Regt., for the operation, provided with scaling ladders, &c Although the distance marched did not exceed five or six miles, the difficulties of the Road were such, that, with the united exertions of Officers and Men, the column could not be formed for the attack before daylight. Confiding however in the valour of the Troops, I ordered the immediate assault of Fort Napoleon. My confidence was fully justified by the event.

The 1st Battalion of the 50th, and one Wing of the 71st Regt, regardless of the Enemy's Artillery and Musketry, escaladed the work in three places, nearly at the same time. The Enemy seemed at first determined, and his fire was destructive, but the ardour of our Troops was irresistible, and the Garrison was driven at the point of the Bayonet through the several intrenchments of the Fort and Tête de Pont, across the Bridge, which having been cut by those on the opposite side of the river, many leaped into the River, and thus perished.

The impression made upon the Enemy's Troops was such, that panick soon communicated itself to those on the right bank of the river, and Fort Ragusa was instantly abandoned, the garrison flying in the greatest confusion towards Naval Moral.

I cannot sufficiently praise the conduct of the 50th and 71st Regiments to whom the assault fell. The cool and steady manner in which they formed and advanced, and the intrepidity with which they mounted the ladders and carried the place, was worthy of those distinguished Corps and the Officers who led them.

Could the attack have been made before day, the 92nd Regt, under Lt. Col. Cameron, and the remainder of the 71st, under the Hon. Lt. Col. Cadogan, were to have escaladed the Tête du Pont, and effected the destruction of the Bridge at the same time that the attack was made on Fort Napoleon. The impossibility of advancing deprived them of this opportunity of distinguishing themselves, but the share which they had in the operations, and the zeal which they displayed, entitles them to my warmest commendation; and I cannot avoid to mention the steadiness and good discipline of the 6th Portuguese Infantry, and two companies of the 60th Regt. under Colonel Ashworth, which formed the reserve to this attack.

Our operations in this quarter were much favoured by a diversion made by Lt. General Chowne, with the Troops under his Orders, against the Castle of Mirabete, which succeeded in inducing the enemy to believe that we should not attack the Forts near the Bridge until we had forced the pass, and thus have made way for our Artillery. The Lt. General conducted this operation, as well as his former advance entirely to my satisfaction. I regret much, that the peculiar situation of Mirabete should have prevented my allowing the gallant Corps under his Orders to follow up an operation which they had commenced, with much spirit, and were so anxious to compleat; *but the possession of these Forts would not have made amends for the valuable blood which must have been shed in taking them.*

I cannot too strongly express how much I am satisfied with the conduct of M General Howard through the whole of this operation, the most arduous part of which has fallen to his share; and particularly with the manner in which he led his brigade to the assault. He was ably assisted by his staff, Brigade Major Wemyss, of the 50th, and Lieut. Battersby, of the 23rd Lt. Dragoons.

To M General Long I am also indebted for his assistance, although his column was not immediately engaged.

Lt Col Stewart, and Major Harrison of the 50th, and Major Cother of the 71st, commanded the three attacks, and led them in a most gallant and spirited manner.

I have received the greatest assistance from Lt Colonel Dickson, of the Royal Artillery, whom with a Brigade of 24 pdrs, a Company of British, and one of Portuguese Artillery, Your Lordship was pleased to put under my Orders.

Circumstances did not permit his guns being brought into play; but his exertions, and those of his Officers and Men during the attack and destruction of the place, were unwearied. In the latter service, Lieut. Thiele, of the Royal German Artillery was blown up; and we have to regret in him a most gallant officer. He had particularly distinguished himself in the assault. Lieut. Wright, of the Royal Engineers has also rendered me very essential service. He is a most intelligent, gallant, and meritorious Officer; and I must not omit also to mention Lieut. Hillier, of the 29th Regt, whose knowledge of this part of the country (in which he has been for some time in observation) proved of great assistance.

Your Lordship will observe from the Return of Ordnance and stores which I have the honor to inclose, that Almaraz has been considered by the Enemy in the light of a most important station, and I am happy to state, that its destruction has been most compleat. The towers of masonry which were in Forts Napoleon and Ragusa have been entirely levelled; the ramparts of both in great measure destroyed, and the whole apparatus of the Bridge together with the work shops, magazines, and every piece of timber which could be found, entirely destroyed.

A colour belonging to the 4th battalion of the Corps Etranger was taken by the 71st Regt and I shall have the honour of forwarding it to your Lordship.

Our loss has not been severe considering the circumstances under which the attack was made. I enclose a list of the killed and wounded. Captain Candler, of the 50th Regt, (the only officer killed in the assault) has, I am sorry to say, left a large family to deplore his loss. He was one of the first to mount the ladder, and fell upon the Parapet after giving a distinguished example to his Men.

I have had frequent occasions to mention to your Lordship in terms of the highest praise the conduct of Lt Col Rooke Assistant Adjutant General. During the whole period I have had a separate command in this country, that officer has been with me, and rendered most essential service to my Corps; on the present expedition he has eminently distinguished himself, and I beg leave particularly to notice his conduct. Your Lordship is also aware of the merits of Lt Col Offeney, my Assist. Quarter Master General, of whose valuable aid I have been deprived during the latter part of this expedition. Though labouring under severe illness, he accompanied me, to the serious detriment of his health, and until it was totally impracticable for him to proceed. Captain Thorn, Det Assist Q M General, succeeded to his duties, and I am indebted to him for his assistance, and also to Major Hill and my personal Staff.

The Marquis de Almeida, Member of the Junta of Estremadura, has done me the honour to accompany me, since I have been in the Province; I have received from him, as well as from the people, the most ready and effectual assistance which it was in their power to bestow.

Major Currie, my Aide de Camp, will deliver to your Lordship this dispatch, and the Colour taken from the Enemy, and will be able to give you any further particulars.

I beg leave to recommend him to your Lordship.

I have the honour to be, &c.

R. Hill, Lt Genl.

I enclose a Return of Prisoners in number 259, including the Governor, one Lt Colonel, and fifteen officers. I also transmit a Return of provisions in the Forts near the Bridge, taken from one signed by the Chief of the French Commissariat, on the 13th of May.[4]

---

4   TNA, WO 1/254, pp.393-409.

Bibliography

Archival Sources

Cumberland Museum of Military Life, Carlisle
    Record of the Second Battalion 34th Regiment, written by William Moxon, LIB-843.
Gloucestershire Archives, Gloucester
    Handwritten Life and Letters of Col. John Chas. Rooke by Sir H. Willoughby Rooke, his
        brother. D1833/F14.
The National Archives (TNA), Kew
    Multiple records in the War Office (WO) archive including:
    WO1 – Secretary-at-War, Secretary of State for War, and Commander-in-Chief, In-letters
    WO12 – General Muster Books and Pay Lists
    WO17 – Monthly Returns to the Adjutant General
    WO25 – Secretary-at-War, Secretary of State for War, and Related Bodies, Registers
    WO27 – Adjutant General and Army Council: Inspection Returns
    WO65 – Printed Annual Army Lists
The British Library (BL Add.MS), London
    The Hill Papers:
    Vol. I, 22 May, 1801-31 Mar. 1812. Correspondence of Lord Hill: Add MS 35059.
    Vol. II, 1 Apr. 1812-10 Aug. 1842. Correspondence of Lord Hill: Add MS 35060
    Vol. III, Letters of General Hill to members of his family. Add MS 35061.
    Vol. IV, Letter-books of General Lord Hill; 6 June, 1808-10 Oct. 1818. Add MS 35062.
National Army Museum (NAM), London
    Photocopy of letter written by Lt James Ker Ross, 92nd Regiment of Foot, to his brother,
        Portalegre 5 Nov 1811. 1980-02-66.
    Bound transcription of the diary of Capt Exham Vincent, 30 Jul 1800-16 Jun 1813. 2006-05-69.
    Photocopies of manuscript transcripts made by Rev E.E. Gubbins of letters and journal written
        by Capt James Gubbins, 13th Light Dragoons 1811-1815. 1992-12-138.
    Narrative of the service of Lt Col Richard Brunton. 1968-07-461.
Archivo Histórico Nacional, Madrid
    Comunicaciones y oficios de varios realizados en su mayoria por el General en Jefe del
        5° Ejército, Francisco Javier Castaños, a cerca de varias actuaciones en Extremadura.
        Diversos-Colecciones,137, N.68
National Records Scotland (NRS), Edinburgh
    Letter to General [Sir John Hope] from Lieutenant Colonel John Cameron, at Campo Maior,
        describing the Battle of Arroyo Molinos. GD1/736/121.
    Letters to Ewen Cameron of Fassifern, his father from Lieutenant Colonel John Cameron.
        GD1/736/122-123.

Published Sources

Anon., *General Orders Spain & Portugal* (London: Egerton 1811/2).

Anon., *Historical Record of the 13th Regiment of Light Dragoons* (London: Parker, 1842).

Anon., *Journal of a Soldier of the 71st* (Edinburgh: W. & C. Tait, 1819).

Anon., *Historical Record of the 13th Regiment of Light Dragoons* (London: Parker, 1842).

Anon., *Vicissitudes in the Life of a Scottish Soldier* (London: Colburn, 1827).

Anon., *Lista dos Officiaes do Exercito em 1811* (Lisbon: Impressão Regia, 1811)

Anon., *Lista dos Officiaes do Exercito em 1813* (Lisbon: Impressão Regia, 1813)

Bamford, A., *With Wellington's Outposts* (Barnsley: Frontline, 2015).

Bamford, A., *Sickness, Suffering and the Sword* (Norman: University of Oklahoma Press, 2013).

Barret, C.R.B., *History of the XIII Hussars* (London: Blackwood, 1911).

Beamish, N.L., *History of the King's German Legion* (London: Thomas & William Boone, 1837).

Bell, G., *Rough Notes by an Old Soldier* (London: Day, 1867).

Bickley, F., *Report on the Manuscripts of Earl Bathurst, preserved a Cirencester Park* (London: HM Stationary Office, 1923).

Blakeney, R., *A Boy in the Peninsular War* (London: Murray, 1899).

Bonaparte, J., *The Confidential Correspondence of Napoleon Bonaparte with his Brother Joseph* (New York: Appleton, 1856).

Brandt, H. von, *In the Legions of Napoleon* (Barnsley: Frontline, 2017).

Brandt, H. von, *The Two Minas and the Spanish Guerrillas* (London: Egerton, 1825).

Broughton, S.D., *Letters from Portugal, Spain, & France* (London: Longman, 1815).

Burnham, R., *Charging Against Wellington: Napoleon's Cavalry in the Peninsula 1807-1814* (Barnsley: Frontline, 2011).

Burnham, R. & McGuigan, R., *Wellington's Brigade Commanders, Peninsula & Waterloo* (Barnsley: Pen & Sword, 2017).

Burnham, R. & McGuigan, R., *The British Army against Napoleon, Facts, Lists, and Trivia 1805-1815* (Barnsley: Frontline Books, 2010).

Cadell, C., *Narrative of the Campaigns of the Twenty-Eighth Regiment* (London: Whittaker, 1835).

Cannon, R., *Historical Record of the 34th, Or the Cumberland Regiment of Foot* (London: Parker, Furnivall, and Parker, 1844).

Cannon, R., *Historical Record of the 9th or the Queen's Royal Regiment of Light Dragoons; Lancers* (London: Parker, 1841).

Clerk, A., *Memoir of Colonel John Cameron* (Glasgow: Murray, 1858).

Costa de Serda, E., *Opérations des Troupes Allemandes en Espagne de 1808 a 1813* (Paris: Dumaine, 1874).

Davies, H.J., *Spying for Wellington* (Norman: University of Oklahoma Press, 2018).

Delavoye, A.M., *Life of Thomas Graham* (London: Richardson, 1880).

Dempsey, G., *Napoleon's Mercenaries* (London: Greenhill, 2002).

Dempsey, G., *Albuera 1811* (Barnsley: Frontline Books, 2008).

Drouet, J.B., *Le Maréchal Drouet, Comte d'Orlon, Vie Militaire* (Paris: Barba, 1844).

Du Casse, A., *Mémoires et Correspondance Politique et Militaire du Roi Joseph* (Paris: Perrotin, 1854).

Du Casse, R., *Le Volontaire de 1793* (Paris: Dillet, 1880).

D'Urban, B., *The Peninsular Journal Of Major-General Sir Benjamin D'Urban: 1808-1817* (Kindle Edition).

Esdaile, C., *Fighting Napoleon* (New Haven: Yale University Press, 2004).

Esdaile, C., *The Peninsular War* (London: Allen Lane, 2002).

Esdaile, C., *The Spanish Army in the Peninsular War* (Nottingham: Partizan, 2012)

Fieffé, E, *Histoire des Troupes Étrangères au Service de France* (Paris: Librairie Militaire, 1854).

Fletcher, I.(ed), *In the Service of the King. The Letters of William Thornton Keep at Home, Walcheren, and in the Peninsula, 1808-1814* (Staplehurst: Spellmount, 1997).

Forrest, A., *Napoleon's Men* (London: Hambledon & London, 2002).

Fortescue, J.W., *A History of the British Army* (London: Macmillan & Co, 1906).

Fraser, E., *The Soldiers Whom Wellington Led* (London: Methuen, 1913).

Fyler, A.E., *The History of the 50th or (The Queen's Own) Regiment* (London: Chapman & Hall, 1895).

Gennequin, P., *The Centurions vs the Hydra: French Counterinsurgency in the Peninsular War (1808-1812)* (Fort Leavenworth: U.S. Army Command & General Staff College, 2011)

Girod de l'Ain, M., *Vie militaire du général Foy* (Paris: Plon, 1900).

Glover, G. (ed.), *The Journal of Sergeant David Robertson* (Godmanchester: Kent Trotman, 2018).

Grasset, A., *Malaga Province Français (1811-12)* (Paris: Lavauzelle, 1910).

Greenhill Gardyne, C., *The Life of a Regiment – The History of the Gordon Highlanders* (Edinburgh: Douglas, 1929).

Gurwood, J., *The General Orders of Field Marshal The Duke of Wellington K.G. in Spain, Portugal & France* (London: Egerton, 1837).

Gurwood, J., *The Dispatches of Field Marshall the Duke of Wellington* (London: John Murray, 1838).

Hall, J.A., *The Biographical Dictionary of British Officers Killed & Wounded, 1808-1814* (London: Greenhill, 1998).

Halliday, A., *Observations on the Present State of the Portuguese Army* (London: Murray, 1811).

Haythornthwaite, P. J., *The Armies of Wellington* (London: Arms & Armour, 1994).

Hill, J., *Wellington's Right Hand* (Stroud: Spellmount, 2012).

Hope, J., *Letters from Portugal, Spain and France* (London, Underwood, 1819).

Hope, J., *The Military Memoirs of an Infantry Officer 1809-1816* (Edinburgh: Anderson & Bryce, 1833).

Iglesias-Rogers, G. *British Liberators in the Age of Napoleon* (London: Bloomsbury, 2013).

Jones, J.T., *Journals of Sieges Carried on by the Army under the Duke of Wellington* (London: Egerton, 1827).

Lendy, A.F. (translator), *On Modern Armies by Marshal Marmont* (London: Mitchell, 1865).

Leslie, J.H., *The Dickson Manuscripts, Series C 1809-11* (London: Royal Artillery, 1905)

Leslie, J.H., *The Dickson Manuscripts, Series C, Vol.VI* (London: FireStep, 2017)

Leith-Hay, A., *Narrative of the Peninsular War* (London: Whittaker, 1832)

Linch, K., *Britain and Wellington's Army* (Basingstoke: Palgrave, 2011)

MacCarthy, J., *Recollections of the Storming of the Castle of Badajos* (Staplehurst: Spellmount, 2001).

MacBride, M., *With Napoleon at Waterloo* (London: Griffiths, 1911).

Marcel, N., *Campagnes du Capitaine Marcel, du 69e de ligne, en Espagne* (Paris: Plon, 1913).

Marmont, A., *Mémoires du Marechal Marmont, Duc de Raguse de 1792 a 1841* (Paris: Perrotin, 1857).

Martinien, A., *Tableaux, par Corps et par Batailles, des Officiers Tués et Blessés Pendant les Guerres de l'Empire (1805-1815)* (Paris, Charles-La Vauzelle, undated)

Martinien, A., *Tableaux, par Corps et par Batailles, des Officiers Tués et Blessés Pendant les Guerres de l'Empire (1805-1815) Supplement* (Paris, Fournier, 1909)

Maxwell, W. H., *Peninsular Sketches* (London: Colburn, 1845).

McGuffie, T.H., *Peninsular Cavalry General* (London: Harrap, 1951)

McGrigor, M., *Wellington's Spies* (Barnsley, Leo Cooper, 2005).

Moore Smith, G.C., *The Life of John Colborne, Field Marshal Lord Seaton* (London: Murray, 1903)

Muir, R., *Salamanca 1812* (New Haven: Yale, 2001).

Mullié, M.C., *Biographie des Célébrités Militaires des Armées de Terre et de Mer de 1789 à 1850* (Paris: Surcy, 1851).

Nafziger, G.F., *The Armies of Spain & Portugal 1808-1814* (Privately published, 1993)

Napier, W., *English Battles & Sieges in the Peninsula* (London, Murray, 1910).

Napier, W., *History of the War in the Peninsula & in the South of France* (London: Warne, 1886)

Oman, C., *A History of the Peninsular War* (Oxford: Clarendon Press, 1902).

Page, J., *Intelligence Officer in the Peninsula* (Staplehurst: Spellmount, 1986).

Patterson, J., *The Adventures of Captain John Patterson* (London: T & W Boone, 1837).

Patterson, J., *Camps and Quarters, or Scenes and Impressions, of Military Life* (London: Saunders & Otley, 1840).

Plon, H., & Dumaine, J., *Correspondance de Napoléon 1er* (Paris: Imprimeur de l'Empereur, 1868).

Reid, S., *Wellington's Highlanders* (Oxford: Osprey, 1992).

Rodriguez Villa, A., *El Teniente General Don Pablo Morillo* (Madrid: Editorial-America, 1920).

Rottenburg, F. de, *Regulations for the Exercise of Riflemen and Light Infantry and Instructions for their Conduct in the Field* (London: Egerton, 1803).

Sarrazin, J., *Histoire de la guerre d'Espagne et de Portugal de 1807 à 1814* (Paris: J.G. Dentu, 1814).

Sherer, M., *Recollections of the Peninsula* (London: Longman, Rees, Orme, Brown, & Green, 1827).

Sidney, E., *The Life of Lord Hill* (London: John Murray, 1845).

Six, G., *Dictionnaire Biographique des Généraux et Amiraux de la Révolution et de l'Empire: 1792-1814* (Paris, Librarie Historique et Nobiliaire, 1934)

Smith, D., *Napoleon's Regiments* (London: Greenhill, 2000).

Teffeteller, G., *The Surpriser, The Life of Rowland, Lord Hill* (Newark: University of Delaware Press, 1983).

Thompson, M.S., *Wellington's Engineers* (Barnsley: Pen & Sword, 2015).

Uffindell, A., *The National Army Museum Book of Wellington's Armies* (London: Sidgwick & Jackson, 2003)

Urban, M., *The Man Who Broke Napoleon's Codes* (London: Faber & Faber, 2001).

Van Eeckhoudt, G., *Les Chevau-Légers Belges du duc d'Arenberg* (Schiltigheim: Le Livre chez Vous, 2002).

Ward, S.G.P., *Wellington's Headquarters* (Barnsley: Pen & Sword, 2017).

Warre, W., *Letters from the Peninsula* (London: Murray, 1909).

Weigall, R. *The Correspondence of Lord Burghersh* (London: Murray, 1912).

Wellington, 2nd Duke of, *Supplementary Despatches, Correspondence and Memoranda of Field Marshal Arthur Duke of Wellington* (London, Murray, 1860)

Wilkin B. & Wilkin R., *Fighting the British* (Barnsley: Pen & Sword, 2018).

Wollocombe, R.H., *With the Guns in the Peninsula* (Barnsley: Frontline, 2017).

C.M. Woolgar (ed.), *Wellington Studies IV* (Southhampton: University of Southampton, 2008).

Wrottesley, G., *The Life and Correspondence of Field Marshal Sir John Burgoyne* (London: Bentley, 1873)

Wyld, J., *Maps and Plans Showing the Principle Movements, Battles and Sieges, in which the British Army was Engaged during the War from 1808 to 1814 in the Spanish Peninsula and South of France* (London: Wyld, 1841)

Journal Articles

Atkinson, C.T., 'The Ninth Queen's Royal Lancers, 1715-1936', *Journal of the Society for Army Historical Research*, Vol.18, No.72 (Winter, 1939), pp.235-8

Gillingham, H.E., 'Spanish Orders Of Chivalry And Decorations Of Honour', *Numismatic Notes and Monographs*, No 31 (1926), pp.1-165.

Goupille, A., 'Mémoires du Capitaine Ballue de la Haye-Descartes', *Bulletin Trimestriel de la Société Archéologique de Touraine*, V.XXXIII, pp.351-65

Mckenzie, A., 'Lieutenant-Colonel Charles Cother (1777-1855, 71st (Highland) Regiment (Light Infantry, and later of the 83rd Regiment', *Journal of the Society for Army Historical Research*, Vol.49, No.197 (Spring, 1971), pp.10-3

Rubio, J.A.P., 'Pablo Morillo: Acciones militares y la contribución de los pueblos de las tierras de Montánchez al esfuerzo de guerra (1811-1813)', *Revista de Estudios Extremeños*, 2013, Tomo LXIX, Número I, pp. 311-336

Ward, S.G.P., 'The Portuguese Infantry Brigades, 1809-1814', *Journal of the Society for Army Historical Research*, Vol.53, No.214 (Summer, 1975), pp.103-12.